C000068630

THE RU(

WHO'S WHO

1990/91

THE RUGBY UNION
WHO'S WHO
1990/91

Compiled and edited by
ALEX SPINK

WILLOW BOOKS
HarperCollins

Willow Books
HarperCollins Publishers,
London

First published in Great Britain in 1990 by
HarperCollins Publishers,
London

A CIP catalogue record for this book is available from the British Library
ISBN 0 00 218390 0

Cover photographs of Brian Moore, Gavin Hastings,
Robert Jones, Brendan Mullin by Russell Cheyne/Allsport
Portraits by Russell Cheyne/Allsport

Typeset in Plantin Light by A.L. Publishing Services, London W3

Printed and bound in Great Britain by
Butler & Tanner Ltd, Frome and London

Contents

Preface

The Rugby Union Who's Who 1990/91 has been born out of the boom in popularity which the sport is currently experiencing. It is a book of the players and for the players who, after all, are the most important ingredient in the recipe that is rugby union.

The territory of the book is International rugby football, as played by the four Home Unions, from Under-21 level through to Full status. Those who played for England, Ireland, Scotland or Wales last season at either Under-21, Under-25 (in Ireland's case), 'B' or Full level, are logged within the pages of what is hoped will become an indispensable reference for rugby fans across Great Britain and Ireland.

Rugby union is entering a new era, a new profile, and it is the players who, lest we forget, are leading it there. It is imperative, therefore, that they are looked after, kept in the sport, and encouraged to continue the progress.

This book does not merely give the players' details – the characters behind Saturday's muddy warriors – it also gives them a voice, to express opinions which, all too often in the past, have not been solicited.

The overwhelming majority have made it abundantly clear that they do not expect to be paid to play, nor would they seek such a scenario. But from top to bottom they ask with one voice why they cannot be reimbursed for working time lost to rugby, and why they should not be permitted to benefit financially from their rugby success away from the field.

The four nations' 1989/90 seasons, as seen through the eyes of the captains – Will Carling (England), Donal Lenihan (Ireland), David Sole (Scotland) and Robert Jones (Wales) – are reviewed between pages x–xviii.

And a comprehensive results section, starting on page 331, gives the run-down on who did what, where and when in 1989/90, the season that was.

On a personal note I would like to extend thanks to the players and club officials within the four Home Unions, without whose co-operation this book would not have been possible. Likewise, to John Griffiths, for his statistics, Russell Cheyne and the AllSport photographic team, Kevin Smyth and Karen Giles.

Alex Spink
1990

Foreword

P. T. BATEMAN
Chief Executive, Save & Prosper Group

It gives us all at Save & Prosper great pleasure to sponsor this first edition of *The Rugby Union Who's Who*, a fascinating compendium of rugby and personal information about the current leading players from the four home Unions.

As major sponsors of this great game, Save & Prosper hope this detailed information on our best players will bring supporters a little closer to their heroes and act as a useful point of reference even to the well-informed.

The Captains review the 1989/90 Season

ENGLAND

Will Carling

As we approached the 1989/90 season, I knew from the contribution made by English players to the British Lions' success in Australia that we had a very strong core to the team. I felt it was a case of building on what we had done in the previous season and establishing a pattern of play.

In that respect Fiji (won 58-23) were the ideal opponents to start the season. That game taught us that moving the ball down the line was not a risk at International level – it could actually be a constructive method of playing. Hence, we went into the Five Nations Championship full of confidence.

Our first appointment was against the Irish at Twickenham (won 23-0) and for two-thirds of the match we were frustrated – caught in the classic Five Nations syndrome of claustrophobic rugby. It took us far longer than we wanted to impose any real authority. But once we did, we did so emphatically.

Our following performances against France (won 26-7) and Wales (won 34-6) were intensely satisfying as we at last put into effect what we had worked on so hard. However, what I found so encouraging was the belief that we were still capable of playing better. We missed a few chances against Wales and I would like to think we can improve on our rucking and general ball retention this season.

The Scottish defeat at Murrayfield (lost 7-13) was a massive disappointment, especially bearing in mind the manner of our previous victories in Paris and at Twickenham. Mentally, we got the build-up all wrong, while the Scots produced their best performance. But we have tried to draw constructive points from the game. The defeat taught us lessons that took time to digest but, hopefully, it might be regarded as a blessing in disguise by the time the World Cup arrives.

We have time to recover before then whereas if something similar happened in the forthcoming Five Nations Championship it might hurt us. Success is important for each of the competing nations. As far as England are concerned, we want to win to confirm to ourselves the ability a lot of people believe we have.

IRELAND

Donal Lenihan

When I took over as captain, midway through the Five Nations Championship, my first task was to shake off the fear of losing prevalent within the side and instill a measure of confidence.

I was obviously concerned because the previous two or three seasons had not been satisfactory for Ireland. But in some way our failings last season might have been a disguised blessing. They spotlighted the need for change, and hastened a change in attitude.

The appointment of Ciaran Fitzgerald as coach, at the end of the season, was a notable step in the right direction because man-management is his strength and that is such an important ingredient in a successful coach.

The season began with the visit of New Zealand to Dublin (lost 6-23). It was very much a one-off for us as no-one had played against them before, and while our performance confirmed that we had a lot of good players it taught us that we had still to get the blend right. The All Blacks exposed our weakness, namely durability. We played well but fell away in the last period of the game.

The same happened against England at Twickenham (lost 0-23).

I felt we did well but it was more of an exercise in containment than going out to beat them. The fear of defeat was greater than our will to win.

That 'fear' probably cost us in our next match against Scotland (lost 10-13), where we played really well and indeed felt we should have won, yet didn't.

The French game (lost 12-31) was amazing. It was the fifth time I had played in Paris and was easily the best performance I had ever seen by an Ireland pack. Unfortunately there was no confidence behind the scrum.

It was a massive relief to beat Wales (won 14-8) and avoid the Wooden Spoon. Realistically, we should have won by 15 points instead of having to hang on desperately at the end but, on the day, victory was more important than the means by which it was achieved.

I feel we now have the nucleus of a good side. We do not have players who have won everything but we are in a better position to compete than at any time in the last eighteen months.

It was significant that we had nine players unavailable last season due to injury. But while we struggled, for that reason, it did allow us to bring in players who would otherwise have remained on the periphery.

Now we have more depth in the squad and, if we can get the organisation and personal commitment right, there is no reason why we cannot compete as successfully as the Scottish side did last season. The framework, which had worried me before, is now in place for the World Cup.

But we don't regard the World Cup as our only priority. We have first got to re-establish ourselves in the Five Nations Championship and use that as a springboard to go on.

We had last summer off, free from tours, which I thought was a wise move. I would be slightly concerned if I was English, for example, in the demand they have placed on their players. They have not had a break for so long and there is only so much you can ask people to do. Ireland preferred to instruct their players to work hard individually last summer, before coming together at the start of this season to begin an eighteen-month build-up to the World Cup.

SCOTLAND

David Sole

I discovered early in the season that we had a side capable of competing against any opponent. We showed, in our performances against pre-Christmas opponents Fiji (won 38-17) and Romania (won 32-0), that we could adapt our game to counter any styles. Those matches might have been in a different league to the Five Nations Championship, but they nevertheless allowed us to gain enormous confidence.

Scotland was a very easy side to captain, because coaches and players reacted and interacted very well, and there were a number of guys who could probably have captained the team. It was that spirit which gave us grounds for such optimism going into the Five Nations campaign.

For all our early season confidence, we did not start our Five Nations campaign impressively against Ireland (won 13-10), although we took heart from the fact that we still collected our first away win in 21 internationals. The atmosphere in the dressing room afterwards was one of great disappointment, but we all felt we could have done a great deal better which was very reassuring. It said a lot about the team's attitude. There were missed opportunities that by the end of the season we were taking.

Our job was made extremely hard by the fact that we were playing nations directly after their games with England. Consequently, Ireland, France and Wales were all looking to bounce back from heavy defeats.

Some of the shine from our win against France (21-0) was unfortunately taken off by the dismissal of their flanker Alain Carminati. After all, not many sides beat France by 21 points. The sending off came at a time when we were getting the upper hand anyway - they were under enormous pressure and were starting to get frustrated.

Next stop was Wales (won 13-9) and what struck me first in Cardiff was the passion with which the Welsh sang their anthem. There had been rumblings of discontent in Wales all season, yet we were met with a great feeling of optimism. Prior to the 1980s we had an abysmal record in Cardiff and we had played enough rugby on our two previous visits to win, yet had come away with nothing. But this year Wales had no-one of that previous calibre and their front row was not up to scratch as far as scrummaging was concerned.

The state of play going into the England game is well known - it was a case of all or nothing. We had been written off by the English, which was a wee bit frustrating to say the least because we felt no-one had rated us even though we were in the same position as England. England had played fantastically well all year but no-one had put them under any pressure – never knocked them down in midfield. We knew those had to be our tactics, rather than running around like headless chickens.

That was why we walked out onto the Murrayfield pitch - to control the aggression. The performance we produced was a tremendous credit to the players. We won (13-7) because we were the hungrier side but never before had I played in a game of such sustained intensity.

The match generated massive interest. It was just a game on the day but it meant so much more than 'just' a game. We have since had letters from Scots all over the word saying they were now able to hold their heads up that much higher than before.

Our performances in New Zealand last summer provided a fitting end to the season. We do not have the strength in depth of other countries so we have to encourage younger players. And this tour was, in many respects, make or break for some of these guys - to find out if they could compete at the top level.

The tour was part of a very good World Cup build-up. Some might have seen it as a gamble but we knew we would learn a great deal more by going to New Zealand than by going to Japan or Zimbabwe and maybe winning all our games. If we are going to improve, we have got to play, and set our standards against, the best.

WALES

Robert Jones

Wales' season got off to the worst possible start – losing to Bridgend. Coach John Ryan had arranged the game as a means of instilling confidence in the team but unfortunately it backfired. We were always going to be on a hiding to nothing but the players did not play with the commitment they should have done and certainly failed to match Bridgend in that department.

However, a lot of positive thoughts came out of the individual club performances against the touring All Blacks and we went into the International confident enough to think not only that we could give a good account of ourselves, but that we had a good chance. In the event we did not play terribly badly but were well beaten (9-34) by a better side.

That took us into the Five Nations Championship and Wales' first ever whitewash. I was heartened by the bags of commitment we showed against France after Kevin Moseley had been sent off in that match. The incident actually seemed to lift our morale and our backs created more than theirs did. And although we lost (19-29), we were most optimistic about our forthcoming visit to Twickenham.

We left for England believing we had sorted our problems out and I guess that made what followed all the more painful. The 6-34 defeat really hurt all the players and coaches and John Ryan took it on himself to resign – a decision which surprised us all as he had not mentioned it to anyone beforehand. But his commitment had always been 100 per cent and he felt he would take the responsibility for the team's failings. His departure was a little bit disappointing but the players had not really helped him.

Ron Waldron brought to the job a more enthusiastic approach. He was immediately regarded as a miracle-worker - the answer to all our problems – but he was never going to be able to turn us around overnight. He will, however, be great for our future – he is a tremendous coach with a fine approach to the game, and he most certainly lifted us after our record Twickenham loss.

Make no mistake, we went out to win every game and played some good rugby on occasions (like Arthur Emyr's try in our 9-13 defeat by Scotland). But just not enough good rugby, because only rarely did we produce the ball our backs would have liked.

I found the season especially frustrating as I had spent the previous summer in the company of the Lions, getting ball where and when I wanted it. Playing for Wales I had to get used to playing behind beaten packs and having to make the most of what limited possession we did get.

However, the end-of-season tour to Namibia ensured that it wasn't all gloom. I watched and listened with great excitement on television and radio back home where I was recovering from injury. The youngsters played very well, gaining valuable experience for the World Cup in the process, and those of us who missed the unbeaten trip know we will have our work cut out to win back our places in the team.

KEY TO INDIVIDUAL STATISTICS
(provided by John Griffiths)

Statistics give year (shown in brackets) in which players made debuts at various levels (U–21, U–25, B, Full) and in the case of full status include comprehensive career appearance and scoring details. At other levels, only last season's statistics have been logged.

Appearances below B-status are only included if they represent the highest level the player has attained.

'Rep' followed by a number indicates the number of times the player came on as a replacement.

Full British Lions details are given, with recognition also made to those who toured but were not capped. The 1986 IRB Centenary match in Cardiff (Lions 7, The Rest 15) has been included as a Lions cap.

Last summer's tour selections (Scotland to New Zealand, Wales to Namibia and England to Argentina) have also been recognised in cases where they represented the player's greatest achievement.

Statistics for England XV refer to Italy 15, England 33, 1 May 1990, Rovigo.

Players who retired from Rugby Union or who switched codes during the season are shown on pages 323–329.

Additional players selected by England to a development squad in preparation for the 1995 World Cup are shown in the Appendix on page 325.

THE PLAYERS A TO Z

Ackford, P.J. England

Full Name: Paul John Ackford
International category: England Full
Club: Harlequins
Position: Lock
Height: 6'6" **Weight:** 17st 4lb
Occupation: Police officer
Born: Hanover, West Germany, 26.2.58
Family: Married
Family links with rugby: Father played for Army
Former clubs: Plymouth Albion, Rosslyn Park, Met Police
International debut: England 28, Australia 19, 1988
Five Nations' debut: England 12, Scotland 12, 1989
Best moment in rugby: Final whistle in decisive third Test, Australia v 1989 Lions
Worst moment in rugby: Losing Grand Slam decider to Scotland (1990)
Most embarrassing moment: Losing ball to Rob Andrew in mauling practice
Most respected opponent: England lock Wade Dooley – because he's bigger than me
Serious injuries: Assorted shoulder and rib injuries
Other sporting achievements: Worst Celebrity-Am golfer on the circuit

	apps.	pts.
England B (1979)		
Last Season	0 caps	0
England (1988)		
Last Season	6 caps	4
Career	11 caps	4
1991	World Cup squad	
Lions 1989	3 Tests	0

KEY Year in brackets: i.e. **(1979)** = year in which player made debut. See also page xix

Best memory last season: Trying to remember lineout calls after being concussed v Fiji
Most improved International player last season: Ireland lock Neil Francis
Suggestions to improve rugby: Introduce a compulsory retiring age of 55 for all alickadoos

Other notable landmarks in rugby career: Spotting Daily Mail Rugby Correspondent Terry O'Connor buying a drink. Being complimented by a back – it must happen one day
Touchlines: Cooking, eating

Adam, D.R.W.   Scotland

Full Name: Douglas **Russell** Wallace Adam
International category: Scotland U-21
Club: Edinburgh Academicals
Position: Centre
Height: 6' **Weight:** 13st 5lb
Occupation: Student
Born: Nassau, Bahamas, 20.7.70
Family: Single
Family links with rugby: Mother's family related to Osler brothers (South African Internationals in 1920s)
International debut (U-21): Scotland 10, Wales 24, 1990
Serious injuries: Post-viral syndrome
Best memory last season: Playing against Wales U-21s at Ayr
Other notable landmarks in rugby career: Toured New Zealand in 1988 with Scottish Schools. Played for Scotland U-19s (wing) and involved with U-21s for two seasons (one on bench). Also played for Edinburgh U-21s. Represented North and Midlands before having played for Edinburgh Academicals first team

Adam R	apps.	pts.
Scotland U-21 (**1990**)		
Last Season	1 cap	0

Aherne, L.F.P.   Ireland

Full Name: Leslie Fergus Patrick
Aherne
International category: Ireland
Full
Club: Lansdowne
Position: Scrum-half
Height: 5'9" **Weight:** 12st 3lb
Occupation: Civil engineer
Born: Cork, 16.3.63
Family: Married
Family links with rugby: Father
played for Leinster
Former clubs: University College
Cork, Dolphin
International debut: Ireland 10,
England 21, 1988
Five Nations' debut: Ireland 21,
France 26, 1989
**Other notable landmarks in
rugby career:** Played for UCC for
four seasons, captaining them to
1984/85 Munster Senior League
title. Made Provincial bow with
Leinster, after breaking into Ireland
team and returning with them from
tour of France. Toured with
Ireland to North America (1989)
and captained Leinster throughout Inter-Pros last season

	apps.	pts.
Ireland (1988)		
Last Season	5 caps	0
Career	12 caps	4

Ainscough, G.C.   England

Full Name: Gerry Christopher
Ainscough
International category: England B
Club: Orrell
Positions: Centre, fly-half
Height: 5'11" **Weight:** 11st 7lb
Occupation: Mechanical engineer
Born: Wigan, 7.8.64
Family: Married
Family links with rugby: Father
and uncle played schoolboy rugby
league for Wigan
International debut: Spain 9,
England B 31, 1989
Best moment in rugby: Dropping
a goal for Orrell from 45 metres,
with 2 minutes remaining in 1988
Lancs Cup semi-final v Waterloo,
to win 9-7

Worst moment in rugby:
Recurrence of back injury (Aug
1989) which sidelined me for six
months of season

	apps.	pts.
England B (1989)		
Last Season	1 cap	0

Most embarrassing moment:
Falling into compost heap whilst
retrieving practice ball prior to
debut for Wigan Schools Rugby League U-11s (1974)
Most respected opponent: Gloucester as a team – locally born players with
great pride and immense will to win
Serious injuries: Prolapsed spinal disc. Torn medial ligaments
Other sporting achievements: Wigan Schools Rugby League, football and
athletics
Best memory last season: Kicking last-minute penalty for Orrell v
Harlequins to win 16–15 in English First Division
Most improved International player last season: England centre Jeremy
Guscott
Suggestions to improve rugby: Simplify rules to reduce number of stoppages
and allow a more flowing game. Increase points awarded for tries and
conversions – decrease points for penalty and dropped goal. Reduce number
of players by eliminating flankers

Other notable landmarks in rugby career: Playing at Wembley (1975) for Wigan Schools Rugby League U-11s. Senior debut for Orrell (1983). Lancashire debut (1985). Helped Lancashire win County final at Twickenham and Orrell win first Lancs Cup (1988). North of England debut and England B tour (1989). Scored 1,200 first-class points in career. Scored 12 points in England B's 32–15 defeat of Spanish Select (1989)
Touchlines: Cricket

Allan, J.   Scotland

Full Name: John Allan
International category: Scotland Full
Club: Edinburgh Academicals
Position: Hooker
Height: 6' **Weight:** 15st
Occupation: Computer programmer
Born: Glasgow, 25.11.63
Family: Single
Family links with rugby: William and Richard (brothers) both play
Former clubs: Glenwood Old Boys, Natal (SA)
International debut: New Zealand 31, Scotland 16, 1990
Best moment in rugby: The happiness on the players' faces when they achieved the 1990 Grand Slam

Worst moment in rugby: Being sidelined for six months after a knee operation
Most respected opponent: Uli Schmidt – totally dedicated to the game
Serious injuries: Snapped knee ligaments

	apps.	pts.
Scotland (**1990**)		
Last Season	1 cap	0
Career	1 cap	0

Other sporting achievements: Softball for Scotland Schools
Best memory last season: Meeting new rugby people

Most improved International player last season: Scotland wing Tony Stanger
Suggestions to improve rugby: Stop negative rugby – prevent players from spoiling the opposition's ball
Other notable landmarks in rugby career: Warmed Scotland's replacements' bench throughout last season. Was also among the reserves for Scotland B against Ireland and France. Toured with Scotland to New Zealand last summer and made debut in first Test at Dunedin

Allen, A.G.   Wales

Full Name: Andrew George Allen
International category: Wales Full
Club: Newbridge
Position: Lock
Height: 6'4" **Weight:** 17st 7lb
Occupation: Sales representative
Born: Newport, 5.4.67
Family: Single with son
Former clubs: Cwmbran, Garndiffaith
International debut: Wales 19, France 29, 1990
Five Nations' debut: As above
Best moment in rugby: Running out onto Cardiff Arms Park on debut
Worst moment in rugby: Wales losing to Ireland in 1990 Wooden Spoon decider
Most embarrassing moment: Walking off after heaviest ever Twickenham loss to England last season
Most respected opponent: Ireland lock Donal Lenihan – superb timing and very athletic
Serious injuries: Broken collarbone, lost four teeth

	apps.	pts.
Wales B (**1989**)		
Last Season	1 cap	0
Wales (**1990**)		
Last Season	3 caps	0
Career	3 caps	0

Other sporting achievements: Cwmbran pairs darts champion
Best memory last season: Wales debut

Most improved International player last season: Me
Other notable landmarks in rugby career: Front jumper capped by Wales Youth in 1986 and toured Canada that year, along with Anthony Clement and David Young. Played U-23 rugby for Monmouthshire and Welsh Counties, and made Wales B debut in 15–28 loss against France last season. Made full debut having played only 38 matches for a Newbridge team I joined at beginning of 1988/89

Andrew, C.R.   England

Full Name: Christopher **Robert** Andrew
International category: England Full
Club: Wasps
Position: Fly-half
Height: 5'9" **Weight:** 11st 4lb
Occupation: Chartered surveyor
Born: Yorkshire, 18.2.63
Family: Married with daughter
Family links with rugby: Brother played for Yorkshire in 1990 Colts County Championship final against Lancashire
Former clubs: Middlesbrough, Cambridge University (Blues: 1982,83,84), Nottingham, Gordon (Australia)
International debut: England 22, Romania 15, 1985
Five Nations' debut: England 9, France 9, 1985
Best moment in rugby: Lions third and decisive Test win v Australia (1989)
Worst moment in rugby: Losing Five Nations' Grand Slam decider 13–7 to Scotland (March 1990)
Most embarrassing moment: Missing 9 out of 10 kicks at goal

	apps.	pts.
England B (**1988**)		
Last Season	0 caps	0
England (**1985**)		
Last Season	6 caps	5
Career	31 caps	129
1991	World Cup squad	
England XV 1989/90	1 app	7
Lions 1989	2 Tests	8

for Nottingham v London Welsh in 4th round of 1985 J P Cup. We lost 12–11

Most respected opponent: Former Scotland fly-half John Rutherford
Other sporting achievements: Played first-class cricket for Yorkshire 2nd XI and Cambridge Univ, 1984 and 1985 (as captain). Scored 101 n.o. for Univ against Notts at Trent Bridge (1984)
Best memory last season: England 34, Wales 6
Most improved International player last season: England scrum-half Richard Hill
Other notable landmarks in rugby career: Set England records for points scored in an International (21) and penalties kicked (6), in England's 21–18 defeat of Wales at Twickenham in 1986. Selected for Lions and Home Unions. Captained England against Romania in Bucharest (May 1989) and Home Unions v France in Paris (1989). Divisional rugby both for North (1985, 1987) and London (1989)

Armstrong, G.   Scotland

Full Name: Gary Armstrong
International category: Scotland Full
Club: Jed-Forest
Position: Scrum-half
Height: 5'8" **Weight:** 13st 7lb
Occupation: Lorry driver
Born: Edinburgh, 30.9.66
Family: Married with child
Family links with rugby: Father played for Jed-Forest. Brother played for Jed-Forest and Scotland U-21s
Former club: Jed Thistle
International debut: Scotland 13, Australia 32, 1988
Five Nations' debut: Scotland 23, Wales 7, 1989
Best moment in rugby: Beating England to win 1990 Grand Slam
Most respected opponent: French scrum-half Pierre Berbizier
Serious injuries: Torn knee and ankle ligaments

Best memory last season: Grand Slam and second Test against All Blacks which Scotland came so close to winning
Most improved International player last season: Scotland lock Chris Gray
Suggestions to improve rugby: Scrap 90-degree wheel law
Other notable landmarks in rugby career: Represented Scotland at U-18, Youth, U-21 and B level

	apps.	pts.
Scotland B (**1987**)		
Last Season	0 caps	0
Scotland (**1988**)		
Last Season	8 caps	0
Career	13 caps	4
Lions 1989		

Arnold, P.   Wales

Full Name: Paul Arnold
International category: Wales Full
Club: Swansea
Position: Lock
Height: 6'5" **Weight:** 15st 4lb
Occupation: Building employee
Born: 28.4.68
Family: Single
International debut: Namibia 9, Wales 18, 1990
Worst moment in rugby: Not being originally picked for Welsh tour to Namibia
Best moment in rugby: Going to Namibia after injured Gareth Llewellyn withdrew
Most respected opponent: Newport's former Welsh lock David Waters
Best memory last season: Playing for Swansea against All Blacks
Most improved International player last season: Wales flanker Alan Reynolds
Other notable landmarks in rugby career: In third season with

	apps.	pts.
Wales U-21 (**1990**)		
Last Season	1 cap	0
Wales (**1990**)		
Last Season	2 caps	0
Career	2 caps	0

Swansea, having progressed through All Whites' youth set-up. Also gained experience playing in New Zealand (summer 1989). Last season played for Wales U-21s in their 24–10 defeat of Scotland at Ayr and followed that with selection for Wales' tour of Namibia, where won selection to full team for both Tests
Touchlines: Sunday soccer

Ashurst, N. England

Full Name: Neil Ashurst
International category: England U-21
Club: Orrell
Position: Flanker
Height: 6'2" **Weight:** 15st 7lb
Occupation: Quantity surveyor
Born: St Helens, Lancs, 12.5.69
Family: Single
Family links with rugby: Brothers play rugby league for Widnes
Former club: West Park
International debut: Netherlands 3, England U-21 24, 1990
Best moment in rugby: Being picked by England U-21s
Most respected opponent: England flanker Peter Winterbottom
Other sporting achievements: Cricket for Lancashire XI
Best memory last season: Scoring hat-trick of tries for Orrell v Vale of Lune
Most improved International player last season: England lock Wade Dooley

	apps.	pts.
England U-21 (1990)		
Last Season	2 caps	0

Suggestions to improve rugby: Referees should be more flexible in their interpretation of laws
Other notable landmarks in rugby career: Started playing aged 11. Represented England Colts four times (1988/89) and twice won England U-21 honours, v Netherlands and French Armed Forces (1989/90)

Back, N.A. England

Full Name: Neil Antony Back
International category: England U-21
Club: Leicester
Position: Openside flanker
Height: 5'10" **Weight:** 13st 7lb
Occupation: Assurance clerk
Born: Coventry, 16.1.69
Family: Single
Former club: Nottingham
International debut (U-21): Romania 13, England 54, 1989
Best moment in rugby: Scoring 3 tries on U-21 debut in Bucharest
Most respected opponent: England flanker Andy Robinson
Serious injuries: Broken arm (aged 16)
Other sporting achievements: Cricket for Coventry and Warwickshire Schools

Best memory last season: Playing for England XV in 33–15 defeat of Italy and scoring try
Most improved International player last season: England fly-half Rob Andrew

	apps.	pts.
England U-21 (**1989**)		
Last Season	3 caps	12
England 1991	World Cup squad	
1995	Development squad	
England XV 1989/90	1 app	4

Suggestions to improve rugby:
Establish worldwide, uniform guidelines concerning amateurism
Other notable landmarks in rugby career: Represented England U-18s (1985–87), England Colts (1987/88), England U-21s (1988–90) and England XV (1990)
Touchlines: Training five days a week for rugby. Weight training, squash, badminton

Bailey, M.D.   England

Full Name: Mark David Bailey
International category: England
Full
Club: Wasps
Position: Wing
Height: 6'2" **Weight:** 13st 8lb
Occupation: College lecturer
Born: Castleford, 21.11.60
Family: Married
Family links with rugby: Father
former secretary of Featherstone
Rovers Rugby League Club
Former clubs: Ipswich, Bedford,
Cambridge University (Blues:
1982,83,84,85)
International debut: South Africa
33, England 15, 1984
Five Nations' debut: England 23,
Ireland 0, 1990
Best moment in rugby: When
Fran Clough knocked-on for
England v Japan in 1987 World
Cup
Worst moment in rugby: The
claret at Ipswich RFC club dinner
Most embarrassing moment:
Every time I play Sevens
Most respected opponent:

	apps.	pts.
England B (1986)		
Last Season	0 caps	0
England (1984)		
Last Season	4 caps	4
Career	7 caps	4

England centre Fran Clough – because of his robust tackling and stinging
wit
Serious injuries sustained: Deeply bruised ego – inoperable
Other sporting achievements: Captain of Suffolk in Minor Counties cricket
championship, 1988,89,90
Best memory last season: Getting married to the delightful Julie
Most improved International player last season: Wasps' England
scrum-half Steve Bates
Suggestions to improve rugby: Keep game amateur
Other notable landmarks in rugby career: After-dinner speaking for
London Division. Played for London between 1981–88, captain in 1987
Touchlines: Enjoy claret and port drinking. Author of *A marginal economy*
(published 1989)

Baldwin, D.N.   England

Full Name: David Neil Baldwin
International category: England B
Club: Sale
Position: Lock
Height: 6'6" **Weight:** 17st 8lb
Occupation: Screen printer
Born: Leeds, 3.9.64
Family: Married with son
Family links with rugby: Four uncles played Union, two played League
Former clubs: Bramley, Wakefield
International debut: England B 18, USSR 10, 1989
Best moment in rugby: Yorkshire's 1989/90 County Championship final defeat of Middlesex
Worst moment in rugby: Yorkshire losing 12–37 to Lancashire in 1988 Championship
Most respected opponent: Former England lock Steve Bainbridge
Other sporting achievements: Soccer for Leeds Schools U-11, U-12, U-15 and U-16 teams. Rugby League for Leeds Schools U-16s
Best memory last season: Selection for England B v USSR
Most improved International player last season: England hooker Brian Moore
Touchlines: Body building

	apps.	pts.
England B (1989)		
Last Season	2 caps	0
England 1995	Development squad	

13

Baldwin, G.P.S. England

Full Name: Gavin Paul Samuel Baldwin
International category: England U-21
Club: Northampton
Position: Prop
Height: 6' **Weight:** 16st 7lb
Occupation: Senior health and fitness instructor
Born: Hereford, 6.12.68
Family: Single
Family links with rugby: Father played for Gloucester Civil Service
Former clubs: Worcester, Nottingham, Loughborough Students
International debut: Netherlands 3, England U-21 24, 1990
Best moment in rugby: Helping English Students beat French and Soviet counterparts in 1989/90 season
Worst moment in rugby: Not being picked for England Schools
Best memory last season: French Students 4, English Students 32
Most improved International player last season: Scotland tight-head prop Paul Burnell
Other notable landmarks in rugby career: Represented Midlands Schools and U-21s, English Students and Universities. Named in England development squad at tail end of 1989/90 season

	apps.	pts.
England U-21 (**1990**)		
Last Season	2 caps	0
England 1995	Development squad	

14

Barley, B.   England

Full Name: Bryan Barley
International category: England B
Club: Wakefield
Position: Centre
Height: 5'10" **Weight:** 13st 7lb
Occupation: Insurance broker
Born: Wakefield, 4.1.60
Family: Married with two
daughters
International debut: England 12,
Ireland 9, 1984
Five Nations' debut: As above
Best moment in rugby: Scoring
try for England v Fiji (Suva 1988)
Worst moment in rugby: Not
being picked for England v France
in 1988 after scoring try to help
England B beat England in Trial
Most respected opponent:
Former French centre Didier
Codorniou
Serious injuries: Two damaged
knees, broken jaw
Best memory last season:
Revenge win over Rugby in Cup
(they beat us in final game of
1988/89 season to prevent our
promotion to English Second
Division)

	apps.	pts.
England B (1988)		
Last Season	1 cap	0
England (1984)		
Last Season	0 caps	0
Career	7 caps	4

Most improved International player last season: England fly-half Rob
Andrew
Suggestions to improve rugby: Make sure skills are coached in practice
rather than concentrate all the time on fitness and game plans
Other notable landmarks in rugby career: Returning to International rugby
after two serious knee operations

Full Name: David Barrett
International category: Scotland B
Club: West of Scotland
Position: Full-back
Height: 5'10" **Weight:** 12st 6lb
Occupation: PE teacher
Born: London, 25.7.63
Family: Married with one child
Former club: Edinburgh University
International debut (B): Scotland
22, Ireland 22, 1989
Best moment in rugby: Glasgow
securing last-minute victory over
Anglo-Scots to win 1990
Inter-District Championship
Worst moment in rugby: Being
relegated from Scottish First
Division last season with West
Most respected opponent:
Former Ireland midfield back Mike
Gibson
Best memory last season:
Glasgow beating touring Fijians as
prelude to winning Championship
Suggestions to improve rugby:
Establish a Scottish knock-out cup

	apps.	pts.
Scotland B (1989)		
Last Season	2 caps	12

Other notable landmarks in rugby career: Being invited to tour Canada
with West in 1983 and subsequently joining club permanently. Switching from
fly-half to full-back in 1988. Represented Scotland B v Ireland and France
last season
Touchlines: Golf, cricket, DIY

Barry, N.   Ireland

Full Name: Nicky Barry
International category: Ireland U-21
Club: Garryowen
Positions: Wing, fly-half
Height: 5'11" **Weight:** 12st 7lb
Occupation: BSc student
Born: 5.1.69
Family: Single
Family links with rugby: All family, except females, play
International debut (U-21): Italy 13, Ireland 22, 1988
Best moment in rugby: Captaining Irish Schools. Touring France with Ireland aged 19
Worst moment in rugby: Losing Munster Senior Cup final
Most embarrassing moment: Once playing a match with no boots
Most respected opponent: Australian wing David Campese – tremendous ability to attack from anywhere on field
Serious injuries: Broken hand
Other sporting achievements: All-Ireland sprint (athletics)

	apps.	pts.
Ireland U-21 (1988)		
Last Season	1 cap	6

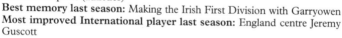

Best memory last season: Making the Irish First Division with Garryowen
Most improved International player last season: England centre Jeremy Guscott
Suggestions to improve rugby: Move season to May and June to allow a faster game of rugby to be played
Other notable landmarks in rugby career: Toured Australia (with Irish Schools), Canada and France (with Ireland)
Touchlines: Greyhound racing

Bateman, A.G.   Wales

Full Name: Allan Glen Bateman
International category: Wales Full
Club: Neath
Position: Centre
Height: 5'9" **Weight:** 12st 7lb
Occupation: Medical laboratory
scientific officer
Born: Measteg, 6.3.65
Family: Married
Family links with rugby: Father
chairman of Maesteg Youth
Former clubs: Maesteg Celtic,
Maesteg
International debut: Wales 9,
Scotland 13, 1990
Five Nations' debut: As above
Best moment in rugby: Winning
first full cap against Scotland
Worst moment in rugby: Neath
losing to 1989 All Blacks in match
we should have won
Most embarrassing moment:
Running into own posts, playing
for Bridgend and District
Most respected opponent: Wales
B centre Colin Laity
Serious injuries: Pulled hamstrings
Other sporting achievements:

	apps.	pts.
Wales B (1989)		
Last Season	1 cap	0
Wales (1990)		
Last Season	4 caps	0
Career	4 caps	0

Soccer for Llynfi Valley U-16s against Scotland Representative XI
Best memory last season: Wales debut at Cardiff Arms Park
Most improved International player last season: All Black centre Walter
Little
Suggestions to improve rugby: Standardise refereeing interpretations
between southern and northern hemispheres
Other notable landmarks in rugby career: Joining Neath from Maesteg in
Dec 1988. Schools final trialist. Two games for Wales Youth (1983). Wales
B debut in 15–28 loss to France last season

Bates, S.M.   England

Full Name: Steven Michael Bates
International category: England
Full
Club: Wasps
Position: Scrum-half
Height: 5'10" **Weight:** 13st
Occupation: Sales executive
Born: Merthyr Tydfil, 4.3.63
Family: Married
Former clubs: West London
Institute, Welwyn
International debut: Romania 3,
England 58, 1989
Best moment in rugby: Winning
first cap in Bucharest
Worst moment in rugby:
Twickenham pitch invasion near
end of Wasps' 1987 John Player
Cup final defeat by Bath. Took
dignity out of occasion as referee
was forced to 'abandon' game
Most respected opponent:
Harlequins' former New Zealand
scrum-half Dave Loveridge
Serious injuries: Broken jaw
(1983/84) and arm (1986 JP Cup
final)
Other sporting achievements:
Soccer for Hertfordshire. Golf
(4-handicap)

England (1989)	apps.	pts.
Last Season	1 cap	0
1990	Tour to Argentina	
Career	1 cap	0
1991	World Cup squad	
England XV 1989/90	1 app	0

Best memory last season: Winning English First Division with Wasps
Most improved International player last season: Scotland scrum-half Gary
Armstrong
Other notable landmarks in rugby career: Joined Wasps (1981) and
immediately represented Herts. English Colleges (1981–83). Toured Japan
with England Students (1982). Played for London Division since 1986.
England U-23 against Spain (1986). England replacement for first time against
1988 Wallabies. Likewise for nine of England's last ten matches. Exception
was Romania when won first cap. Flew out to Argentina as replacement for
England last summer
Touchlines: Photography – built own darkroom

Blair, A.G.   Ireland

Full Name: Ashley Graham Blair
International category: Ireland U-25
Club: Dungannon
Position: Scrum-half
Height: 6' **Weight:** 12st 8lb
Occupation: PE teacher
Born: Dungannon, 20.10.64
Family: Single
Family links with rugby: Uncle played for Dungannon
International debut: Ireland U-25 12, US Eagles 10, 1990
Best moment in rugby: Ulster debut v 1989 All Blacks
Worst moment in rugby: Being left out of Irish Schools team
Most embarrassing moment: Terribly mis-cueing a penalty from touch in front of large school crowd
Most respected opponent: Irish scrum-half Nigel Carr
Other sporting achievements: Irish League B Division football with Dungannon Swifts
Best memory last season: Playing v All Blacks and US Eagles

	apps.	pts.
Ireland U-25 (**1990**)		
Last Season	1 cap	0

Most improved International player last season: Ireland full-back Kenny Murphy
Suggestions to improve rugby: Listen to players and recognise their commitment
Other notable landmarks in rugby career: Top points scorer and club record holder with Dungannon – 237 (1986–89)
Touchlines: Travelling

Booth, A.H.   Wales

Full Name: Andrew Howell Booth
International category: Wales B
Club: Cardiff
Position: Scrum-half
Height: 5'10" **Weight:** 12st 10lb
Occupation: Student
Born: Swansea, 8.12.68
Family: Single
Family links with rugby: Father
played for West Wales
Former clubs: UC Swansea, Neath
International debut (B): France
28, Wales 15, 1989
Best moment in rugby:
Replacement for Wales v 1989 All
Blacks (lost 9-34)
Worst moment in rugby: Being
dropped from any team
Most respected opponent: Wales
scrum-half Robert Jones
Serious injuries sustained:
Cracked ankle ligaments
Best memory last season: Wales
v New Zealand
Suggestions to improve rugby:
Boost confidence of all players at
all times leading up to a match – criticise constructively

	apps.	pts.
Wales B (1989)		
Last Season	1 cap	0

Other notable landmarks in rugby career: West Wales U-11s, Welsh
Schools U-15s, U-18s, U-21s, Students (scored 15 points), Wales B. Played
for Cardiff v 1989 All Blacks. 1989 Cambridge Blue. Wales replacement last
season

Boyle, L.S.   England

Full Name: Laurence Stuart Boyle
International category: England
U-21
Club: Moseley
Position: Centre
Height: 5'10" **Weight:** 13st 1lb
Occupation: Student
Born: Warwick, 29.1.70
Family: Single
Family links with rugby: Brother
played for England U-16s
Former club: Leamington
International debut: French
Armed Forces 16, England U-21s
23, 1990
Best moment in rugby: Winning
first cap at England U-16 level
Worst moment in rugby: Losing
to Bath in semi-final of 1989/90
Pilkington Cup
Most respected opponent:
Former England fly-half Les
Cusworth – leadership skills
Other sporting achievements:
Athletics all-rounder for
Warwickshire. Javelin at
All-England Championships

England U-21 (1990)	apps.	pts.
Last Season	1 cap	0

Best memory last season: The mistake by David Campese that cost Australia
the Lions' series
Most improved International player last season: England fly-half Rob
Andrew
Suggestions to improve rugby: At representative level, tell people who have
been dropped where they went wrong and how they can improve
Other notable landmarks in rugby career: England U-16 Schools v Italy.
England B U-18 Schools v Japan. Warwickshire Colts v Sweden. Midland
Colts v Italy. Midland U-21s v NZ U-21s

Bradley, M.T.   Ireland

Full Name: Michael Timothy Bradley
International category: Ireland Full
Club: Constitution
Position: Scrum-half
Height: 5'10" **Weight:** 13st 5lb
Occupation: Freight agent
Born: Cork, 17.11.62
Family: Single
Family links with rugby: Father played for Constitution
International debut: Ireland 9, Australia 16, 1984
Five Nations' debut: Scotland 15, Ireland 18, 1985
Best moment in rugby: Winning 1985 Triple Crown with Ireland
Worst moment in rugby: Ireland losing 3-35 to England at Twickenham in 1988, having led 3-0 at half-time
Most respected opponent: Australian scrum-half Nick Farr-Jones
Serious injuries: Torn ankle ligaments (1990)
Best memory last season: Being recalled by Ireland for Wooden Spoon decider against Wales

	apps.	pts.
Ireland B (**1983**)		
Last Season	0 caps	0
Ireland (**1984**)		
Last Season	1 cap	0
Career	23 caps	16

Most improved International player last season: Ireland full-back Kenny Murphy
Suggestions to improve rugby: Players should receive bonus payments for International matches and reimbursement for loss of earnings
Other notable landmarks in rugby career: Played four games for Irish Schools and captained them on 1980 tour of Australia. Captained Irish U-19s and U-21s. Completed journey up representative ladder with appearances for U-25s and B (1983 v Scotland). Chosen as replacement for Ireland in 1984 before having played Provincial rugby for Munster
Touchlines: Golf, anything that moves

23

Breckenridge, G.M. — Scotland

Full Name: George McLean Breckenridge
International category: Scotland B
Club: Glasgow High/Kelvinside
Position: Fly-half
Height: 6' **Weight:** 12st 2lb
Occupation: Sales representative
Born: Glasgow, 5.9.64
Family: Single
Family links with rugby: Brother played for Glasgow Schools
Former club: St Medard de Guizeres (Fr)
International debut (B): France 31, Scotland 9, 1990
Best moment in rugby: Scotland B debut in Oyonnax
Worst moment in rugby: Sitting out for nine months after damaging knee ligaments in 1987
Most embarrassing moment: Playing in 1990 Kilmarnock Sevens, went to touch ball down for try, but it bounced off knee and back over my head. Fortunately still got decisive touch

	apps.	pts.
Scotland B **(1990)**		
Last Season	1 cap	0

Most respected opponent: Former All Black John Schuster
Serious injuries: Damaged knee ligaments
Other sporting achievements: Golf (5-handicap): seventh in 1981 Dumbartonshire County Boys Strokeplay Golf Championship
Best memory last season: GHK beating champions Kelso 12–9
Most improved International player last season: Scotland fly-half Craig Chalmers
Other notable landmarks in rugby career: Played for Glasgow in win against Fiji and helped them win Inter-District Championship (both 1989/90)
Touchlines: Reading, travel

Brewster, A.K.   Scotland

Full Name: Alex Kinloch Brewster
International category: Scotland
Full (squad)
Club: Stewart's Melville FP
Positions: flanker, loose-head prop
Height: 5'11½" **Weight:** 15st 7lb
Occupation: Farmer
Born: Bangour, 3.5.54
Family: Married with four children
Family links with rugby: Twin
brother David plays
International debut: England 26,
Scotland 6, 1977
Five Nations' debut: As above
Best moment in rugby: Beating
England by record score (33–6) in
1986
Worst moment in rugby: Scottish
defeat by Japan (Tokyo 1989)
Most embarrassing moment:
Being dropped by Scotland in
1981/82 after first victory in
fourteen games against France
Most respected opponent:
Scotland prop Iain Milne
Serious injuries: Damaged knee
ligaments

	apps.	pts.
Scotland (1977)		
Last Season	0 caps	0
Career	6 caps	0

Best memory last season: Grand Slam
Most improved International player last season: Scotland wing Tony
Stanger
Suggestions to improve rugby: Play ball on ground – would make it more
quickly available and give more continuity to game
Other notable landmarks in rugby career: Won caps at flanker and prop.
Led Edinburgh to back-to-back Scottish District Championships. Captained
Scotland to Japan in 1989

Bridges, C.J.   Wales

Full Name: Christopher Jeffrey Bridges
International category: Wales Full
Club: Neath
Position: Scrum-half
Height: 5'11" **Weight:** 13st
Occupation: Labourer
Born: Pontypridd, 31.8.68
Family: Married with son
Former club: Beddau
International debut: Namibia 9, Wales 18, 1990
Best moment in rugby: Scoring try on full Welsh debut
Worst moment in rugby: Losing to Llanelli in 1988 Welsh Cup final
Most respected opponent: Former Wales scrum-half Jonathan Griffiths
Other sporting achievements: Cricket for Glamorgan U-15s. Won players' golf tournament in Namibia
Best memory last season: Receiving Welsh cap in Cardiff on return from Namibian tour
Most improved International player last season: Wales centre Allan Bateman

	apps.	pts.
Wales B (**1989**)		
Last Season	1 cap	0
Wales (**1990**)		
Last Season	2 caps	4
Career	2 caps	4

Suggestions to improve rugby: Quite enough changes have already been made to Welsh rugby
Other notable landmarks in rugby career: Captained Welsh Youth (1986/87), toured New Zealand with U-19s (1987), Canada with Wales B (1989) and Namibia with Wales (1990). Also represented U-21s and twice a Five Nations' replacement
Touchlines: Golf (25/26-handicap)

Brown, C.J.   Scotland

Full Name: Calum John Brown
International category: Scotland U-21
Club: Jed-Forest
Position: Flanker
Height: 5'10" **Weight:** 13st 7lb
Occupation: Agricultural engineer
Born: Jedburgh, 19.9.68
Family: Single
Family links with rugby: Father played for Jed-Forest and captained club for two seasons
International debut (U-21): Scotland 10, Wales 24, 1990
Best moment in rugby: Being picked for Scotland U-21
Worst moment in rugby: Breaking leg playing for South U-21s v Glasgow U-21s
Most embarrassing moment: Coming on twice as a replacement in vital match against Kelso. Injured player decided to stay on first time but then changed his mind and I returned, to crowd's great amusement

	apps.	pts.
Scotland U-21 (**1990**)		
Last Season	1 cap	0

Most respected opponent: Eric Paxton (ex-Scotland) – hard player who always gave 100 per cent
Serious injuries sustained: Broken elbow, leg
Best memory last season: Beating Stirling County in crunch match
Most improved International player last season: Scotland captain David Sole
Other notable landmarks in rugby career: Being in the winning team when Jed-Forest won the Border League
Touchlines: Enjoy keep-fit, shooting, travelling abroad

Bryant, D.J.   Wales

Full Name: David John Bryant
International category: Wales B
Club: Bridgend
Position: Flanker, No.8
Height: 6'2" **Weight:** 15st
Occupation: Student
Born: Bridgend, 21.2.67
Family: Single
International debut: New Zealand 52, Wales 3, 1988
Five Nations' debut: Scotland 23, Wales 7, 1989
Best moment in rugby: Scoring try for Bryntirion v Brynteg school derby match – 50 yarder down cheering touchline
Worst moment in rugby: Vainly chasing Irish No.8 Noel Mannion up Cardiff touchline (1989) – so near yet so far – he scored and Ireland beat Wales 19–13
Most embarrassing moment: Losing game for Wales U-18s v Ireland, in gale force wind, when I sliced an intended clearance over my own head and opposition gratefully accepted scoring gift
Most respected opponent: New Zealand flanker Michael Jones – class of his own

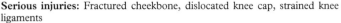

	apps.	pts.
Wales B (1987)		
Last Season	2 caps	0
Wales (1988)		
Last Season	0 caps	0
Career	4 caps	0

Serious injuries: Fractured cheekbone, dislocated knee cap, strained knee ligaments
Other sporting achievements: Welsh Schools cricket cap and basketball squad member. County junior men's squash team
Best memory last season: Captaining Bridgend for first time
Most improved International player last season: England hooker Brian Moore
Suggestions to improve rugby: Decide which way game is to go. Is it to remain a strictly amateur sport with associated deceit, or adopt semi-professionalism

Other notable landmarks in rugby career: Captained Welsh Schools to 12–10 win against New Zealand. Toured with Wales to New Zealand, and captained Welsh team in Students World Cup in France (both 1988)

Bryson, D. Scotland

Full Name: David Bryson
International category: Scotland B
Club: Gala
Position: Scrum-half
Height: 5'8" **Weight:** 12st 7lb
Occupation: Textile executive
Born: Galashiels, 5.5.58
Family: Married with two daughters
International debut (B): France 44, Scotland 4, 1982
Best moment in rugby: Captaining victorious Gala team at Gala Sevens
Worst moment in rugby: Missing out on a Scottish tour because of injury suffered playing soccer
Most embarrassing moment: Speaking to a local radio correspondent without realising the programme was live on air
Most respected opponent: Former Scotland No.8 Donny McLeod – hard and uncompromising, but not dirty

	apps.	pts.
Scotland B (1982)		
Last Season	2 caps	0

Serious injuries: Torn ligaments (shoulder, knee and ankle), broken collarbone, dislocated shoulder
Other sporting achievements: Played cricket for Gala and South of Scotland. Reduced golf handicap from 14 to 6 in five years
Best memory last season: Watching Scotland beat England in Grand Slam decider
Most improved International player last season: Scotland No.8 Derek White
Suggestions to improve rugby: Play more in spring/autumn and implement winter break (Dec-Feb)

Other notable landmarks in rugby career: Hold Scottish record for points scored in a National League match – 34 (3 tries and all 11 conversions attempted). Captained Gala seasons 1984/85, 1989/90. Nearing 300 games for club. Highest try-scorer in Gala's history excluding wings. Capped by Scottish Schools three times. Toured with Scotland to North America (1985)
Touchlines: Passion for Chinese cookery, woodwork, gardening, snooker and horse racing. Spent numerous summer holidays at Newmarket

Buckett, I.   Wales

Full Name: Ian Buckett
International category: Wales
(Namibia squad)
Club: Swansea
Position: Prop
Height: 6'1" **Weight:** 16st 7lb
Occupation: Student
Born: Hollywell, 23.12.67
Family: Single
Former clubs: Swansea
University, Wrexham
Best moment in rugby: Playing
for Swansea against 1989 All Blacks
Worst moment in rugby: Missing
Swansea's game against Barbarians
after catching foot in a lawnmower
Most respected opponent:
Former Wales prop David Young
Serious injuries: Broken toe in
three places in above accident
Best memory last season: Being
selected to tour Namibia
**Most improved International
player last season:** Welsh lock
Paul Arnold

Wales (1990)	Tour to Namibia

Other notable landmarks in rugby career: Represented Welsh Schools U-15s and U-18s and Wales U-21s. Toured Namibia with Wales last summer

Buckton, J.R.   England

Full Name: John Richard Buckton
International category: England B
Club: Saracens
Position: Centre
Height: 6'2" **Weight:** 12st 11lb
Occupation: Computer manager
Born: Hull, 22.12.61
Family: Single
Family links with rugby: Two
brothers (Peter and Nick) play for
Liverpool St Helens
Former clubs: Hull and East
Riding, Marist Old Boys
International debut: England 28,
Australia 19, 1988
Best moment in rugby: Coming
on as last-minute replacement v
1988 Wallabies to win first cap
Worst moment in rugby: Getting
injured with England in Australia
immediately prior to first Test
(1988)
Most embarrassing moment:
Missing Yorkshire/Lancashire
County game while stuck on train
from London to Manchester
Most respected opponent:
Saracens' centre Lawrence Smith
(in training)
Best memory last season:
Saracens' performances on debut
in English First Division

	apps.	pts.
England B (1988)		
Last Season	2 caps	0
England (1988)		
Last Season	0 caps	0
Career	1 cap	0
1990	Tour to Argentina	
1991	World Cup squad	
England XV 1989/90	1 app	4

Most improved International player last season: England No.8 Mike
Teague
Suggestions to improve rugby: Pay players
Other notable landmarks in rugby career: Winning 1987 County
Championship with Yorkshire. Helping Saracens win English Second Division
(1988/89). Last season played twice for England B (v USSR and France) and
helped England XV defeat Italy 33–15 in Rovigo. Spent summer touring
Argentina with England
Touchlines: Stamp collecting, travel

Budd, M.   Wales

Full Name: Michael Budd
International category: Wales B
Club: Bridgend
Position: Flanker
Height: 6'1" **Weight:** 15st
Occupation: Sales manager
Born: Cardiff, 24.5.63
Family: Married with two sons
Family links with rugby:
Grandfather and uncle played
district rugby
Former club: St Josephs
International debut (B): Wales
12, France 18, 1989
Best moment in rugby:
Captaining Bridgend to 23–15 win
over Wales XV (1989)
Worst moment in rugby: Giving
away a penalty that could have
presented Aberavon with a place in
1989/90 Schweppes final. But they
missed and Bridgend won semi-final
Most respected opponent:
Former Wales scrum-half David
Bishop – most complete player ever
come up against. Could have
played any number of positions

	apps.	pts.
Wales B (1988)		
Last Season	2 caps	0

Serious injuries: Twisted pelvis, pulled hamstrings
Best memory last season: Schweppes Cup final – despite losing 10–16 to
Neath
Most improved International player last season: England fly-half Rob
Andrew
Suggestions to improve rugby: Pump more money into grass roots of game
Other notable landmarks in rugby career: Played for Wales Youth 1980/81,
and captained 1981/82 team. Made senior Bridgend debut aged 18. Toured
USA with Bridgend (1990). Won 3 caps for Wales B

Burnell, A.P.   Scotland

Full Name: Andrew Paul Burnell
International category: Scotland
Full
Club: London Scottish
Position: Tight-head prop
Height: 6'1" **Weight:** 16st
Occupation: Sales executive
Born: Edinburgh, 29.9.65
Family: Single
Former clubs: Marlow, Leicester
International debut: England 12,
Scotland 12, 1989
Five Nations' debut: As above
Best moment in rugby: Beating
England to win 1990 Grand Slam
Worst moments in rugby:
Missing 1989 Japan tour for
operation, losing to France in
1989, London Scottish getting
relegated from English Second
Division (1988/89)
Most respected opponent:
Scotland prop David Sole – good
scrummager, great ball player,
superb captain
Serious injuries: Serious back
injury, requiring surgery
Best memory last season:
Winning Grand Slam

	apps.	pts.
Scotland B (**1988**)		
Last Season	0 caps	0
Scotland (**1989**)		
Last Season	6 caps	0
Career	9 caps	0

Most improved International player last season: Scotland lock Chris
Gray
Suggestions to improve rugby: More recognition from the Unions to the
amount of time required away from work to meet the standards required to
play international rugby
Other notable landmarks in rugby career: Scoring on first team debut for
Leicester. Promotion with London Scottish (1989/90) as English Third
Division champions. Toured New Zealand with Scotland last summer

Bursey, D.J.W.   Ireland

Full Name: David James William
Bursey
International category: Ireland
U-21
Club: Old Wesley
Position: Lock
Height: 6'4" **Weight:** 17st
Occupation: Family motor business
Born: Dublin, 2.10.68
Family: Single
Former club: Wesley College
International debut: Italy 9,
Ireland 10, 1989
Best moment in rugby: Winning
first U-21 cap in Treviso, Italy
(Sept 1989)
Worst moment in rugby:
Breaking jaw at club level
Serious injuries: Broken jaw, nose
Best memory last season: Ireland
U-21s' 13–13 draw with New
Zealand
**Most improved International
player last season:** Ireland
full-back Kenny Murphy
Suggestion to improve rugby:
New All-Ireland League
Touchlines: American football,
fishing, motor racing

	apps.	pts.
Ireland U-21 (**1989**)		
Last Season	2 caps	0

Busby, J.D.   Scotland

Full Name: James **Derek** Busby
International category: Scotland B
Club: Glasgow High/Kelvinside
Position: Flanker
Height: 6'2½" **Weight:** 15st
Occupation: Sales representative
Born: Glasgow, 1.5.66
Family: Single
Family links with rugby: Brother played for Scottish Schoolboys
Former club: Hillhead
International debut (B): Scotland 22, Ireland 22, 1989
Best moment in rugby: Scoring try on B debut
Worst moment in rugby: Returning fighting fit from Hillhead tour to Denver (aged 18) only to tear ankle ligaments in first Glasgow training session (out for eight weeks)
Most respected opponent: Former Wales fly-half Jonathan Davies
Serious injuries: Broken bone in back (1986), torn ankle ligaments

	apps.	pts.
Scotland B (**1989**)		
Last Season	2 caps	4

Best memory last season: Winning Inter-District Championship with Glasgow
Most improved International player last season: Scotland wing Tony Stanger
Other notable landmarks in rugby career: Reached final of Haig Sevens at Murrayfield with Glasgow. Played twice for Scotland Schools (1984/85) and three seasons for Scotland U-21s (captain in 1987). Won second B cap in 9-31 loss to France
Touchlines: Golf (19-handicap)

Buzza, A.J. England

Full Name: Alan Jan Buzza
International category: England B
Club: Wasps
Position: Full-back
Height: 6'2" **Weight:** 13st
Occupation: Student
Born: Beverley, 3.3.66
Family: Single
Family links with rugby: Father played for Hertfordshire
Former clubs: Redruth, Bath, Cambridge University
International debut (B): France 15, England 15, 1990
Best moment in rugby: Captaining Cambridge to 22–13 defeat of Oxford in 1989 Varsity match
Worst moment in rugby: Cornwall losing 9-13 to Durham in 1988 English County final
Most embarrassing moment: Kick from mark in B match v France which went along ground
Most respected opponent: Loughborough's Ian Harris
Serious injuries: Ankle ligaments (1990)

	apps.	pts.
England B (**1990**)		
Last Season	1 cap	0
England 1991	World Cup squad	
1995	Development squad	

Other sporting achievements: Cambridge University cricket Blue (1989). Minor Counties Cricket for Cornwall and for Minor Counties U-25s
Best memory last season: Lifting Bowring Bowl at Twickenham
Most improved International player last season: England fly-half Rob Andrew
Other notable landmarks in rugby career: Played for England Schools 18 group, Combined England Students, UAU, Cornwall, South West. England replacement for 23–0 defeat of Ireland (1990)

Callard, J.E.B.   England

Full Name: Jonathan Edward Brooks Callard
International category: England B
Club: Bath
Position: Full-back
Height: 5'10" **Weight:** 12st 7lb
Occupation: PE teacher
Born: Leicester, 1.1.66
Family: Single
Family links with rugby: Brother Nigel plays for Newport
Former clubs: Newport, St Mary's College
International debut: Spain 9, England B 31, 1989
Best moment in rugby: Bath's 48–6 defeat of Gloucester in 1990 Pilkington Cup final
Worst moment in rugby: Newport losing to Fiji after I had missed five kicks at goal
Most embarrassing moment: Bath losing to Saracens last season in English First Division and missing kicks at goal that would have reversed result

	apps.	pts.
England B (1989)		
Last Season	1 cap	4
England 1995	Development squad	

Most respected opponent: Leicester's former England fly-half Les Cusworth
Serious injuries: Torn cartilage (1989/90)
Other sporting achievements: Junior county cricket for Monmouthshire
Best memory last season: Pilkington Cup final and beating Wasps in League
Most improved International player last season: England scrum-half Richard Hill
Suggestions to improve rugby: Neutral observers in stands to guard against violent play. Reimbursement for loss of earnings
Other notable landmarks in rugby career: Represented Wales at Schools level (U-15, U-16, U-18) and went on to play for Wales U-20s, U-21s and U-23s before moving from Newport to Bath and electing to adopt English qualification. Toured Spain with England B (summer 1989) and Moscow with Crawshays
Touchlines: Golf

Carling, W.D.C.   England

Full Name: William David Charles Carling
International category: England Full
Club: Harlequins
Position: Centre
Height: 5'11" **Weight:** 14st 2lb
Occupation: Runs own business: 'Inspirational Horizons'
Born: Bradford-on-Avon, Wiltshire, 12.12.65
Family: Single
Family links with rugby: Father played for Cardiff
Former club: Durham University
International debut: France 10, England 9, 1988
Five Nations' debut: As above
Best moment in rugby: England beating Australia 28–19 in my first game as captain
Worst moment in rugby: Losing 1990 Grand Slam decider to Scotland
Most embarrassing moment: Not touching down try for Harlequins v Rosslyn Park at the Save & Prosper Middlesex Sevens
Most respected opponent: French centre Denis Charvet
Serious injuries: Fracture of leg (1989)

	apps.	pts.
England B (1987)		
Last Season	0 caps	0
England (1988)		
Last Season	7 caps	8
Career	19 caps	12
1990	Tour to Argentina	
1991	World Cup squad	
England XV 1989/90	1 app	0

Best memory last season: Manner of England's defeat of Wales
Most improved International player last season: Scotland lock Damian Cronin
Suggestions to improve rugby: General level of coaching in English club rugby must be raised. We are too stuck in our ways at present. We must learn from other countries
Notable landmark in rugby career: Turning in one of my best performances, playing for Durham against Lancashire, in front of the then Northern Division selectors Geoff Cooke and Dave Robinson
Touchlines: Painting – sketching and inks

Chalmers, C.M.   Scotland

Full Name: Craig Minto Chalmers
International category: Scotland
Full
Club: Melrose
Position: Fly-half
Height: 5'10" **Weight:** 12st 10lb
Occupation: Marketing
representative for South of Scotland
Electricity Board
Born: Galashiels, 15.10.68
Family links with rugby: Father
coaches at Melrose
International debut: Scotland 23,
Wales 7, 1989
Five Nations' debut: As above
Best moment in rugby: Winning
1990 Grand Slam by beating
England
Worst moment in rugby: Being
dropped by 1989 Lions, after
playing in first Test
Most respected opponent: NZ
Fly-half Grant Fox
Serious injuries: Torn knee
cartilage
Best memory last season: Winning
Grand Slam and Scotland's
performance against New Zealand in
second Test

	apps.	pts.
Scotland B (**1988**)		
Last Season	0 caps	0
Scotland (**1989**)		
Last Season	7 caps	33
Career	11 caps	40
Lions 1989	1 Test	6

**Most improved International
player last season:** Scotland wing Tony Stanger
Suggestions to improve rugby: None. Don't change a successful recipe
Other notable landmarks in rugby career: Youngest player ever to
represent Scotland B – scored a try and drop goal on full debut. Earned
selection to 1989 Lions tour of Australia and kicked 6 points in first Test.
Represented Scotland at U-15, U-18, U-19, U-21 and B levels
Touchlines: Golf (12-handicap)

Chilcott, G.J.   England

Full Name: Gareth James Chilcott
International category: British Lion/England Full (squad)
Club: Bath
Position: Prop
Height: 5'9" **Weight:** 16st 4lb
Occupation: MD of car hire company
Born: Bristol, 20.11.56
Family: Married
Family links with rugby: Father played
Former club: Old Redcliffians
International debut: England 3, Australia 19, 1984
Five Nations' debut: Ireland 13, England 10, 1985
Best moments in rugby: Winning first of six English Cups with Bath (1984 v Bristol). Selection for 1989 Lions
Worst moment in rugby: Being dropped for disciplinary reasons after England's 1987 defeat by Wales in Cardiff
Most embarrassing moment: Getting overtaken by a six-foot banana when England team competed in Great North Race (half-marathon)

	apps.	pts.
England B (1988)		
Last Season	0 caps	0
England (1984)		
Last Season	1 cap	0
Career	14 caps	0
Lions 1989		

Most respected opponents: Former Wales prop Graham Price and Wasps' England tight-head Jeff Probyn
Serious injuries: Broken nose, dislocated both knees
Best memory last season: Picking up Pilkington Cup after beating Gloucester 48–6 in Twickenham final
Best international comeback last season: England scrum-half Richard Hill
Suggestions to improve rugby: Look after players better. Rugby is about players and always should be
Other notable landmarks in rugby career: Representative rugby began with Somerset Colts and continued with full county team after joining Bath. Also played for South West. Along with Richard Hill, hold distinction of having

appeared in all six Bath Cup final wins. Toured Australia with 1989 Lions and was a replacement when England won 58–3 in Romania (May 1989)
Touchlines: Golf, snooker

Childs, G.C. England

Full Name: Graham Christopher Childs
International category: England Full (squad)
Club: Wasps
Position: Centre
Height: 6' **Weight:** 13st 5lb
Occupation: Advertising/marketing
Born: Fareham, Hants, 3.4.68
Family: Single
Family links with rugby: Father and brother played for Worthing
Former clubs: Worthing, Poverty Bay (NZ), Northern
International debut (B): France 15, England 15, 1990
Best moment in rugby: Making England B debut in Paris
Worst moment in rugby: North losing to London in 1989/90 English Divisional Championship
Most respected opponent: England B centre Bryan Barley
Best memory last season: Playing first game for Northern Division

	apps.
England B (**1989/90**)	Rep 1
England 1990	Tour to Argentina
1995	Development squad

Most improved International player last season: England centre Jeremy Guscott
Suggestions to improve rugby: Relax laws on amateurism
Other notable landmarks in rugby career: Played mini-rugby at Worthing. Represented South of England Schools and, later, Northumberland in English County Championship. Spent first part of last summer playing for Poverty Bay in New Zealand and then toured Argentina with England before returning home to join Wasps

Clarke, B.B.   England

Full Name: Benjamin Bevan Clarke
International category: England
B (squad)
Club: Saracens
Position: No.8
Height: 6'5" **Weight:** 17st
Occupation: Student
Born: Bishop's Stortford, 15.4.68
Family: Single
Family links with rugby: Father
played for Bishop's Stortford and is
club President
Former club: Bishop's Stortford
International debut: French
Students 4, England Students 32,
1990
Best moment in rugby: Saracens
beating Bath last season in English
First Division
Worst moment in rugby:
Damaging shoulder and missing
England XV's game against an Italy
XV (May 1990)
Most respected opponent: Bath's
England back row David Egerton
Serious injuries: Sprung shoulder
joint, torn ligaments

	apps.
England B **(1989/90)**	Rep 1
England 1995	Development squad

Best memory last season: Beating Bath at Southgate
Most improved International player last season: England scrum-half
Richard Hill
Other notable landmarks in rugby career: Represented Hertfordshire
Colts, U-21 and full teams while with Stortford. Since joining Saracens at start
of last season, have played for London Division, Public School Wanderers,
Penguins, and England Students, and been a replacement for England B
Touchlines: Golf, squash, hockey

Clement, A.   Wales

Full Name: Anthony Clement
International category: Wales Full
Club: Swansea
Positions: Fly-half, full-back
Height: 5'9" **Weight:** 13st 8lb
Occupation: Contract hire consultant
Born: Swansea, 8.2.67
Family: Married
Family links with rugby: Father played for Bonymaen. Brother played for Llanelli
Former club: Morriston Youth
International debut: Wales 46, US Eagles 0, 1987
Five Nations' debut: England 3, Wales 11, 1988
Best moment in rugby: Scoring 2 tries for Wales on debut
Worst moment in rugby: Being dropped by Wales for second time (before 1988/89 Five Nations' Championship) when playing well
Most respected opponent: Newport's former Welsh fly-half Paul Turner
Serious injuries: Hamstring strain
Ambition: To play for Wales at full-back – more of a future for me there

	apps.	pts.
Wales B (**1987**)		
Last Season	0 caps	0
Wales (**1987**)		
Last Season	5 caps	3
Career	10 caps	11
Lions 1989		

Best memory last season: Helping Wales beat Australia 16–10 in quarter-finals of Hong Kong Sevens
Most improved International player last season: Wales lock Paul Arnold
Suggestions to improve rugby: None, now that leagues have been introduced
Other notable landmarks in rugby career: After playing six games for Wales Youth (1984), joined Swansea (1985) and captained Wales U-20s. Also represented Wales U-21s, B and Barbarians. Toured South Africa with World XV (1989)
Touchlines: Soccer, cricket

Clinch, P.D.   Ireland

Full Name: Paul Daniel Clinch
International category: Ireland B
Club: Lansdowne
Position: Centre
Height: 6'3" **Weight:** 13st 12lb
Occupation: Pharmaceutical
product manager
Born: Aldershot, 25.3.61
Family: Single
Family links with rugby: Great
grandfather played for Ireland and
Lions (1890s) and was IRFU
President. Grandfather
represented Ireland and Lions
(1920s). Father played for Dublin
Univ and Wanderers
Former club: Dublin University
International debut (B):
Scotland 22, Ireland 22, 1990
Best moment in rugby: Helping
Ireland beat France in unofficial
Test (Auch, 1988)
Worst moment in rugby: Being
dropped
Most respected opponent: 'Doc
Ivers' – great speed and eye for a gap

	apps.	pts.
Ireland B (**1989**)		
Last Season	1 cap	0

Serious injuries: Broken leg, ribs and wrists. Torn ankle and knee ligaments
Other sporting achievements: Cricket for Dublin University
Best memory last season: Lansdowne qualifying for All-Ireland Premier
Divison
Most improved International player last season: Ireland flanker Pat
O'Hara
Suggestions to improve rugby: Go professional
Other notable landmarks in rugby career: Represented and captained
Combined Irish Universities (1982–85). Played for (since 1985) and captained
(1989) Leinster. Captained Ireland U-25s (1986). Played four unofficial
Internationals for Ireland
Touchlines: Fourth generation of Clinch family to gain 'colours' for Trinity
College, Dublin

Clohessy, P.   Ireland

Full Name: Peter Clohessy
International category: Ireland B
Club: Young Munster
Position: Tight-head prop
Height: 5'10" **Weight:** 15st
Occupation: MD suspended
ceiling company
Born: Limerick, 22.3.66
Family: Married
Family links with rugby:
Grandfather captained Garryowen
to 1931/32 Cup victory
Former club: Garryowen
International debut: Ireland
U-25 21, Italy 16, 1988
Best moment in rugby: Playing
for Munster v 1989 All Blacks
(lost 3-21)
Worst moment in rugby: Being
sent off in U-20 Cup final v
Shannon – hopefully for last time
Most embarrassing moment:
Marking a ball I caught on my
10-yard line in 1987 League final
against Shannon
Serious injuries: Slipped disc –
out for most of 1987 season

	apps.	pts.
Ireland B (1989)		
Last Season	1 cap	0

Best memory last season: Playing against New Zealand
Most improved International player last season: Ireland full-back Kenny
Murphy
Suggestions to improve rugby: Banish 90-degree scrum wheel law
Other notable landmarks in rugby career: Playing for Munster aged 21.
Helping Ireland draw 22–22 with Scotland in B International at Murrayfield
last season

Clough, F.J.   England

Full Name: Francis John Clough
International category: England B
Club: Wasps
Position: Centre
Height: 6'1" **Weight:** 14st 7lb
Occupation: University research scientist
Born: Wigan, 1.11.62
Family: Single
Former clubs: Orrell, Cambridge University
International debut: England 25, Ireland 20, 1986
Five Nations' debut: As above
Best moment in rugby: Cambridge beating Oxford 15–10 in 1987 Varsity match
Worst moment in rugby: Missing England's 1990 summer tour to Argentina after breaking leg playing Sevens
Most embarrassing moment: Holder of world knock-on record for England v Japan in 1987 World Cup
Most respected opponent: Peter Williams
Serious injuries: Broken leg (1990), ruptured Achilles tendon, recurrent dislocated shoulder

	apps.	pts.
England B (1985)		
Last Season	2 caps	8
England (1986)		
Last Season	0 caps	0
Career	4 caps	0
1991	World Cup squad	
England XV 1989/90	1 app	0

Other sporting achievements: England Schools Rugby League U-16s and U-19s
Best memory last season: London beating North at Otley in English Divisional Championship
Most improved International player last season: England centre Will Carling
Other notable landmarks in rugby career: Won four Cambridge Blues (1984,85,86,87), captaining team in 1987. Played for England B three times, twice last season. Came on as replacement in England's 33–15 defeat of Italy last May. Picked for England's 1991 World Cup squad

Collings, P.   England

Full Name: Paul Collings
International category: England B (squad)
Club: Bristol
Position: Flanker
Height: 6'1" **Weight:** 14st
Occupation: Pensions analyst
Born: Bristol, 2.1.67
Family: Single
Family links with rugby: Father played and was chairman of Old Redcliffians
Best moment in rugby: Seeing Bristol's Andy Blackmore scoring from our 22 v Cardiff at Arms Park
Worst moment in rugby: Hearing Andy Blackmore go on about it
Most embarrassing moment: Dropping certain try-scoring pass v Gloucester
Most respected opponent: England No.8 Dean Richards
Serious injuries sustained: Cauliflower ear and nose

England B (1989/90)	apps.
	Rep 1

Other sporting achievements: Soccer trials for Bristol Rovers and Bristol City
Best memory last season: Winning Dubai Exiles Sevens with Cambrian Thistles
Most improved International player last season: England's other No.8 Mike Teague
Other notable landmarks in rugby career: Selected as replacement for England B v Fiji (Nov 1989). 1988 season when Bristol reached Twickenham finals of John Player Cup and Middlesex Sevens
Touchlines: Five-a-side football

Collins, P.C.   Ireland

Full Name: Paul Cornelius Collins
International category: Ireland
Full
Club: London Irish
Position: Flanker
Height: 6'3" **Weight:** 15st 7lb
Occupation: Chartered
accountant
Born: Cork, 7.12.59
Family: Married with a son
Former clubs: University College
Cork, Highfield, Lansdowne
International debut: Ireland 46,
Canada 19, 1987 World Cup
Five Nations' debut: Ireland 10,
Scotland 13, 1990
Best moment in rugby:
Captaining Munster against 1989
All Blacks
Most respected opponent:
Ireland flanker Phil Matthews
Other sporting achievements:
Inter-County Gaelic football for
Cork
Best memory last season:
Munster v New Zealand
**Most improved International
player last season:** Ireland
full-back Kenny Murphy

	apps.	pts.
Ireland B (1989)		
Last Season	1 cap	0
Ireland (1987)		
Last Season	1 cap	0
Career	2 caps	0

Suggestions to improve rugby: Reimburse players for time lost to rugby.
Credit employers for their understanding with publicity in programmes or
a couple of tickets
Other notable landmarks in rugby career: Capped three times by Irish
Schools (v Australia, England and Scotland). Played five years for Irish
Universities and once for Ireland B, in 22–22 draw with Scotland last
season. Five times a replacement for the Full team
Touchlines: Golf, squash

48

Collins, R.G.   Wales

Full Name: Richard (**Richie**)
Graham Collins
International category: Wales
Full
Club: Cardiff
Position: Flanker
Height: 6'1" **Weight:** 14st 4lb
Occupation: Policeman
Born: Cardiff, 2.3.62
Family: Single
Former clubs: Pontypridd,
Newport, South Wales Police
International debut: Wales 19,
England 12, 1987
Five Nations' debut: As above
Best moment in rugby: Wales
winning 1988 Triple Crown in
Ireland
Worst moments in rugby:
Wales' defeats last season against
England and Ireland
Most respected opponent:
Scotland flanker Finlay Calder
Other sporting achievements:
Welsh basketball International
Best memory last season:
Cardiff beating Llanelli in Welsh
Cup

	apps.	pts.
Wales B (1986)		
Last Season	0 caps	0
Wales (1987)		
Last Season	3 caps	0
Career	14 caps	0

Most improved International player last season: England fly-half Rob
Andrew
Other notable landmarks in rugby career: Played initially to sharpen
reflexes and bulk-up for basketball. Spent season playing Wellington club
rugby in New Zealand before returning to join Pontypridd, and Newport, with
whom played in 1986 Welsh Cup final. Made Wales debut as replacement at
Cardiff in 1987

Full Name: Ian Corcoran
International category: Scotland B
Club: Gala
Position: Hooker
Height: 5'11" **Weight:** 13st 5lb
Occupation: Carpet fitter/upholsterer
Born: Edinburgh, 11.5.63
Family: Single
Family links with rugby: Two brothers play for Gala
International debut (B): France 31, Scotland 9, 1990
Best moment in rugby: Scoring first Scotland try of 1989 tour of Japan
Worst moment in rugby: Being dropped from senior Scotland squad (replacement v Fiji and Romania) after France B game
Most respected opponent: Former Gala and Scotland International Kenny Lawrie
Serious injuries: Damaged knee ligaments required operation (missed 1988 season)

	apps.	pts.
Scotland B (1990)		
Last Season	1 cap	0

Other sporting achievements: Cricket for Gala
Best memory last season: Gala beating centenary club Heriot's FP
Most improved International player last season: Scotland tight-head prop Paul Burnell
Suggestions to improve rugby: Players remunerated for working time lost to game
Other notable landmarks in rugby career: Promoted to Scotland B last season, having previously earned 1 cap for Scotland U-21s
Touchlines: Squash, badminton

Couper, J.A.   Scotland

Full Name: John Alan Couper
International category: Scotland
U-21
Club: Glasgow High/Kelvinside
Position: Loose-head prop
Height: 5'10" **Weight:** 15st 2lb
Occupation: Bank officer
Born: Glasgow, 21.10.69
Family: Single
International debut (U-21):
Scotland 10, Wales 24, 1990
Best moment in rugby: Scoring
2 tries for Scotland U-21s v
Combined Services (1989)
Worst moment in rugby:
Scotland U-21s' 1990 defeat by
Wales at Ayr
Most respected opponent:
Scotland loose-head prop and
captain David Sole
Serious injuries: Pulled muscles
in back
Other sporting achievements:
Cricket for Scotland U-15s and
U-16s

	apps.	pts.
Scotland U-21 (1990)		
Last Season	1 cap	0

Best memory last season: GHK
beating Boroughmuir in Scottish First Division
Most improved International player last season: Scotland lock Chris Gray
Other notable landmarks in rugby career: Represented Scotland U-18s
and U-19s against Italy. Unused replacement for Scottish Students against
Welsh and English counterparts

Cronin, D.F.   Scotland

Full Name: Damian Francis
Cronin
International category: Scotland
Full
Club: Bath
Position: Lock
Height: 6'6" **Weight:** 17st
Occupation: Sales executive
Born: Wegberg, West Germany,
17.4.63
Family: Single
Family links with rugby: Father
is president of Ilford Wanderers
Former club: Ilford Wanderers
International debut: Ireland 22,
Scotland 18, 1988
Five Nations' debut: As above
Best moment in rugby: Winning
1990 Grand Slam with Scotland
Worst moments in rugby:
Snapping knee ligaments. Bath's
3-4 defeat by Moseley in
quarter-finals of 1987/88 John
Player Cup
Most respected opponent:
Wales lock Robert Norster
Serious injuries: Ligament
damage in both knees. Staple put
in right knee

	apps.	pts.
Scotland B (1987)		
Last Season	0 caps	0
Scotland (1988)		
Last Season	8 caps	4
Career	17 caps	8

Other sporting achievements: Drove in celebrity race round Brands Hatch
Best memory last season: Scotland's Grand Slam
Suggestions to improve rugby: Look seriously at commercialisation of rugby
in support of players
Other notable landmarks in rugby career: Returned to rugby after
fracturing base of spine aged 22. Built reputation in Scotland with
performances for Anglo-Scots, having become eligible thanks to Lothian-based
grandparents. Helped 1987 Anglo's beat French at Cupar and was included
in Scottish XV which achieved a similar feat. Toured with Scotland to
Zimbabwe (1988) and captained team v Mashonaland District

Crossan, K.D.   Ireland

Full Name: Keith Derek Crossan
International category: Ireland
Full
Club: Instonians
Position: Wing
Height: 5'7" **Weight:** 11st 4lb
Occupation: Banker
Born: Belfast, 29.12.59
Family: Married with two children
Family links with rugby: Uncle
captained Ireland
International debut: Ireland 21,
Scotland 12, 1982
Five Nations' debut: As above
Best moment in rugby: Being
selected to tour South Africa with
Ireland (1981)
Worst moment in rugby:
Withdrawing from Ireland's
match against Australia (1984)
because of illness
Most embarrassing moment:
Being sick on pitch (too much
alcohol previous night) after
scoring 2 tries for Instonians
against Trinity

Ireland (1982)	apps.	pts.
Last Season	5 caps	0
Career	33 caps	44

Most respected opponent:
Former England wing Mike Harrison – always scores against me, either for
Yorkshire or England
Serious injuries: Broke jaw in two places (1985, out for three months)
Best memory last season: Tackling Rory Underwood into touch during
Ireland's match against England (try subsequently given)
Most improved International player last season: Ireland full-back Kenny
Murphy
Suggestions to improve rugby: Change playing season so don't have to play
in depths of winter. Standardise refereeing interpretations
Other notable landmarks in rugby career: Within one game of equalling
Trevor Ringland's Irish record number of caps for wing (34), and within one
Ulster appearance of equalling Willie Anderson's all-time record of 71 caps.
Ever-present for Ireland in 1987 World Cup. Toured with Ireland to North

America (1989). Total of 11 Irish tries is third on all-time list behind George Stevenson and Brendan Mullin
Touchlines: Try to treat rugby as a 'sport' but this is becoming more difficult as more pressure is put on winning at all costs

---

Cunningham, V.J.G.   Ireland

Full Name: Vincent John Gerald Cunningham
International category: Ireland U-25
Club: St Mary's College
Position: Centre
Height: 5'11½" **Weight:** 13st 2lb
Occupation: Accountancy student
Born: Dublin, 14.3.67
Family: Single
Family links with rugby: Father played for St Mary's
International debut: Ireland 10, England 21, 1988
Best moment in rugby: Winning first cap in Millennium match
Worst moment in rugby: Breaking hand in training last season to miss Ireland's tour to North America
Most respected opponent: French centre Philippe Sella
Serious injuries: Broken hand
Other sporting achievements: Irish schoolboy cricket international
Best memory last season: Coming on as replacement for Leinster against New Zealand

	apps.	pts.
Ireland U-25 (**1990**)		
Last Season	1 cap	4
Ireland (**1988**)		
Last Season	0 caps	0
Career	2 caps	2

Most improved International player last season: Ireland full-back Kenny Murphy
Suggestions to improve rugby: Broken time payments
Other notable landmarks in rugby career: Beating France on Irish tour two seasons ago. Replacement four times for Ireland, in addition to 2 caps

against England and Italy. Scored Ireland U-25s try in 12–10 defeat of US Eagles in Limerick last season
Touchlines: Enjoy horse racing at Leopardstown and Phoenix Park

Cusani, D.A.   England

Full Name: David Anthony Cusani
International category: England (XV)
Club: Orrell
Positions: Lock, No.8
Height: 6'7" **Weight:** 17st 7lb
Occupation: Travel agent
Born: Wigan, Lancs, 16.7.59
Family: Married with two sons
Family links with rugby: Brother Charles plays for Orrell. Uncle played for Lancashire
Former clubs: Wigan, Liverpool St Helens
International debut: Ireland 17, England 0, 1987
Five Nations' debut: As above
Best moment in rugby: Winning sole England cap
Worst moment in rugby: Final whistle of debut game – I knew I was for chop
Most respected opponent: Former England lock Steve Bainbridge
Serious injuries: Knee cartilage – sidelined for two years
Best memory last season: Helping Lancashire beat Middlesex in County Championship final
Most improved International player last season: England lock Paul Ackford
Suggestions to improve rugby: Broken time payments for players

	apps.	pts.
England B (1982)		
Last Season	0 caps	0
England (1987)		
Last Season	0 caps	0
Career	1 cap	0
England XV 1989/90	1 app	0

55

Other notable landmarks in rugby career: Represented Lancashire Colts before touring Italy with England U-23s in 1982. England B debut v Ireland in Belfast ((1983). Toured South Africa with England (1984). Earned surprise recall last season as No.8 in England XV which beat Italy 33–15
Touchlines: Organising rugby tours through agency

Danaher, P.P.A.   Ireland

Full Name: Philip Paul Anthony Danaher
International category: Ireland Full
Club: Garryowen
Position: Full-back
Height: 5'11" **Weight:** 13st 10lb
Occupation: Insurance consultant
Born: Limerick, 5.10.65
Family: Single
Former clubs: Abbeyfeale, Lansdowne
International debut: Ireland 22, Scotland 18, 1988
Five Nations' debut: As above
Best moment in rugby: Winning Schools medal
Worst moment in rugby: Being dropped second time round after France 1990
Most embarrassing moment: Touching ball down behind line and conceding 5-yard scrum against Wales (ref was wrong!)
Most respected opponent: French full-back Serge Blanco – naturally brilliant

	apps.	pts.
Ireland (1988)		
Last Season	2 caps	0
Career	8 caps	6

Serious injuries: Broken both ankles, serious hamstring injuries
Other sporting achievements: Badminton at national level while at school. Played Gaelic Football at county level
Best memory last season: Getting into First Division of new Irish National League with Garryowen

Most improved International player last season: England centre Will Carling

Suggestions to improve rugby: Improve coaching of schools and age-group levels

Other notable landmarks in rugby career: Joining Lansdowne and being coached properly for first time. Toured with Ireland to France and North America in 1989

Davies, J.D.   Wales

Full Name: John David Davies
International category: Wales (World Cup squad)
Club: Neath
Position: Tight-head prop
Height: 5'11" **Weight:** 16st
Occupation: Farmer
Born: Carmarthen, 1.2.69
Family: Single
Family links with rugby: Cousin plays for Cwmgwrach
Former club: Cwmgwrach
International debut (U-21): Wales 26, Scotland 18, 1989
Best moment in rugby: Playing for Neath v Llanelli at the Gnoll (1989/90)
Worst moment in rugby: Not being selected for Wales U-19 tour of New Zealand
Most respected opponent: Wales prop Brian Williams (in training)
Best memory last season: Watching Neath play All Blacks
Most improved International player last season: New Zealand prop Steve McDowell

Wales 1991   World Cup Squad

Suggestions to improve rugby: Keep game amateur but look after players better

Other notable landmarks in rugby career: Played for Wales Youth (1987–89) before breaking into Wales U-21 team (1988/89)

Touchlines: Hunting, shooting

Davies, N.G.   Wales

Full Name: Nigel Gareth Davies
International category: Wales
(World Cup squad)
Club: Llanelli
Positions: Centre, wing
Height: 6' **Weight:** 13st 7lb
Occupation: Senior quality
engineer
Born: Llanelli, 29.3.65
Family: Married
Family links with rugby: Father
played for Trimsaran
Former club: Trimsaran
International debut: New Zealand
54, Wales 9, 1988
Five Nations' debut: Scotland 23,
Wales 7, 1989
Best moment in rugby: Scoring
2nd of 2 tries for Wales in 24–6
win over Western Samoa (1988)
Worst moment in rugby: Being
dropped after Samoan game
Most respected opponent:
England wing Simon Halliday – so
hard to mark
Other sporting achievements:
County tennis player (member of
Llanelli LTC)

	apps.	pts.
Wales B (**1986**)		
Last Season	0 caps	0
Wales (**1988**)		
Last Season	0 caps	0
Career	4 caps	8

Best memories last season: Captaining Llanelli against Swansea and Cardiff
Most improved International player last season: Scotland lock Damian
Cronin
Suggestions to improve rugby: Broken time payments. More consideration
should be given to players' families
Other notable landmarks in rugby career: Graduated from Trimsaran
Youth to Wales Youth. Toured Italy with Wales B (1986/87)
Touchlines: Reading, music, motocross

Davies, P.T.   Wales

Full Name: Phillip Thomas Davies
International category: Wales Full
Club: Llanelli
Positions: Lock, flanker, prop,
No.8
Height: 6'3" **Weight:** 18st
Occupation: Sales representative
Born: Seven Sisters, 19.10.63
Family: Married with two
daughters
Family links with rugby: Wife
Caroline is Jonathan Davies' sister
Former clubs: Seven Sisters,
South Wales Police
International debut: Wales 24,
England 15, 1985
Five Nations' debut: As above
Best moment in rugby:
Captaining Llanelli to 1988
Schweppes Cup final win v Neath
Worst moment in rugby: Wales'
1990 whitewash
Most embarrassing moment:
Having ball knocked from grasp by
Kenfig Hill centre while touching
down in Cup last season
Most respected opponent:
French back row Laurent Rodriguez
Serious injuries: Broken
cheekbone

	apps.	pts.
Wales B (1987)		
Last Season	0 caps	0
Wales (1985)		
Last Season	4 caps	4
Career	25 caps	16

Other sporting achievements: Swam for West Wales Schools
Best memory last season: Llanelli beating Neath 27–21 at Stradey Park
Most improved International player last season: Scotland lock Chris Gray
Suggestions to improve rugby: Remuneration for time spent away from
work for rugby
Other notable landmarks in rugby career: First played for Wales at
16-group. Former policeman who broke into full Welsh squad in 1984. Had
jaw broken by punch in fiery 1987 clash with England. Dropped after playing
in World Cup and became Wales B captain. Now back in Welsh team and
have retained place throughout traumas of past two seasons. Also represented
Crawshays and Barbarians

Davies, S.L.   England

Full Name: Stewart Lyn Davies
International category: England
U-21
Club: Rosslyn Park
Position: Hooker
Height: 5'11" **Weight:** 14st 7lb
Occupation: Sales consultant
Born: Farnborough, Hants, 5.1.69
Family: Single
Family links with rugby: Father
played
Former clubs: Farnborough,
Camberley
International debut: Netherlands
3, England U-21 24, 1990
Best moment in rugby: Making
debut in English First Division for
Rosslyn Park v Wasps last season
Worst moment in rugby: Rosslyn
Park losing heavily in League
match to Gloucester
Most respected opponent:
England development squad
member Troy Thacker (Leicester
hooker) – after playing him it felt
like every bone in my body was
broken

	apps.	pts.
England U-21 (**1990**)		
Last Season	2 caps	0

Serious injuries: Dislocated knee cap
Other sporting achievements: Swimming, cricket and football for school
Best memory last season: Making England debut in Netherlands
Most improved International player last season: England flanker Peter
Winterbottom
Suggestions to improve rugby: Concentrating on playing more expansive
game, whilst improving rucking and ball retention skills
Notable landmark in rugby career: Joining Park from Camberley (1987)

Davies, W.S.M.   Wales

Full Name: William **Simon** Morgan Davies
International category: Wales (World Cup squad)
Club: Llanelli
Position: Centre
Height: 5'11" **Weight:** 14st 7lb
Occupation: Farmer
Born: Carmarthen, 19.1.67
Family: Single
International debut (B): Wales 12, France 18, 1988
Best moment in rugby: Winning 1988 Welsh Cup final with Llanelli
Worst moment in rugby: Being left out of Llanelli team to play Neath in 1989 Cup final
Most respected opponent: England centre/wing Simon Halliday
Other sporting achievements: Beat European champion Colin Jackson into second place in U-16 100m hurdles in Welsh AAA Championships
Best memory last season: Representing Barbarians v East Midlands

	apps.	pts.
Wales B (1988)		
Last Season	0 caps	0
Wales 1991	World Cup squad	

Most improved International player last season: Wales scrum-half Robert Jones
Suggestions to improve rugby: Players and employers should be compensated for time lost to work due to rugby
Other notable landmarks in rugby career: Played for Wales Schools (once), Youth (once), U-21s (twice) and B (once)
Touchlines: Shooting, golf

Davis, E.   England

Full Name: Everton Davis
International category: England B
Club: Harlequins
Position: Wing
Height: 5'9" **Weight:** 11st 10lb
Occupation: Senior computer
analyst
Born: Leicester, 30.5.60
Family: Single
Former clubs: Leicester,
Twickenham
International debut: England B
12, Fiji 20, 1989
Best moment in rugby: Winning
1988 John Player Cup final with
Harlequins and then returning to
Twickenham seven days later to
win Middlesex Sevens
Worst moment in rugby:
Dropping first pass on England B
debut
Most respected opponent:
England B wing Tony Underwood
– small and elusive like myself
Serious injuries: Groin injury
(required operation and sidelined
me for half of 1988/89 season)

	apps.	pts.
England B (1989)		
Last Season	2 caps	0
England 1995	Development squad	

Other sporting achievements: England Schools sprinter
Best memory last season: Winning English Divisional Championship with
London
Most improved International player last season: England centre Jeremy
Guscott
Other notable landmarks in rugby career: Toured Spain with England B
(summer 1989) and also represented them in 18–10 win over Soviet Union
at Northampton (Dec 1989)

Davis, J.   England

Full Name: Julian Davis
International category: England U-21
Club: Bristol
Position: Scrum-half
Height: 5'7" **Weight:** 11st 7lb
Occupation: Draughtsman
Born: Lydney, 1.10.68
Family: Single
Family links with rugby: Father is a referee
Former club: Lydney
International debut: Netherlands 3, England U-21 24, 1990
Best moment in rugby: Playing Dutch at Hilversum
Worst moment in rugby: Tearing knee ligaments playing at school
Most respected opponent: Former Wales scrum-half David Bishop
Serious injuries: Torn knee ligaments
Other sporting achievements: Cricket for Lydney
Best memory last season: Earning a regular place in Bristol first team

	apps.	pts.
England U-21 (**1990**)		
Last Season	1 cap	0
England 1995	Development squad	

Most improved International player last season: England centre Will Carling
Suggestions to improve rugby: Improve training facilities for players
Other notable landmarks in rugby career: Helped Lydney beat Berry Hill in 1987 Gloucestershire Cup final. Member of England Colts squad and bench reserve for England U-21s v Romania (1989) and French Armed Forces (1990)
Touchlines: Squash

De Glanville, P.R.   England

Full Name: Philip Ranulph de Glanville
International category: England U-21
Club: Bath
Position: Centre
Height: 6' **Weight:** 13st
Occupation: Pol/econ student
Born: Loughborough, 1.10.68
Family: Single
Family links with rugby: Father played for Loughborough and Rosslyn Park. Now MD of Rhino scrum machines
International debut (U-21): Romania 13, England 54, 1989
Best moment in rugby: Replacement for England B in 44–0 defeat of Italy (1989)
Worst moment in rugby: English Students losing 16–6 to Welsh in Cardiff (1989)
Most embarrassing moment: Losing match for Durham Univ on Canadian tour when dropped a goalbound penalty effort beneath posts, and Univ of Victoria scored try from resultant scrum
Most respected opponent: England B centre Fran Clough

	apps.	pts.
England U-21 (**1989**)		
Last Season	2 caps	8
England B (**1989**)		
Last Season	0 caps	0
England 1991	World Cup squad	
1995	Development squad	

Serious injuries: Broken arm, dislocated collarbone
Best memory last season: England Students beating French 32–4 away
Most improved International players last season: England half-backs Richard Hill and Rob Andrew
Suggestions to improve rugby: Retain County Championship as a meaningful entity
Other notable landmarks in rugby career: Toured Australia with Bath last summer. Scored 2 tries v Romania on U-21 debut
Touchlines: Windsurfing

De Maid, M.W.   Wales

Full Name: Matthew William de
Maid
International category: Wales
U-21 (squad)
Club: Cardiff
Position: Scrum-half
Height: 5'8" **Weight:** 12st
Occupation: Student
Born: Cardiff, 20.11.69
Family: Single
Family links with rugby: Second
uncle, Don Hayward, played for
Wales and Lions
Best moment in rugby: Making
debut for Welsh Schools in 9-6
defeat of French (1988)
Worst moment in rugby: Being
dropped by Welsh Schools
Best memory last season:
Making Cardiff first team debut
against Pontypool
**Most improved International
players last season:** Wales wing
Arthur Emyr and England centre
Will Carling

	apps.
Wales U-21 (1989/90)	Rep 1

Other notable landmarks in rugby career: Represented Welsh Schools
(1988) and played for Wales U-21s against Combined Services last season.
Selected as bench reserve for International against Scotland at Ayr (April
1990)
Touchlines: Studying law

Delaney, L.   Wales

Full Name: Laurance Delaney
International category: Wales Full
Club: Llanelli
Position: Prop
Height: 5'11" **Weight:** 16st 7lb
Occupation: Welder
Born: Llanelli, 8.5.56
Family: Married with son and daughter
Former club: New Dock Stars
International debut: Wales 13, Ireland 19, 1989
Five Nations' debut: As above
Best moment in rugby: Winning first cap
Worst moment in rugby: Being dropped by Wales after 6-34 defeat by England (1990)
Most respected opponent: Former Wales prop Ian Stephens
Serious injuries: Muscular spasms in back (1986)
Best memory last season: Playing 450th game for Llanelli v London Welsh on Boxing Day
Most improved International player last season: Wales hooker Kevin Phillips

	apps.	pts.
Wales B (1985)		
Last Season	1 cap	0
Wales (1989)		
Last Season	1 cap	0
Career	4 caps	0

Suggestions to improve rugby: Broken time payments for players
Other notable landmarks in rugby career: Capped by Wales Youth (1974/75) and twice by Wales B (1983). Joined Llanelli in 1977. Finally won full cap in 1989, following knee-ligament injury to then incumbent David Young
Touchlines: Sea fishing (best: 31lb tope)

Dinneen, L.M.   Ireland

Full Name: Leonard Michael Dinneen
International category: Ireland U-25 (squad)
Club: Constitution
Position: Prop
Height: 6'2" **Weight:** 16st 7lb
Occupation: Building Society employee
Born: London, 14.12.66
Family: Single
Family links with rugby: Father played for London Irish, Old Crescent and Munster. Three brothers played for Bective Rangers and Old Crescent
Former club: Wanderers
International debut (U-18s): Scotland 13, Ireland 26, 1984
Best moment in rugby: Winning 1988/89 Munster Cup with Constitution
Worst moment in rugby: Losing 1985 Munster Schools Cup final with Crescent

	apps.
Ireland U-25 (**1989/90**)	Rep 1

Most respected opponent: Former Ireland prop Phil Orr
Best memory last season: Being selected for Ireland U-25 bench v US Eagles, 1990
Suggestions to improve rugby: Worldwide uniformity in refereeing decisions, rules and interpretation
Other notable landmarks in rugby career: Captained Irish Schools v New Zealand at Cork in 1985 (lost 3-17). Joined Constitution in 1987
Touchlines: Golf (18-handicap)

Dods, M.   Scotland

Full Name: Michael Dods
International category: Scotland
U-21 (squad)
Club: Gala
Positions: Full-back, wing
Height: 5'11" **Weight:** 11st
Occupation: Senior storekeeper
Born: Galashiels, 30.12.68
Family: Single
Family links with rugby: Brother
Peter plays for Gala, Scotland and
British Lions
Former club: Gala Wanderers
International debut (U-21):
Scotland 21, Combined Services 4,
1990 (non-cap)
Best moment in rugby: Being
picked for Scotland U-21s
Worst moment in rugby:
Breaking collarbone before final
Scotland U-19s' trial for
International against Italy

	apps.
Scotland U-21 (**1989/90**)	Rep 1

Most embarrassing moment:
Missing penalty goal from in front
of posts against Hawick in Border
League
Most respected opponent: Scotland wing Tony Stanger
Serious injuries sustained: Broken collarbone (1988), nose (1990)
Best memory last season: Beating Heriot's in final game of season
Most improved International player last season: Scotland prop Paul
Burnell
Suggestions to improve rugby: Let players receive money from advertising
etc. and better compensation when away from work on tour
Other notable landmarks in rugby career: Represented Scottish Schools
at 15 and 18 age-groups. Played for Gala 1st XV when only 17. Kicked
conversion in U-21 match against Combined Services
Touchlines: Golf, shooting. Restoring an old house

Dods, P.W.   Scotland

Full Name: Peter William Dods
International category: Scotland
Full (squad)
Club: Gala
Positions: Full-back, centre
Height: 5'9" **Weight:** 12st
Occupation: Joiner
Born: Galashiels, 6.1.58
Family: Married with two
daughters
Family links with rugby: Brother
Michael plays for Gala
Former club: Gala Wanderers
International debut: Scotland 13,
Ireland 15, 1983
Five Nations' debut: As above
Best moment in rugby:
Scotland's 1984 Grand Slam
Most respected opponent:
French full-back Serge Blanco
Serious injuries: Broken bones in
back, cheekbone
Best memory last season: Being
part of Scotland's Grand Slam
squad
**Most improved International
player last season:** England
fly-half Rob Andrew
Other notable landmarks in

	apps.	pts.
Scotland B (1979)		
Last Season	0 caps	0
Scotland (1983)		
Last Season	0 caps	0
Career	19 caps	186
Lions 1989		

rugby career: Scotland's 1984 Grand Slam full-back. After five years in
International wilderness, returned in 1989 when Gavin Hastings was
injured and scored 36 points in Five Nations to earn place on Lions tour.
Scored in every game played for Scotland and has represented them in
France, New Zealand, Romania, Australia, United States and Spain. Once
scored 43 points in a game (v Alberta)

Doggart, G.   England

Full Name: George Doggart
International category: England B
Club: Aspatria
Position: Scrum-half
Height: 5'10" **Weight:** 12st
Occupation: Electrician
Born: Workington, 22.5.64
Family: Single
Former clubs: British Steel,
Wigton, Sale
International debut: England B 9,
Australia 37, 1988
Best moment in rugby: Coming
on as replacement for England B v
touring Wallabies
Worst moment in rugby:
Breaking collarbone playing in
America (1988)
Most embarrassing moment:
Aspatria's 7-39 Pilkington Cup
defeat by Wasps (1988/89)
Most respected opponent:
Former England scrum-half Nigel
Melville
Serious injuries sustained:
Broken leg, collarbone

	apps.	pts.
England B (1989)		
Last Season	1 cap	4

Other sporting achievements: County football, basketball
Best memory last season: Captaining Aspatria to Cumbria Cup
Most improved International player last season: England fly-half Rob
Andrew
Suggestions to improve rugby: Allow wheeling scrums only if ball is taken
against head
Other notable landmarks in rugby career: Captained England Colts
(1982/83). Three caps for North of England, thirty caps for Cumbria

Dooley, W.A.   England

Full Name: Wade Anthony Dooley
International category: England
Full
Club: Preston Grasshoppers
Position: Lock
Height: 6'8" **Weight:** 17st 9lb
Occupation: Police constable
Born: Warrington, 2.10.57
Family: Married with one daughter
Family links with rugby: Father
played rugby league. Brother also
plays for Grasshoppers
Former club: Fylde
International debut: England 22,
Romania 15, 1985
Five Nations' debut: England 9,
France 9, 1985
Best moment in rugby: British
Lions series win in Australia (1989)
Worst moment in rugby:
England losing Grand Slam match
to Scotland (1990)
Most embarrassing moment:
Being banned for one match for
part in violent Wales v England
match (1987)
Most respected opponent:
England lock Paul Ackford
Serious injuries: Torn medial
ligament (right knee)

England (1985)	apps.	pts.
Last Season	8 caps	0
Career	36 caps	8
1990	Tour to Argentina	
1991	World Cup squad	
Lions 1986		
1989	2 Tests	0

Other sporting achievements: Blackpool police division volleyball
champions
Best memory last season: Lions tour
Most improved International player last season: Paul Ackford
Suggestions to improve rugby: Trust funds for International players. Relax
regulations on players earning money from promoting goods, sponsors for
players etc.
Touchlines: All types of music except jazz. Watching old black and white
movies. Fell walking with pet Airedale dog. Eating out. Passion for gardening

Dow, J.L.   Scotland

Full Name: John Lachlan Dow
International category: Scotland U-21 (squad)
Club: Gordonians
Position: Hooker
Height: 5'9" **Weight:** 13st 12lb
Occupation: Electrician
Born: Aberdeen, 8.9.68
Family: Single
Family links with rugby: John (father, MBE) played senior rugby (1947–65), referee (Scottish First Division), International touch judge (Scotland v New Zealand, 1969 and 1972), past president of Gordonians
Best moment in rugby: Scoring winning try in third/fourth play-off of Universities European Cup, Clermont Ferrand (May 1989)
Worst moment in rugby: North and Midlands U-21 losing to Edinburgh (1990)

	apps.
Scotland U-21 **(1989/90)**	Rep 1

Most embarrassing moment: Every time I lose a strike against the head
Most respected opponent: Fellow Scotland U-21 squad member Gordon Peterson – hard and fast
Best memory last season: Selection for U-21 squad
Most improved International player last season: England hooker Brian Moore
Suggestions to improve rugby: Tighter control by referees in order to stamp out violence
Other notable landmarks in rugby career: North and Midlands U-21 (1986–90)
Touchlines: Basketball, skiing, cricket, hill walking

Duncan, M.D.F.   Scotland

Full Name: Matthew Dominic
Fletcher Duncan
International category: Scotland
(Japan tour)
Club: West of Scotland
Position: Wing
Height: 5'10½" **Weight:** 14st
Occupation: Local government
officer
Born: Glasgow, 29.8.59
Family: Married with child
Family links with rugby:
Grandfather played amateur rugby
league for Hunslet
International debut: Scotland 18,
France 17, 1986
Five Nations' debut: As above
Best moment in rugby: Winning
first full cap
Worst moment in rugby:
Scotland losing 12–21 to England
(1987)
Most respected opponent:
Scotland wing Iwan Tukalo
Serious injuries: Ankle and
shoulder operations
Other sporting achievements:
Scottish U-16 300m champion
(still hold record). Swam for
Glasgow Schools

	apps.	pts.
Scotland B (**1985**)		
Last Season	0 caps	0
Scotland (**1986**)		
Last Season	0 caps	0
Career	18 caps	28

Best memory last season: Watching Scotland win Grand Slam
Most improved International players last season: Scotland duo Paul
Burnell and Tony Stanger
Suggestions to improve rugby: Relax laws to allow players to earn money
away from game (dinners, endorsing products etc.)
Other notable landmarks in rugby career: Started playing aged 16. Injured
between 1979–84. Made Scotland B debut in 1985/86 season. Toured Japan
with Scotland in summer 1989
Touchlines: Golf

Dunlea, F.J.   Ireland

Full name: Fergus John Dunlea
International category: Ireland
(Canada tour)
Position: Full-back
Height: 5'10" **Weight:** 14st
Occupation: Dentist
Born: Dublin, 25.2.64
Family: Single
Former clubs: Trinity College,
Lansdowne
International debut: Wales 13,
Ireland 19, 1989
Five Nations' debut: As above
Best moment in rugby: Scoring
try against Scotland at Murrayfield
Most respected opponent:
Scotland full-back Peter Dods
Serious injuries: Badly concussed
for Ireland against USA, and
Leinster against All Blacks (both
1989)
Other sporting achievements:
Gaelic football for Dublin Schools
Best memory last season:
Touring North America with
Ireland
**Most improved International
players last season:** Scotland
centres Sean Lineen and Scott Hastings

Ireland (1989)	apps.	pts.
Last Season	0 caps	0
Career	3 caps	4
1989	Tour to Canada	

Suggestions to improve rugby: Impose 30-second time limit for all kicks.
Increase worth of tries
Other notable landmarks in rugby career: Represented Leinster Schools,
Irish Universities, U-21s and U-25s. Played both non-cap Internationals in
North America last summer

Dunn, K.A.   England

Full Name: Kevin Anthony Dunn
International category: England B
Club: Gloucester
Position: Hooker
Height: 5'9" **Weight:** 13st 10lb
Occupation: Bricklayer
Born: Gloucester, 5.6.65
Family: Married with daughter
Family links with rugby: Father
played for Gloucester Spartans
Former clubs: Gloucester
Spartans, Lydney, Warathas (Aus)
International debut: England B 9,
Australia 37, 1988
Best moment in rugby: Being
selected to England set-up for
Australian game (1988)
Worst moment in rugby:
Gloucester losing 6-48 to Bath in
1990 Pilkington Cup final
Most respected opponent: All of
them
Best memories last season:
Being in with a chance of winning
League and Cup double with
Gloucester. Playing at Twickenham
(in Cup final) for first time

	apps.	pts.
England B (1988)		
Last Season	1 cap	0
England 1995	Development squad	

Most improved International player last season: England centre Jeremy
Guscott
Suggestions to improve rugby: Scrap 90-degree scrum wheel law. Clamp
down on crooked feeds by scrum-halves
Other notable landmarks in rugby career: Played five times for England
B and warmed B bench on six occasions. Unused replacement for Full England
team against Australia (1988)
Touchlines: Shooting, cricket

Edmunds, D.A.   Wales

Full Name: David **Alan** Edmunds
International category: Wales Full
Club: Neath
Position: Wing
Height: 5'11" **Weight:** 12st
Occupation: Carpenter
Born: Neath, 8.10.61
Family: Married with son and
three daughters
Former clubs: Neath Athletic,
Aberavon
International debut: Ireland 14,
Wales 8, 1990
Five Nations' debut: As above
Best moment in rugby: Coming
on as replacement for David Evans
in 57th minute at Lansdowne Road
to win first cap
Worst moment in rugby: Neath
losing 1988/89 Welsh Cup final
Most respected opponent: Wales
wing Glenn Webbe
Serious injuries: Torn medial
knee ligaments
Other sporting achievements:
Cricket for Neath Athletic
Best memory last season: Scoring
try for Neath against All Blacks

	apps.	pts.
Wales B (1989)		
Last Season	1 cap	0
Wales (1990)		
Last Season	1 cap	0

Most improved International player last season: Wales centre Allan
Bateman
Suggestions to improve rugby: Relax laws regarding reimbursing players
for loss of earnings
Other notable landmarks in rugby career: Played two seasons of Welsh
Youth (1980–81), having left school aged 15. Played for Glamorgan Schools.
Made Wales B debut in last season's 15–28 defeat in France

Edwards, B.   Scotland

Full Name: Brian Edwards
International category: Scotland B
Club: Boroughmuir
Position: Centre
Height: 6' **Weight:** 13st 10lb
Occupation: Contracts engineer
Born: Dunfermline, 3.12.59
Family: Married with two children
Former club: Alloa
International debut (B): Italy 3, Scotland 26, 1988
Best moment in rugby: North and Midlands beating Glasgow in 1984 at Hughenden
Worst moment in rugby: Sitting on bench watching Japan beat Scotland 28–24 in Tokyo (1989)
Most embarrassing moment: Being unable to make try-line, playing v Edinburgh in 1989/90 Scottish Inter-District Championship, following best break of season
Most respected opponent: Former Scotland centre Jim Renwick

	apps.	pts.
Scotland B (1988)		
Last Season	2 caps	0

Serious injuries: Torn medial ligaments in knee
Other sporting achievements: Golf (9-handicap)
Best memory last season: Boroughmuir beating Pontypool away prior to Wales-Scotland International
Most improved International player last season: Scotland wing Tony Stanger
Suggestions to improve rugby: Cut points for a penalty and ensure referees send off all players who indulge in foul play
Other notable landmarks in rugby career: District debut for North and Midlands (1981), followed by Edinburgh district debut v Fiji (1982). Toured North America with Scotland (1985) and Zimbabwe with Public School Wanderers (1986). Played in both Scotland's B games last season, v Ireland and France
Feats: Managing to see wife and children between September and May

Full Name: Mark Walter Edwards
International category: Wales B
Club: Cardiff
Position: No.8
Height: 6'6" **Weight:** 18st 4lb
Occupation: Transport manager
Born: Senghenydd, 26.3.63
Family: Single
Family links with rugby: Father
played for Senghenydd
Former clubs: Senghenydd, Cross
Keys
International debut (B): France
28, Wales 15, 1990
Best moment in rugby: Winning
first cap for Wales B at La Teste
(Nov 1989)
Worst moment in rugby: Hearing
nothing after sitting on bench
throughout 1987 Welsh Trial
Most embarrassing moment:
Having to change shorts in front of
packed stand during Cardiff's game
with 1989 All Blacks
Most respected opponent:
Bridgend's Wales back row Owain
Williams

	apps.	pts.
Wales B (1989)		
Last Season	1 cap	0

Best memory last season: Scoring try for Cardiff in 15–25 defeat by touring
New Zealanders at Arms Park
Most improved International player last season: Cardiff's Wales fly-half
David Evans
Suggestions to improve rugby: Introduce broken time payments
Other notable landmarks in rugby career: Only took up game at age of
17. Captained Cross Keys in 1986/87 season
Touchlines: Squash, eating out, cooking

Egerton, D.W.   England

Full Name: David William Egerton
International category: England Full
Club: Bath
Positions: No.8, flanker
Height: 6'5" **Weight:** 16st 10lb
Occupation: Broker consultant
Born: Pinner, Middlesex, 19.10.61
Family: Single
Family links with rugby: House called 'Scrummage'. Brother Andy plays for Saracens. Former dog called 'Superlative wing-forward'. Father played for Wasps 3rd XV
Former clubs: Salisbury, Loughborough Students, Wasps (3rd XV)
International debut: Ireland 10, England 21, 1988
Five Nations' debut: England 23, Ireland 0, 1990

Best moments in rugby: Winning first cap in Millennium match. Helping England beat 1988 Australians
Worst moment in rugby: Being integrated so slowly into England team

	apps.	pts.
England B (1986)		
Last Season	0 caps	0
England (1988)		
Last Season	3 caps	4
Career	7 caps	4
1990	Tour to Argentina	

Most embarrassing moment: 'Scored' try on 22-metre line playing for Bishop Wordsworth's School
Most respected opponents: Former England forwards John Hall (in training) and Andy Ripley (in prime)
Serious injuries: Fractured lower back, dislocated knee cap
Other sporting achievements: Shot put for Dorset and Wilts
Best memory last season: Bath beating Gloucester 48–6 in Pilkington Cup final
Most improved Internationals last season: England No.8 rival Mike Teague and International referee Fred Howard
Suggestions to improve rugby: Game needs clear guidance. At moment it is being pulled in all sorts of directions. Involve current players in law changes

Other notable landmarks in rugby career: Influence of coaches Steve Ralph-Bowman (school) and Jack Rowell (Bath). Won 1984 UAU title with Loughborough against Brian Moore's Nottingham. Unused member of England's 1987 World Cup squad. England's first-choice No.8 for opening Five Nations' game against Ireland (scored try) but dropped when Mike Teague returned from injury

Touchlines: Country and Western music fan (esp. Johnny Cash), enjoy playing acoustic guitar. Researcher in ergonomics. Like to read science articles and fiction

---

Emyr, A. Wales

Full Name: Arthur Emyr (Jones)
International category: Wales Full
Club: Swansea
Position: Wing
Height: 6'2½" **Weight:** 14st 10lb
Occupation: Welsh language freelance TV and radio broadcaster
Born: Bangor, 27.7.62
Family: Married
Family links with rugby: Two brothers played for Penarth (and younger, for Swansea)
International debut: Wales 12, England 9, 1989
Five Nations' debut: As above
Best moment in rugby: Scoring first try for Wales against Scotland (1990)
Worst moment in rugby: Knee injury, suffered against Maesteg (1987), which required two operations
Most respected opponent: New Zealand wing John Kirwan
Serious injuries: Damaged knee
Other sporting achievements: Welsh International 4 x 100m athlete

	apps.	pts.
Wales B (**1985**)		
Last Season	1 cap	4
Wales (**1989**)		
Last Season	7 caps	12
Career	8 caps	12

Best memory last season: Swansea's game against All Blacks at St Helen's
Biggest international nuisance last season: Scotland flanker John Jeffrey
Suggestions to improve rugby: More consideration for players and their employers. Current amateur regulations are a farce
Other notable landmarks in rugby career: Career disrupted by serious knee injury (1987) which sidelined me for fourteen months. In and out of Welsh squad since 1983 but finally won first cap in Wales' 1989 defeat of England. Also represented Welsh Universities, Welsh Students, Barbarians, Wales B. At Sevens, have represented Wales, and Barbarians in Hong Kong

---

Essien, D.N.   England

Full Name: David Nicholas Essien
International category: England U-21
Club: Bristol
Positions: Full-back, wing
Height: 6' **Weight:** 13st 7lb
Occupation: Student
Born: Lagos, Nigeria, 11.9.69
Family: Single
Family links with rugby: Brother played for Richmond last season
Former club: Taunton
International debut (U-21): Romania 13, England 54, 1989
Best moment in rugby: End of training session
Worst moment in rugby: Start of training session
Most respected opponent: England wing Rory Underwood
Serious injuries: Torn hamstring
Other sporting achievements: Capped twice in 1987 for English Schools cricket
Best memory last season: Making England U-21 debut in Bucharest
Most improved International player last season: England fly-half Rob Andrew

	apps.	pts.
England U-21 (1989)		
Last Season	1 cap	4

Other notable landmarks in rugby career: Scored one of England U-21s' 10 tries v Romania

---

Evans, D.W.   Wales

Full Name: David Wyn Evans
International category: Wales Full
Club: Cardiff
Positions: Fly-half, centre
Height: 5'9" **Weight:** 12st 11lb
Occupation: Finance representative
Born: Wootton Bassett, Wilts,
1.11.65
Family: Married
Family links with rugby: Father
captained Carnegie College
Former clubs: Swansea and
Oxford Universities, Aberaman
International debut: France 31,
Wales 12, 1989
Five Nations' debut: As above
Best moment in rugby: Wales
defying odds to beat England 12–9
at Cardiff (1989)
Worst moment in rugby: Wales
losing 6-34 to England at
Twickenham (1990)
Most respected opponent:
French centre Philippe Sella
Serious injuries: Dislocated and
fractured shoulder, concussion
**Most improved International
player last season:** England centre
Jeremy Guscott

	apps.	pts.
Wales B (**1989**)		
Last Season	1 cap	0
Wales (**1989**)		
Last Season	5 caps	3
Career	7 caps	3

Suggestions to improve rugby: Reduce number of games played by top players
Other notable landmarks in rugby career: Partnered Robert Jones at half-back three times for 1984 Welsh Schools, scoring 16 points in 20–0 defeat of France. Also represented Welsh Students, Welsh Universities, Swansea University (1988 UAU final) and Oxford University (1988 Blue). Toured

Fiji, Australia, New Zealand and USA with Oxbridge, Japan with Oxford, and Canada with Wales B
Touchlines: Learning to speak Welsh and to play Spanish guitar

Evans, I.C. Wales

Full Name: Ieuan Cenydd Evans
International category: British Lions/Wales Full
Club: Llanelli
Position: Wing
Height: 5'10" **Weight:** 13st
Occupation: Sales representative
Born: Pontardulais, 21.3.64
Family: Single
Family links with rugby: Father played for Aberavon
Former club: Carmarthen Quins
International debut: France 16, Wales 9, 1987
Five Nations' debut: As above
Best moment in rugby: Scoring try that clinched Test series for 1989 Lions in Australia
Worst moment in rugby: Wales' mis-conceived 1988 tour to New Zealand
Most respected opponent: Australian wing David Campese – can never let him out of your sight
Serious injuries: Recurring dislocated shoulder, broken leg
Best memory last season: Lions tour
Most improved International player last season: England hooker Brian Moore

	apps.	pts.
Wales B (1985)		
Last Season	0 caps	0
Wales (1987)		
Last Season	0 caps	0
Career	18 caps	28
Lions 1989	3 Tests	4

Suggestions to improve rugby: Broken time payments. When ball is kicked to touch, allow throw-in to be taken anywhere behind mark
Other notable landmarks in rugby career: Playing career severely hampered by injury. Returned with triumphant 1989 Lions from Down Under

but was then forced to miss whole of last season through injury. Played in five matches in 1987 World Cup, scoring 4 tries in 40–9 defeat of Canada
Touchlines: Tennis, cricket, squash, golf

Evans, I.L. Wales

Full Name: Iwan **Luc** Evans
International category: Wales U-21
Club: Bridgend
Positions: Full-back, centre
Height: 5'8½" **Weight:** 12st
Occupation: Dental student
Born: Treherbert, 13.6.71
Family: Single
Family links with rugby: Father played for Swansea
Former clubs: Treherbert, Treorchy
International debut (U-21): Scotland 10, Wales 24, 1990
Best moment in rugby: Helping Bridgend beat Wales last season
Worst moments in rugby: Welsh Schools losing 6-9 to Irish after I missed late penalty. Watching England's Dusty Hare kick late penalty to beat Wales in 1980
Most embarrassing moment: Having to run across field to catch kick while changing shorts, playing for Bridgend against Gloucester

	apps.	pts.
Wales U-21 (**1990**)		
Last Season	1 cap	7

Most respected opponent: Wales centre Allan Bateman
Other sporting achievements: Welsh Schools 400m hurdler
Best memory last season: Playing in Welsh Cup final for Bridgend
Most improved International player last season: Scotland prop David Sole
Other notable landmarks in rugby career: Represented Welsh Schools (U-18) in 1989 and Wales U-21s last season when only 18

Evans, R.L.   Wales

Full Name: Richard (Ricky) Lloyd Evans
International category: Wales B (squad)
Club: Llanelli
Position: Loose-head prop
Height: 6'3" **Weight:** 16st 7lb
Occupation: Fireman
Born: Cardigan, 23.6.61
Family: Married with son and daughter
Former clubs: Cardigan, Army
International debut: Nova Scotia 3, Wales B 70, 1989 (non-cap)
Best moment in rugby: Playing for Wales B in above match
Worst moment in rugby: Being only a replacement for Llanelli v 1989 All Blacks
Most embarrassing moment: Came on as replacement flanker for Llanelli and used hands to push ball back between legs at scrum

Wales B 1989   Tour to Canada

Most respected opponent: Former Wales prop David Young
Serious injuries: Broken leg
Other sporting achievements: Long boat rowing for Aberporth LBC
Best memory last season: Playing for Wales B
Most improved International player last season: Wales flanker Mark Perego
Suggestions to improve rugby: Referees must hold tighter disciplinary reins and not use sin-bin as easy-option
Other notable landmarks in rugby career: Spent nine years in Army (16–25) and then two years playing in Pembrokeshire League for Cardigan. Broke leg against Cambridge University in only sixth game for Llanelli. Toured Canada with Wales B (1989). Also represented Crawshays

Excell, S.C.   England

Full Name: Simon Charles Excell
International category: England
U-21 (squad)
Club: Northampton
Position: Hooker
Height: 5'7" **Weight:** 15st
Occupation: Plumber/heating
engineer
Born: Ipswich, 28.1.69
Family: Single
Family links with rugby: Brothers
play for Woodbridge and Colchester
Former clubs: Southwold,
Woodbridge
Best moment in rugby: Phone
call from England U-21s last season
Worst moment in rugby: Losing
in semi-finals of 1987/88 U-21
County Championship with
Eastern Counties
Most respected opponent:
Harrogate and Yorkshire U-21s' D.
Batty

	apps.
England U-21 (**1989/90**)	Rep 1

Other sporting achievements:
Cricket for Southwold in Dairy
Times Suffolk League
Best memory last season: Eastern Counties winning U-21 County final at
Twickenham
Most improved International player last season: England fly-half Rob
Andrew
Other notable landmarks in rugby career: Successive Twickenham final
victories with Eastern Counties (1988/89, 1989/90). Selected to England U-21
squad while playing junior rugby with Woodbridge. Joined Northampton last
summer
Touchlines: Water sports

Fallon, J.A.   England

Full Name: James (Jim) Anthony
Fallon
International category: England B
Club: Bath
Position: Wing
Height: 6'1" **Weight:** 15st
Occupation: Builder
Born: Windsor, 27.3.65
Family: Single
Family links with rugby: Father
won Oxford Blue, was travelling
reserve for Ireland and coach to
England 16 Group
Former clubs: Tinmouth, Oxford
Polytechnic, Libourne (Fr),
Richmond
International debut (B): France
15, England 15, 1990
Best moment in rugby: Playing
for England B

Worst moment in rugby:
Richmond losing in first round of
1988/89 Middlesex Sevens at
Twickenham

	apps.	pts.
England B (**1990**)		
Last Season	1 cap	0
England 1995	Development squad	

Most respected opponent:
England wing Rory Underwood
Best memory last season:
Scoring 3 tries for South and
South West v Midlands in English Divisional Championship
Most improved International player last season: England scrum-half
Richard Hill
Suggestions to improve rugby: Relax amateur laws
Other notable landmarks in rugby career: Played for Tinmouth first team
as a Colt. Joined Richmond when came to London for work and, from there,
won divisional and national B honours

Farquharson, G.C.   Scotland

Full Name: Grant Charles
Farquharson
International category: Scotland
U-21 (squad)
Club: Jed-Forest
Position: Scrum-half
Height: 5'7" **Weight:** 10st 7lb
Occupation: Joiner
Born: Jedburgh, 19.8.69
Family: Single
Former club: Powerhouse (Aus)
Best moment in rugby: Display
for Jed-Forest (Scottish Second
Division champions) in defeat of
Kelso (First Division champions)
in play-off for 1987/88 Border
League
Most embarrassing moment:
Former Scotland forward Bill
Cuthbertson lifting me onto his
shoulders at line-out during
fund-raising match at Riverside
between Jed and International XV
Serious injuries: Badly strained
back playing for South of Scotland
U-21s

	apps.
Scotland U-21 (**1989/90**)	Rep 1

Best memory last season: Playing for Powerhouse in Melbourne during
summer
Other notable landmarks in rugby career: Represented Scotland at U-15,
U-18 and U-19 level and was unused replacement for U-21s in 10–24 defeat
by Wales last season

Fealey, S. Wales

Full Name: Steve Fealey
International category: Wales
(Namibia tour)
Club: Newbridge
Position: Scrum-half
Height: 5'5" **Weight:** 10st 12lb
Occupation: Carpenter
Born: Tredegar, 22.8.64
Family: Married with child
Former club: Tredegar
Best moment in rugby: Being
selected to tour Namibia with
Wales last summer
Worst moment in rugby: Missing
all of Newbridge's centenary season
due to injury
Most embarrassing moment:
Catching neck on roped-off cricket
pitch while playing rugby at youth
level
Most respected opponent: Ray
Giles
Serious injuries: Dislocated
collarbone

Wales 1990   Tour to Namibia

Other sporting achievements:
Soccer for Merthyr U-15s
Best memory last season: Scoring hat-trick of tries on Welsh debut in
Namibia
Most improved International player last season: Scotland prop David
Sole
Suggestions to improve rugby: Make training more interesting
Other notable landmarks in rugby career: Joining Newbridge. Winning
Dubai Sevens with Crawshays. Scored 4 tries in 3 games for Wales in Namibia

Finegan, R.A.J.   Ireland

Full Name: Ross Arthur John
Finegan
International category: Ireland
U-21
Club: University College Dublin
Position: Flanker
Height: 6'1½" **Weight:** 14st 6lb
Occupation: Student
Born: Dublin, 29.8.69
Family: Single
Family links with rugby: Uncle
played for Leinster and is a past
President
International debut (U-21): Italy
9, Ireland 10, 1989
Best moment in rugby:
Captaining Leinster U-21s to
victory over New Zealand U-21s
last season – their only defeat
Worst moment in rugby: Being
injured
Most embarrassing moment:
Missing tackle on Tony
Underwood, playing for Irish
Students against English Students
in 1987

	apps.	pts.
Ireland U-21 (**1989**)		
Last Season	2 caps	0

Most respected opponent:
England B wing Tony Underwood
Serious injuries: Broken bone in elbow, pulled hamstrings
Other sporting achievements: Leinster U-15 shot put champion
Best memory last season: Scoring 2 tries for Irish Universities in win over
English Universities at Sunbury
Most improved International player last season: Ireland No.8 Noel
Mannion
Suggestions to improve rugby: Country-wide training scheme in Ireland –
a uniform approach, rather than a provincial one
Other notable landmarks in rugby career: Twice represented Irish Schools
(U-18s), touring Australia in 1987. Played for Leinster at U-20 level and both
Province and Ireland (twice) U-21s
Touchlines: Cross-channel sailing

Fitzgerald, D.C.   Ireland

Full Name: Desmond Christopher
Fitzgerald
International category: Ireland
Full
Club: Lansdowne
Position: Prop
Height: 6'1" **Weight:** 17st 3lb
Occupation: Computer
programmer
Born: Dublin, 20.12.57
Family: Married with son and two
daughters
Former club: Dublin University
International debut: England 12,
Ireland 9, 1984
Five Nations' debut: As above
Best moment in rugby: Playing
for 1986 Lions in Cardiff
Worst moment in rugby: Being
dropped by Ireland for first time
after 1984 season (missed 1985
Triple Crown)
Most respected opponent:
Former Wales prop Jeff Whitefoot
Serious injuries: Dislocated both
shoulders, broke ribs, torn
hamstrings
Other sporting achievements:
1980/81 British and Irish
Universities heavyweight boxing
champion. Ex-competitive wrestler

	apps.	pts.
Ireland B (1983)		
Last Season	0 caps	0
Ireland (1984)		
Last Season	5 caps	0
Career	22 caps	0
Lions 1986		

Best memory last season: Coming on for Ireland against New Zealand (first
game back since 1988)
Most improved International player last season: England fly-half Rob
Andrew
Suggestions to improve rugby: Address pro-am dilemma. With levels of
expectation constantly increasing, administrators must decide how to reward
players of future
Other notable landmarks in rugby career: Injuries postponed Ireland B
debut for three years, finally coming in 1983. Toured Romania with Leinster

(1980) and South Africa with Ireland (1981). Represented Ireland at loose and tight-head
Touchlines: Golf (18-handicap), shooting

Fitzgerald, J.J.   Ireland

Full Name: John Joseph Fitzgerald
International category: Ireland Full
Club: Young Munster
Position: Loose-head prop
Height: 5'11" **Weight:** 16st 7lb
Occupation: Business development executive (banking)
Born: London, 31.8.61
Family: Married with one daughter (Nicole)
Family links with rugby: Younger brother plays for Shannon
Former club: Tokoroa (NZ)
International debut: Ireland 22, Scotland 18, 1988
Five Nations' debut: As above
Best moment in rugby: Scoring try against Scotland in 1990 Five Nations' Championship
Worst moment in rugby: Being dropped by Ireland in 1988
Most respected opponent: French prop Pascal Ondarts – tough and durable
Best memory last season: Winning Ulster Senior Cup with Young Munster

	apps.	pts.
Ireland (1988)		
Last Season	3 caps	4
Career	5 caps	4

Most improved International player last season: Ireland flanker Pat O'Hara
Other notable landmarks in rugby career: Playing in Parc des Princes
Touchlines: Enjoyed living in New Zealand for four months during summer 1989; way of life and manner in which they approach rugby was very interesting

Ford, S.P.   Wales

Full Name: Stephen Paul Ford
International category: Wales Full
Club: Cardiff
Position: Right wing
Height: 6' **Weight:** 12st 7lb
Occupation: Carpet fitter
Born: Cardiff, 15.8.65
Family: Single with son
Family links with rugby: Phil
(brother) plays Rugby League for
Leeds and Great Britain
Former clubs: Glamorgan
Wanderers, Rumney
International debut: Ireland 14,
Wales 8, 1990
Five Nations' debut: As above
Best moment in rugby: Scoring
try in first International
Worst moment in rugby: Being
banned for two and a half years
after having Rugby League trial
with Leeds
Most respected opponent: New
Zealand wing John Kirwan
Serious injuries sustained:
Damaged Achilles tendon
Best memory last season:
Scoring 7 tries for Wales B in 47–0
win v Saskatchewan (Canadian
tour) – Welsh record

	apps.	pts.
Wales B (**1989**)		
Last Season	1 cap	4
Wales (**1990**)		
Last Season	3 caps	4
Career	3 caps	4

Most improved International player last season: Wales fly-half David
Evans
Suggestions to improve rugby: Bring money into game

Francis, N.P.   Ireland

Full Name: Neil Patrick Francis
International category: Ireland
Full
Club: Blackrock College
Position: Lock
Height: 6'6" **Weight:** 17st 3lb
Occupation: Banker
Born: Dublin, 17.3.64
Family: Single
Former clubs: London Irish,
Manly (Aus)
International debut: Ireland 32,
Tonga 9, 1987 (World Cup)
Five Nations' debut: Scotland 37,
Ireland 21, 1989
Best moment in rugby: Winning
1981 Schools Cup final with
Blackrock
Worst moment in rugby: Being
dropped by Ireland on 1989 North
American tour
Most respected opponent:
French forward Laurent Rodriguez
Serious injuries: Broken vertebrae
(out two years)
Other sporting achievements:
Javelin for Ireland (national junior
and senior champion)

Ireland (1987)	apps.	pts.
Last Season	3 caps	0
Career	8 caps	4

Best memory last season: Ireland beating Wales to avoid Wooden Spoon
Most improved International player last season: Ireland flanker Pat
O'Hara
Other notable landmarks in rugby career: Represented Irish Schools five
times (1981–82). Rejoined Blackrock from London Irish in 1989. Made full
Ireland debut in 1987 World Cup but not called upon again until Oct 1988
when played against Western Samoa, scoring a try. Sole Irish representative
in Home Unions team which played Rest of Europe at Twickenham in aid of
Romania last season

Gallick, K.   Ireland

Full Name: Keith Gallick
International category: Ireland U-21
Club: Queen's University, Belfast
Position: No.8
Height: 6'3½" **Weight:** 16st 4lb
Occupation: Student
Born: Londonderry, 15.1.69
Family: Single
Former club: City of Derry
International debut (U-21): Ireland 10, Italy 9, 1989
Best moment in rugby: Scoring a try for Irish Students v US Eagles in 19–18 win last season
Worst moment in rugby: Losing to Bangor in Ulster Bank's Schools Cup semi-finals
Most embarrassing moment: Swapping an Irish tracksuit for an appalling Zimbabwean one after a game against the African nation
Most respected opponent: Former England fly-half Les Cusworth
Serious injuries: Torn knee ligaments

	apps.	pts.
Ireland U-21 (**1989**)		
Last Season	2 caps	0

Best memory last season: Scoring against US Eagles
Most improved International player last season: England hooker Brian Moore
Suggestions to improve rugby: Implement a more organised system of attracting children from non-rugby playing schools into the game
Other notable landmarks in rugby career: Captained Ulster U-20s. Two U-21 caps, one Irish Students', and six Irish Universities'
Touchlines: Weight training

Galwey, M.J.   Ireland

Full Name: Michael Joseph Galwey
International category: Ireland B
Club: Shannon
Position: Lock
Height: 6'4" **Weight:** 17st
Occupation: Sales representative
Born: County Kerry, 8.10.66
Family: Single
Former club: Castle Island
International debut (B): Scotland
22, Ireland 22, 1989
Best moment in rugby: Scoring a
try in Munster Cup final
Worst moment in rugby: Losing
1988/89 Munster Cup final to
Constitution
Most respected opponent:
Ireland lock Donal Lenihan
Serious injuries sustained:
Damaged Achilles tendon
Other sporting achievements:
Winner of All-Ireland Gaelic
Football medal with Kerry in 1986
Best memory last season:
Playing against the All Blacks at
Musgrave Park

	apps.	pts.
Ireland B (**1989**)		
Last Season	1 cap	0

Most improved International player last season: Ireland full-back Kenny
Murphy
Other notable landmarks in rugby career: Being selected to play with
Munster U-20 XV whilst a member of Castle Island. Winning the Munster
Senior Cup in three successive seasons, and being awarded a Shannon RFC
cap for the achievement. Playing for Ireland U-25s against United States (won
12–10) in March 1990
Touchlines: Fishing the Kerry Lakes

Glasgow, I.C.   Scotland

Full Name: Iain **Cameron** Glasgow
International category: Scotland Full (squad)
Club: Heriot's FP
Positions: Full-back, wing
Height: 5'7½" **Weight:** 11st 7lb
Occupation: Trainee chartered surveyor
Born: Bridge of Allan, 24.2.66
Family: Single
Family links with rugby: Father played ten times for Scotland. Brother Anthony has played for Army and Blackheath
Former clubs: Edinburgh Wanderers, Howe of Fife, St Andrew's Univ, Cambridge Univ
Best moment in rugby: Scoring 39 points for Scotland XV in record 91–8 defeat of Kanto on 1989 tour of Japan (4 short of Peter Dods' Scottish record for a tour match)

	apps.
Scotland	Rep 2
Scotland B **(1989/90)**	Rep 1

Worst moments in rugby: Scotland XV losing 1989 unofficial Test 24–28 to Japan in Tokyo. Disastrous 1990 Scottish Trial
Most respected opponents: Wales fly-half David Evans, Australian wing Ian Williams and former Scotland flanker Finlay Calder
Serious injuries: Broken cheekbone (five weeks before 1988 Varsity match)
Other sporting achievements: Scottish Junior decathlon champion
Best memory last season: Selected as Scotland reserve for pre-Trial Internationals against Fiji and Romania
Most improved International player last season: Scotland lock Chris Gray
Other notable landmarks in rugby career: Played on right wing for Cambridge in 1988 Varsity match. Toured Fiji, Australia and New Zealand with Oxbridge (1989). Represented Scotland at Schools, U-21 and Student level. Played in 1988 Student World Cup
Touchlines: Golf (11-handicap), tennis

Goodey, R. Wales

Full Name: Richard Goodey
International category: Wales B
(squad)
Club: Pontypool
Positions: Lock, No.8
Height: 6'4" **Weight:** 16st
Occupation: Postman
Born: Chepstow, 17.7.65
Family: Married
Family links with rugby: Brother
plays for Chepstow
Former clubs: Caldicot, Chepstow
Best moment in rugby: Scoring
winning try for Pontypool at
Cardiff (1988/89)
Worst moment in rugby: Tearing
ankle ligaments at Cardiff (1988/89)
Most respected opponent: Wales
lock Phil Davies
Serious injuries: Torn ankle
ligaments (required operation)
Other sporting achievements:
Soccer for Chepstow RFC
Best memory last season:
Beating Llanelli at Pontypool

	apps.
Wales B (1989/90)	Rep 1

Suggestions to improve rugby: Let rucks continue bit longer where possible
Other notable landmarks in rugby career: Played for Ron Waldron's XV
v Lord Mayor's XV (1989/90). Also represented Monmouthshire U-23s and
senior team. Selected as reserve for Wales B v France last season

Graham, G.   Scotland

Full Name: George Graham
International category: Scotland B
Club: Stirling County
Position: Loose-head prop
Height: 5'7" **Weight:** 15st 10lb
Occupation: Army PTI instructor
Born: Stirling, 19.1.66
Family: Married with child
Former club: London Scottish
International debut (B): Scotland 37, Italy 0, 1987
Best moment in rugby: Scoring try on Scotland B debut
Worst moment in rugby: Being dropped by Scotland B (1987)
Most embarrassing moment: Having shorts ripped clean off after scoring try for Stirling
Most respected opponent: Scotland prop Iain 'the Bear' Milne
Best memory last season: Stirling beating Kelso and Hawick for first time. Last time we played Hawick, County lost 98–0
Most improved International player last season: Scotland tight-head Paul Burnell

	apps.	pts.
Scotland B (1987)		
Last Season	2 caps	0

Other notable landmarks in rugby career: Played in two Inter-Services Championship-winning Army teams. Also played for Combined Services. Represented Scotland U-19, U-21 and B (four times) teams
Touchlines: Volleyball, table tennis, basketball

Gray, C.A. Scotland

Full Name: Christopher Anthony Gray
International category: Scotland Full
Club: Nottingham
Position: Lock
Height: 6'5" **Weight:** 16st 7lb
Occupation: Dental surgeon
Born: Haddington, 11.7.60
Family: Single
Family links with rugby: Older brother played and introduced me to game
Former club: Edinburgh Academicals
International debut: Scotland 23, Wales 7, 1989
Five Nations' debut: As above
Best moment in rugby: Winning 1990 Five Nations' Grand Slam
Worst moment in rugby: Losing to Japan 28–24 in unofficial Test (1989). Losing to France 3-19 in Paris (1989)
Most respected opponent: England lock Paul Ackford – excellent in set-piece and very useful in open play

	apps.	pts.
Scotland B (**1986**)		
Last Season	0 caps	0
Scotland (**1989**)		
Last Season	8 caps	8
Career	12 caps	8

Other sporting achievements: Golf (6-handicap)
Best memory last season: Winning Grand Slam
Most improved International player last season: Scotland prop Paul Burnell
Suggestions to improve rugby: Better communications between top administrators and players. Continued communication between players and all level of referees
Other notable landmarks in rugby career: Played for Notts/Lincs/Derby in 1985 English County Championship final. Captained Anglo-Scots in 1987 Scottish Inter-District Championship. Won 4 caps for Scotland B. Captained Scotland XV against Goshawks (Zimbabwe, 1988). Captained Nottingham (1989/90). Played for Barbarians. Scored first tries for Scotland last season against Fiji and New Zealand (first Test)

Gregory, G.D.   England

Full Name: Guy Darren Gregory
International category: England U-21
Club: Nottingham
Position: Fly-half
Height: 6' **Weight:** 13st
Occupation: Student of urban land economy
Born: Chalfont, 13.1.69
Family: Single
Former club: Wasps
International debut: Netherlands 3, England U-21 24, April 1990
Best moment in rugby: Playing for England U-21
Worst moment in rugby: Wasps wing Raphael Tsagane's death in car crash, April 1990
Most respected player: England fly-half Rob Andrew – showed a lot of class and taught me a great deal
Other sporting achievements: Captain of Hertfordshire Schools cricket XI. Hockey for East of England Schools
Best memory last season: Wasps clinching English First Division title

	apps.	pts.
England U-21 (**1990**)		
Last Season	1 cap	12

Most improved International player last season: Rob Andrew
Suggestions to improve rugby: Some form of payment to players at top level
Other notable landmarks in rugby career: Joined Wasps in 1987. Played at Twickenham in 1989 Middlesex Sevens. Played for British Polytechnics. Captained Wasps Colts (1987/88). Scored 12 points (3c, 2p) v Netherlands at Hilversum

Griffiths, M.   Wales

Full Name: Mike Griffiths
International category: Wales Full
Club: Cardiff
Position: Loose-head prop
Height: 6' **Weight:** 16st 7lb
Occupation: Builder
Born: Tonypandy, 18.3.62
Family: Married with two sons
Family links with rugby: Brother
plays for Ystrad Rhondda
Former clubs: Ystrad Rhondda,
Bridgend
International debut: Wales 24,
Western Samoa 6, 1988
Five Nations' debut: Scotland 23,
Wales 7, 1989
Best moment in rugby: Winning
first Welsh cap against touring
Samoans
Worst moment in rugby: Wales
losing 6-34 to England at
Twickenham last season
Most respected opponents:
England prop Jeff Probyn (for his
technique) and Scotland prop Iain
Milne (for his size and strength)
Serious injuries: Broken ribs,
fractured arm, twisted shoulder
muscles, damaged ankle and knee
ligaments

	apps.	pts.
Wales B (**1988**)		
Last Season	0 caps	0
Wales (**1988**)		
Last Season	4 caps	0
Career	11 caps	0
Lions 1989		

Other sporting achievements: Accomplished soccer player (centre-back)
Best memory last season: Being only Welsh representative in Home Unions'
team which played Europe at Twickenham on behalf of Romanian appeal
Most improved International player last season: Scotland tight-head Paul
Burnell
Suggestions to improve rugby: Look after players better
Other notable landmarks in rugby career: Started career in back-row but
moved to front of scrum shortly before joining Bridgend. Moved to Cardiff
for new challenges and found them: playing for Crawshays, Wales B, Wales
and 1989 Lions

Guscott, J.C.   England

Full Name: Jeremy Clayton Guscott
International category: England Full
Club: Bath
Position: Centre
Height: 6'1" **Weight:** 13st 5lb
Occupation: Public relations officer
Born: Bath, 7.7.65
Family: Married
International debut: Romania 3, England 58, 1989
Five Nations' debut: England 23, Ireland 0, 1990
Best moment in rugby: Try scored for 1989 Lions v Australia in second Test
Worst moment in rugby: Being dropped by Bath for semi-finals of 1989/90 Pilkington Cup
Most embarrassing moment: Any time I miss a tackle
Most respected opponent: All of them
Best memory last season: Beating Gloucester 48–6 in Pilkington Cup final
Most improved International player last season: England No.8 Mike Teague

	apps.	pts.
England B (1988)		
Last Season	0 caps	0
England (1989)		
Last Season	6 caps	28
Career	6 caps	28
1991	World Cup squad	
Lions 1989	2 Tests	4

Suggestions to improve rugby: Allow players to earn money through off-field activities. Scrap 90-degree scrum wheel law
Other notable landmarks in rugby career: Started career with Bath's mini-section as a wing, aged 7. In 1989 won 2 caps for England B, marked full England debut in Bucharest with 3 tries and gained an invitation from Lions. Scored crucial try in Brisbane to keep Lions in hunt
Touchlines: Golf

Hackney, S.T. England

Full Name: Stephen Thomas Hackney
International category: England B
Club: Nottingham
Position: Wing
Height: 5'11" **Weight:** 13st 4lb
Occupation: PE Student
Born: Stockton-on-Tees, 13.6.68
Family: Single
Former clubs: Stockton, West Hartlepool, Loughborough Students
International debut: England B 9, Australia 37, 1988
Best moment in rugby: Loughborough winning 1988 UAU final v Swansea
Worst moment in rugby: 1986 English Schools losing 7-10 to Scots (last-minute penalty by Craig Chalmers) to deny us Schools Grand Slam
Most embarrassing moment: Having 'disco dancing' named as my main hobby in four England Schools' programmes
Most respected opponent: Australian wing David Campese – outstanding attacking ability and unpredictability

	apps.	pts.
England B (1988)		
Last Season	1 cap	4
England 1995	Development squad	

Serious injuries: Dislocated shoulder, medial ligament tear (right knee)
Other sporting achievements: Cleveland county U-19 100–200m champion. North East U-19 100m and long jump champion
Best memory last season: Spain 9, England B 31
Most improved International player last season: England fly-half Rob Andrew
Suggestions to improve rugby: Scrap 90-degree scrum wheel law
Other notable landmarks in rugby career: Played for Barbarians and England Students in inaugural Students' World Cup (1988)

Hall, M.R.   Wales

Full Name: Michael Robert Hall
International category: Wales Full
Club: Cardiff
Positions: Centre, wing
Height: 6'1" **Weight:** 14st 2lb
Occupation: Surveyor
Born: Bridgend, 13.10.65
Family: Single
Former clubs: Bridgend, Maesteg,
Cambridge University
International debut: New
Zealand 52, Wales 3, 1988
Five Nations' debut: Scotland 23,
Wales 7, 1989
Best moments in rugby:
Selection for 1989 British Lions.
1990 Hong Kong Sevens with
Barbarians
Worst moment in rugby:
England 34, Wales 6 (Feb 1990)
Most embarrassing moment:
Wales' record defeat at
Twickenham (1990)
Most respected opponent:
French centre Philippe Sella
Serious injuries: Hamstring tears
Other sporting achievements:
Schoolboy honours at county level
in soccer, basketball and cricket

	apps.	pts.
Wales B (1987)		
Last Season	0 caps	0
Wales (1988)		
Last Season	4 caps	0
Career	12 caps	8
Lions 1989	1 Test	0

Best memory last season: Do not have one – had an awful season
Most improved International player last season: England scrum-half
Richard Hill
Suggestions to improve rugby: Simplify rules. Market game properly. Ban
all rugby writers who have never played
Other notable landmarks in rugby career: Past captain of British
Universities, Welsh Students and Wales U-21s. Two Blues at Cambridge
(1987,88). Wales B against France in 1987 (lost 0-26). 1989 Lions against
Australia in first Test (lost 12–30). Toured with Wales to New Zealand (1988)
and to South Africa (1989) with World XV. Winning try against England
(1989)
Touchlines: Golf

Halliday, S.J.   England

Full Name: Simon John Halliday
International category: England Full
Club: Bath
Positions: Centre, wing
Height: 6' **Weight:** 13st 12lb
Occupation: Stockbroker
Born: Haverfordwest, 13.7.60
Family: Married with a daughter
Family links with rugby: Father played for Royal Navy
Former clubs: Oxford University, Harlequins
International debut: England 21, Wales 18, 1986
Five Nations' debut: As above
Best moment in rugby: Listening to Twickenham crowd singing in second half of England's 1988 defeat of Ireland when we recovered a 0-3 half-time deficit to win 35-3
Worst moment in rugby: Fractured dislocation of left foot, sustained playing for Somerset v Middlesex in 1983 County Championship, which cost me three years of International rugby
Most embarrassing moment (almost!): Leg bandage slipped down to my ankle as I broke through to score for England against Australia (1988). Had my journey been any longer the support would have tripped me up
Most respected opponent: Former Wales centre Ray Gravell – very tough to knock down
Serious injuries sustained: Aforementioned leg injury (1983), torn hamstrings
Other sporting achievements: Oxford cricket Blue (1980). Proud owner of first-class century (113 n.o. v Kent). Played for Dorset and Minor Counties
Best memory last season: England beating Wales 34–6 at Twickenham
Most improved International player last season: England wing Rory Underwood

	apps.	pts.
England B (1985)		
Last Season	0 caps	0
England (1986)		
Last Season	4 caps	0
Career	16 caps	4

Suggestions to improve rugby: Recognition of time players spend away from work – pro-rata compensation. Show players what they are doing is appreciated. Present situation is embarrassing

Other notable landmarks in rugby career: Played for Dorset & Wilts U-19s. Won three rugby Blues at Oxford (1979,80,81). Captained South West to victories over USA and Australia (both 1988). Represented Bath in five Cup finals and emerged a winner on each occasion

---

Halpin, G.F.   Ireland

Full Name: Garrett Francis Halpin
International category: Ireland Full
Club: Wanderers
Position: Tight-head prop
Height: 5'11" **Weight:** 17st 4lb
Occupation: Insurance official
Born: Dublin, 14.2.66
Family: Single
Former club: Rockwell College
International debut: England 23, Ireland 0, 1990
Five Nations' debut: As above
Best moment in rugby: Winning first full cap, at Twickenham
Worst moment in rugby: Losing place after above match
Other sporting achievements: Irish International hammer thrower – American Indoor Collegiate champion. Represented Ireland in 1987 World Athletics Championships (Rome)
Best memory last season: Winning Leinster League and Cup double with Wanderers

	apps.	pts.
Ireland (**1990**)		
Last Season	1 cap	0
Career	1 cap	0

Other notable landmarks in rugby career: Joining Wanderers on return from a sports scholarship with University of Manhattan in New York. Played four times for Ireland Schools. Toured North America with Ireland (1989), scoring try in defeat of Mid West in Chicago

Hamlin, M.P. England

Full Name: Michael Paul Hamlin
International category: England B
Club: Gloucester
Position: Fly-half
Height: 5'11" **Weight:** 12st
Occupation: Building consultant
Born: Gloucester, 10.3.60
Family: Married with two
daughters
Family links with rugby: Brother
played for Cheltenham
Former clubs: Coney Hill,
Cheltenham
International debut: Spain 9,
England B 31, 1989
Best moment in rugby:
Captaining Gloucester for past two
seasons
Worst moment in rugby: Final
two weeks of last season when
League and Cup double dream
evaporated
Most respected opponent:
Former England fly-half Les
Cusworth
Serious injuries: Broken
collarbone, ankle

	apps.	pts.
England B (1989)		
Last Season	1 cap	7
England 1995	Development squad	

Best memory last season: Gloucester's League performances away from
Kingsholm
Most improved International player last season: England fly-half Rob
Andrew
Other notable landmarks in rugby career: Broke into England set-up for
first time when selected to tour Spain with England B in summer of 1989
Touchlines: Squash, cricket, DIY

Hannaford, M.P. England

Full Name: Marcus Paul Hannaford
International category: England B
Club: Gloucester
Position: Scrum-half
Height: 6' **Weight:** 13st 7lb
Occupation: Fencing contractor
Born: Bristol, 27.4.63
Family: Married
Family links with rugby: Father played for Gloucester. Uncle played for Bristol, England and Barbarians
Former clubs: Widden Old Boys, Longlevens, Old Cryptians
International debut (B): Italy v England, 1986
Best moment in rugby: Scoring try for England B on first appearance
Worst moments in rugby: Two John Player Cup semi-final defeats by Bath
Most respected opponent: Former Wales scrum-half David Bishop

	apps.
England B (1986)	
Last Season	Rep 1

Serious injuries: Damaged shoulder ligaments (forced to pull out of 1987 World Cup squad) and knee ligaments
Other sporting achievements: Cricket and soccer for Gloucester Schools
Best memory last season: Giving people of Gloucester a day out at Twickenham and representing City in Pilkington Cup final
Most improved International player last season: England flanker Mickey Skinner
Suggestions to improve rugby: Introduce home and away format into English Leagues in order to make it a true test
Other notable landmarks in rugby career: Captained Gloucester (1988/89). Former member of England U-18 and U-23 squads. Recalled to England senior training squad this season three years after withdrawing from 1987 World Cup squad through injury. Replacement in Paris last season when England B drew 15–15 with France
Touchlines: Snooker, darts, golf

Harley, J.R.   Ireland

Full Name: James Robert Harley
International category: Ireland U-21
Club: Queen's University, Belfast
Position: Wing
Height: 5'9" **Weight:** 10st 9lb
Occupation: Student
Born: Nairobi, Kenya, 23.9.68
Family: Single
Family links with rugby: Father played for Harlequins in Kenya
Former club: Imperial College London
International debut (U-21): Ireland 10, Italy 9, 1989
Best moments in rugby: Beating US Eagles 19–18 with Irish Students (March 1990), and being selected for Ulster v 1989 All Blacks
Worst moment in rugby: Having to pull out of New Zealand game through injury
Most embarrassing moment: Forgetting kit for match and having to wear one six sizes too big
Most respected opponent: England B wing Tony Underwood

	apps.	pts.
Ireland U-21 (1989)		
Last Season	2 caps	0

Other sporting achievements: Irish Schools 400m Runner-up. Rowed at Irish Schools Championships
Best memory last season: Beating US Eagles
Most improved International player last season: England fly-half Rob Andrew
Suggestions to improve rugby: Set up professional organising body with sole function to promote game in way that makes it attractive to all spheres of life, especially to those not from a rugby-playing background or school
Other notable landmarks in rugby career: Played for Irish Schools, U-21s and Universities

Full Name: Alun Harries
International category: Wales B
Club: Newbridge
Position: Wing
Height: 5'9" **Weight:** 12st 7lb
Occupation: Technical services engineer
Born: 28.9.67
Family: Single
Family links with rugby: Father, grandfather and uncle all played for Newbridge
Former club: Abercarn
International debut (B): France 28, Wales 15, 1989
Best moment in rugby: Winning Dubai Sevens with Crawshays
Most embarrassing moment: Dived over ball when should have scored, playing for Newbridge against Abertillery in 1987
Most respected opponent: Wales wing Steve Ford – very elusive
Serious injuries: Torn hamstring
Other sporting achievements: Welsh junior men athletics, local cricketer

	apps.	pts.
Wales B (1989)		
Last Season	1 cap	0

Best memory last season: Being selected for Wales B in France
Most improved International player last season: England centre Jeremy Guscott
Suggestions to improve rugby: Broken time payments
Other notable landmarks in rugby career: Represented Wales U-20s (1986/87) and Wales B (1989/90). Member of 1987/88 Welsh U-21 squad
Touchlines: Cardiff Devils ice hockey supporter, adequate skier

Harriman, A.T.　　　　　England

Full Name: Andrew Tuoyo
Harriman
International category: England
(development squad)
Club: Harlequins
Position: Right wing
Height: 6'2" **Weight:** 12st 8lb
Occupation: Chartered surveyor
Born: Lagos, Nigeria, 13.7.64
Family: Single
Former club: Cambridge
University
International debut: England 28,
Australia 19, 1988
Best moment in rugby: Being
informed of England selection
Worst moment in rugby: Playing
while injured for Barbarians v West
Midlands (1989)
Most embarrassing moment:
Being tackled from behind by a
Portuguese prop during Estoril
Sevens
Most respected opponent:
Former Rosslyn Park wing, now
Great Britain Rugby League star,
Martin Offiah – always aware of
opportunities

England (1988)	apps.	pts.
Last Season	0 caps	0
Career	1 cap	0
1995	Development squad	

Serious injuries: Right knee cartilage and ligaments
Other sporting achievements: Great Britain U-16 tennis doubles champion.
Cambridge athletics Blue
Best memory last season: Watching England play best rugby of Five
Nations' Championship
Most improved International player last season: England centre Jeremy
Guscott
Suggestions to improve rugby: Allow players to reap off-field benefits to
compensate for time and hard work given to game
Other notable landmarks in rugby career: Cambridge Blue (1985). Three
Middlesex Sevens trophies – unbeaten in any Sevens game (more than 15
tournaments) since joining Harlequins. 1988 John Player Cup win v Bristol.
Helped London beat 1988 Australians 21–10. Played for Barbarians
Touchlines: Tennis, squash, fives, travelling, listening to music

Harris, M.A.   England

Full Name: Michael Anthony
Harris
International category: England
U-21
Club: Wasps
Position: Flanker
Height: 6'4" **Weight:** 16st 7lb
Occupation: Sports shop manager
Born: London, 7.9.67
Family: Single
Family links with rugby: Uncle
played for Royal Navy
Former club: Blackheath
International debut (U-21):
Romania 13, England 54, 1989
Best moment in rugby: Playing
for first ever England U-21 team
Worst moment in rugby: Being
concussed for 4½ hours during a
game on tour in New Zealand
Most respected opponent:
England flanker Mickey Skinner
Serious injuries: Concussion
Best memory last season:
Scoring for Blackheath in the
Middlesex Sevens at Twickenham

	apps.	pts.
England U-21 (**1989**)		
Last Season	1 cap	0
England 1995	Development squad	

Suggestions to improve rugby:
Law changes should be made to help the players rather than make game
harder – stop tactical fouls by wheeling and collapsing scrums
Other notable landmarks in rugby career: Played at every England level
from U-16s to U-21s. Left Blackheath for Wasps last summer
Touchlines: Tattoos

Harrison, M.E.   England

Full Name: Michael Edward
Harrison
International category: England
Full (squad)
Club: Wakefield
Position: Wing
Height: 5'10" **Weight:** 12st
Occupation: Assistant bank
manager
Born: Barnsley, 9.4.56
Family: Married with three children
International debut: New
Zealand 18, England 13 (first
Test), 1985
Five Nations' debut: Scotland 33,
England 6, 1986
Best moments in rugby: Being
picked by England for NZ 1985.
England beating Scotland in my
first game as captain
Worst moment in rugby:
Wakefield losing to Rugby in
1988/89 to miss promotion to
English Second Division
Most embarrassing moment:
Trying to reply in Japanese at
after-match function in 1987
(Japanese President's XV against
New Zealand)

	apps.	pts.
England B (1985)		
Last Season	0 caps	0
England (1985)		
Last Season	Rep 1	
Career	15 caps	28

Most respected opponent: Former England wing Mike Slemen –
complete footballer
Other sporting achievements: Represented Yorkshire Schools at athletics
Best memory last season: Wakefield beating Gosforth away from home in
Pilkington Cup
Most improved International player last season: England hooker Brian
Moore
Suggestions to improve rugby: Increased encouragement to get ex-players
into refereeing in order to get a more uniform approach
Other notable landmarks in rugby career: Tries in first two Internationals,
v New Zealand. Captained North to Divisional Championship, Yorkshire to
County Championship title, and England. New Wakefield captain

Hartley, G.J.   England

Full Name: Gary James Hartley
International category: England B
Club: Nottingham
Positions: Centre, wing
Height: 6' **Weight:** 13st
Occupation: Chartered surveyor
Born: Lytham St Annes, Lancs,
5.5.62
Family: Married with one child
Family links with rugby: Father
was a Cambridge Blue who played
for Fylde and Lancashire
Former club: Fylde
Best moment in rugby: Winning
in Paris on England B debut
Worst moment in rugby:
Nottingham losing to Leicester for
ninth consecutive time last season
Most respected opponent:
Former England centre Paul
Dodge – marvellous defender
Serious injuries: Fractured larynx,
bruised left kidney, severed nerves
in arm
Other sporting achievements:
Soccer trialist with Manchester
United. MCC cricket trialist

	apps.	pts.
England B (1988)		
Last Season	0 caps	0
	Tour to Spain	

Best memory last season: Scoring 3 tries in 63–3 defeat of a Basque XV
on England B's 1989 tour of Spain
Most improved International player last season: England fly-half Rob
Andrew
Suggestions to improve rugby: None. Would not be playing rugby if wanted
it any different
Other notable landmarks in rugby career: Played four games for England
Students (1984–86), one for England U-23s (1985). Captained England B to
32–15 win over Spanish Select (1989). Missed International against Spain
with bruised kidney
Touchlines: Waterskiing

Full Name: Andrew **Gavin**
Hastings
International category: Scotland
Full
Club: Watsonians
Position: Full-back
Height: 6'2" **Weight:** 14st 9lb
Occupation: Agency surveyor
Born: Edinburgh, 3.1.62
Family: Single
Family links with rugby: Clifford
(father) played No.8 for Edinburgh
XV and Watsonians; Scott
(brother) plays for Watsonians,
Scotland and British Lions;
Graeme (brother) plays centre for
Melbourne RFC and Victoria State
(Australia); Ewan (brother) plays
on wing for Watsonians
Former clubs: Cambridge
University, London Scottish
International debut: Scotland 18,
France 17, 1986
Five Nations' debut: As above
Best moment in rugby: Winning
1990 Grand Slam. 1989 British
Lions' 2-1 series win in Australia
Worst moments in rugby: Varsity
match 1985 (lost 6-7), England 21,
Scotland 12 (1987), British Lions
first Test (1989)

	apps.	pts.
Scotland B (1983)		
Last Season	0 caps	0
Scotland (1986)		
Last Season	8 caps	47
Career	26 caps	269
Lions 1986		
1989	3 caps	28

Most embarrassing moment: Missing plane home from Ireland after B
international
Most respected opponent: The All Blacks, because of their record
Other sporting achievements: Appearing on TV in Trail Blazers (1988)
and Pro-Celebrity Golf (1990)
Best memory last season: Beating England
Most improved International player last season: Scotland wing Tony
Stanger
Suggestions to improve rugby: Get fit and stay fit. Practise your weaknesses

Notable landmarks in rugby career: Going to Cambridge University. Won 5 caps for Scotland B before establishing Scottish record with 6 penalty goals on full debut. Hold Scottish points-scoring record with 255 points in 24 major Internationals, and Scottish record for most points scored in a Five Nations' season (52 in 1986). Toured with Scotland to North America (1985), the 1987 World Cup (where I scored 62 points in 4 games), and New Zealand (May 1990). Scored go-ahead try in second Test for 1989 Lions and 15 points in the Third. Played in 1989 Home Unions' 29–27 win over France (scored 22 points) and for 1989 Barbarians against All Blacks. Led London Scottish to English Third Division Championship last season

Touchlines: Playing golf with Sam Torrance against Ronan Rafferty and Peter Alliss – most nervous I've ever been in my life, including winning first cap at Murrayfield

Hastings, S. Scotland

Full Name: Scott Hastings
International category: Scotland Full
Club: Watsonians
Positions: Centre, wing, full-back
Height: 6'1½" **Weight:** 14st 7lb
Occupation: Advertising account executive
Born: Edinburgh, 4.12.64
Family: Fiancée
Family links with rugby: Clifford (father) played No.8 for Edinburgh XV and Watsonians; Gavin (brother) plays for Watsonians, Scotland and British Lions; Graeme (brother) plays centre for Melbourne RFC and Victoria State (Australia); Ewan (brother) plays on wing for Watsonians

Former clubs: Newcastle, Northern
International debut: Scotland 19, France 18, 1986
Five Nations' debut: As above
Best moments in rugby: British Lions Test series win; winning 1990 Grand Slam with Scotland; playing in Hong Kong Sevens

Worst moment in rugby:
Sustaining hamstring injury on first appearance in 1987 World Cup (55–28 win v Romania)
Most embarrassing moment: My 1987 World Cup injury
Most respected opponent: Fellow Scotland centre Sean Lineen – he can drink!
Serious injuries: Torn hamstring

	apps.	pts.
Scotland B (1985)		
Last Season	0 caps	0
Scotland (1986)		
Last Season	8 caps	0
Career	25 caps	16
Lions 1989	2 Tests	0

Best memory last season: Sunday session after winning Grand Slam
Most improved International player last season: Scotland wing Tony Stanger
Suggestions to improve rugby: Make it 13-a-side!
Other notable landmarks in rugby career: John O'Groats. All rugby tours. 1989/90 captain of Watsonians. With Gavin became the first Scottish brothers to play together in a Lions Test. Played for Barbarians against 1989 All Blacks, and Home Unions against Europe in April 1990. Helped Edinburgh to three Inter-District Championship 'grand slams' between 1986–88. Former captain of Scottish Schools. Played three times for Scotland U-21s
Touchlines: Bandit golfer, watching films, viticulture

Hay, J.A.   Scotland

Full Name: James Alan Hay
International category: Scotland B
Club: Hawick
Position: Hooker
Height: 5'10" **Weight:** 14st 4lb
Occupation: Finishing manager for knitwear company
Birthplace: Hawick, 8.8.64
Family: Susan (wife)
Family links with rugby: Father played for Hawick and South. Father-in-law played for Hawick before switching to Rugby League
Former clubs: Hawick Wanderers, Hawick Linden
International debut (B): Scotland 14, France 12, 1989

Best moment in rugby: Making debut for Hawick v Tynedale (1982)

Worst moment in rugby: Being dropped from Scottish squad last season. Dressing-room scene after Hawick had lost fifth successive National League game

	apps.	pts.
Scotland B (**1989**)		
Last Season	0 caps	0

Most embarrassing moment: Debut for South of Scotland – being awarded South tie after coming on as a replacement for last 10 seconds

Most respected opponent: Scotland hooker Kenny Milne – genuine, modest man who has had to work for everything he has achieved

Best memory last season: Scoring hat-trick of tries against Boroughmuir

Most improved International player last season: Kenny Milne

Suggestions to improve rugby: Become more professional at club level

Other notable landmarks in rugby career: Made Hawick debut aged 17. Member of winning Public School Wanderers' Seven at London Welsh Centenary tournament. First time on Scottish bench (1989). Toured with Scotland to Zimbabwe (1988) and Japan (1989). Scored only Scottish try in 24–28 defeat by Japan in Tokyo

Haycock, P.P.   Ireland

Full Name: Paul Philip Haycock

International category: Ireland (Canada squad)

Club: Terenure College

Position: Wing

Height: 5'11" **Weight:** 13st 2lb

Occupation: Company director

Born: Dublin, 19.5.58

Family: Married with two sons

International debut: Ireland 3, England 16, 1989

Five Nations' debut: As above

Best moment in rugby: Winning first cap against England

Worst moment in rugby: Being one of only two players in Irish World Cup squad not to play a game in 1987 tournament

Most respected opponent:
England wing Rory Underwood
Serious injuries: Dislocated knee
cap playing for Leinster against
Munster (1989)
Best memory last season:
Scoring first ever try for Ireland,
playing against Mid West on North
American tour

	apps.	pts.
Ireland B (1982)		
Last Season	0 caps	0
Ireland (1989)		
Last Season	0 caps	0
Career	1 cap	0
1989	Tour of Canada	

Most improved International player last season: Ireland full-back Kenny
Murphy
Other notable landmarks in rugby career: Helping Terenure win Irish
League for first time (1984). Scoring winning try against rivals St Mary's in
1984 League semi-final. Played for Leinster since 1980 and made Ireland B
debut in 1982

Hayward, B.   Wales

Full Name: Byron Hayward
International category: Wales
U-21 (squad)
Club: Newbridge
Position: Fly-half
Height: 5'8" **Weight:** 11st 10lb
Occupation: Factory worker
Born: Cardiff, 22.2.69
Family: Single with son
Former clubs: Abertillery, Newport
Best moment in rugby: Selection
as captain of Wales Youth
Worst moment in rugby: Being
overlooked by Wales U-21s against
Scotland (1990)
Most embarrassing moment:
Newbridge losing to Abertillery last
season
Most respected opponent:
Newport's Welsh fly-half Paul
Turner

	apps.
Wales U-21 (1989/90)	Rep 1

Other sporting achievements: Water polo for Abertillery. Completing half marathon
Best memory last season: Joining Newbridge
Most improved International player last season: Wales wing Arthur Emyr
Suggestions to improve rugby: Welsh selectors to look more at Gwent players
Other notable landmarks in rugby career: Won 6 caps for Wales Youth. Raised £250 for charity by doing 1,000 press-ups in 45 minutes
Touchlines: Water sports

Henderson, W.M.C.   Scotland

Full Name: William Marr **Crawford** Henderson
International category: Scotland U-21
Club: Madrid Arquitectura, Spain
Position: Wing
Height: 6'1" **Weight:** 13st 3lb
Occupation: Student
Born: London, 11.2.69
Family: Single
Family links with rugby: Father played at London Scottish
Former clubs: Durham University, London Scottish
International debut (U-21): Scotland 10, Wales 24, 1990
Best moment in rugby: Winning Spanish League title last season
Most embarrassing moment: Being tap-tackled in semi-finals of 1989 Middlesex Sevens, playing for London Scottish v Harlequins
Most respected opponent: New Zealand wing John Kirwan
Other sporting achievements: Sprinted for South of England at schools level
Best memory last season: Scotland winning Grand Slam

	apps.	pts.
Scotland U-21 (1990)		
Last Season	1 cap	0

Most improved International player last season: Scotland lock Damian Cronin
Notable landmarks in rugby career: Joint top try-scorer in Spanish League last season with 16. Played five times for Scotland U-21s. Played for 1987 England Schools v Scottish Schools
Touchlines: Hoping to gain a commission with Royal Scots

Hennebry, P.J.   Ireland

Full Name: Paul Joseph Hennebry
International category: Ireland U-25
Club: Terenure College
Position: Fly-half
Height: 6'1" **Weight:** 13st
Occupation: Area sales manager (catering)
Born: Dublin, 12.4.65
Family: Married
International debut: Ireland U-25 12, US Eagles 10, 1990
Best moment in rugby: Scoring 8 points in above match
Worst moment in rugby: Lansdowne beating Terenure 29–0 in 1988/89 Leinster Senior Cup final
Most respected opponent: Former Ireland fly-half Paul Dean
Serious injuries: Chipped bone in neck (aged 17)
Other sporting achievements: Class III tennis for Dublin against Belfast

	apps.	pts.
Ireland U-25 (**1990**)		
Last Season	1 cap	8

Best memory last season: First Leinster cap against Llanelli and scoring 4 points in 33–12 win
Most improved International player last season: Ireland full-back Kenny Murphy
Suggestions to improve rugby: More help and guidance for junior clubs from senior counterparts. Very few top clubs produce their own players

Other notable landmarks in rugby career: Asked to play for Terenure senior team while a fifth XV player (Jan 1986). Played for Leinster U-23s before graduating to senior team and gaining Irish recognition

---

Heslop N.J.   England

Full Name: Nigel John Heslop
International category: England
Full
Club: Orrell
Position: Wing
Height: 5'10" **Weight:** 12st 7lb
Occupation: Police officer
Born: Hartlepool, 4.12.63
Family: Married
Family links with rugby: Brother plays rugby league for Leeds Poly
Former clubs: Waterloo, Liverpool
International debut: Argentina 12, England 25, 1990
Best moment in rugby: Helping England XV defeat Italy XV 33–15 (1990)
Most embarrassing moment: Tackled by stray dog while playing for Liverpool
Most respected opponent: England wing Rory Underwood
Serious injuries: Dislocated elbow (1986)
Other sporting achievements: Sprinted in Police Championships
Best memory last season: Winning County Championship with Lancashire
Most improved International player last season: England centre Jeremy Guscott
Suggestions to improve rugby: Give me more ball

	apps.	pts.
England B (**1989**)		
Last Season	2 caps	0
England (**1990**)		
Last season	2 caps	4
Career	2 caps	4
1990	Tour to Argentina	
1995	Development squad	
England XV 1989/90	1 app	0

Other notable landmarks in rugby career: Played England Colts (1980) but then waited nine years for B cap, on summer tour to Spain. Played for England XV in Rovigo last May as a prelude to touring Argentina with England

---

Hewitt, J.A.   Ireland

Full Name: John Arthur Hewitt
International category: Ireland B
Club: London Irish
Position: Centre
Height: 6' **Weight:** 12st 8lb
Occupation: Teacher
Born: Carrickfergus, 21.11.60
Family: Single
Family links with rugby: Related to Hewitt family who all played for Ireland
Former club: North of Ireland
International debut: South Africa 23, Ireland 15, 1981
Worst moment in rugby: Tearing ankle ligaments the week before I was due to play for Ireland against Australia on my 21st birthday (1982)
Serious injuries: Broken ankle, torn ankle ligaments, dislocated shoulder (twice)
Other sporting achievements: Ulster First Division tennis player
Best memory last season: Representing Ulster against New Zealand
Other notable landmarks in rugby career: Won 2 full caps on

	apps.	pts.
Ireland B (1989)		
Last Season	1 cap	0
Ireland (1981)		
Last Season	0 caps	0
Career	2 caps	0

1981 tour of South Africa, coming on as replacement in each Test. Also played in unofficial Test against Fiji, and represented Ireland U-25s, and Ireland B last season against Scotland

Hill, R.J.   England

Full Name: Richard John Hill
International category: England Full
Club: Bath
Position: Scrum-half
Height: 5'7" **Weight:** 12st 3lb
Occupation: Financial consultant
Born: Birmingham, 4.5.61
Family: Married with son and daughter
Former clubs: Exeter University, Salisbury
International debut: South Africa 33, England 15, 1984
Five Nations' debut: Ireland 13, England 10, 1985
Best moment in rugby: Scoring first try for England, in 34–6 defeat of Wales (1990)
Worst moment in rugby: Being banned (as captain) following England's violent clash with Wales (Cardiff 1987)
Most embarrassing moment: Having pass intercepted by Philippe Sella, who ran in to score from 65 yards, during England's 15–19 Twickenham defeat by France (1987)
Most respected opponent: Former Wales scrum-half David Bishop – he could win matches on his own

	apps.	pts.
England B (**1986**)		
Last Season	0 caps	0
England (**1984**)		
Last Season	7 caps	4
Career	16 caps	4
1990	Tour to Argentina	
1991	World Cup squad	
Lions 1986		

Serious injuries: Knee operation (summer 1990)
Best memories last season: Being recalled to England team for first time since 1987 World Cup; beating Gloucester 48–6 in Pilkington Cup final
Most improved International player last season: England half-back partner Rob Andrew
Suggestions to improve rugby: Establish an Anglo-Welsh championship to strengthen fixture lists. Home and away system in League
Other notable landmarks in rugby career: Kept out of England Colts by Nigel Melville but represented England Students whilst at Exeter University.

Joined Bath and played England final Trial (1983) and won first full cap following season. Share, with Gareth Chilcott, the distinction of having played in all six of Bath's Cup final teams. Captained England four times (1986–87)

Hitchen, N. England

Full Name: Neil Hitchen
International category: England B
Club: Orrell
Position: Hooker
Height: 5'9" **Weight:** 14st 10lb
Occupation: Farmer
Born: Nantwich
Family: Married with one daughter
Former club: Crewe & Nantwich
International debut: Spain 9, England B 31, 1989
Best moment in rugby: Orrell beating Gloucester 16–10 in quarter-finals of 1987/88 John Player Cup
Worst moment in rugby: Orrell losing 31–7 at home to Bath in 1987/88 Cup semi-finals
Most respected opponent: Former England hooker Graham Dawe – strong, fast and skilful
Serious injuries: Broken leg
Most improved International player last season: England flanker Mickey Skinner
Suggestions to improve rugby: Improve fitness, promote game better

	apps.	pts.
England B (1989)		
Last Season	2 caps	0

Other notable landmarks in rugby career: Played over 300 games for Orrell. Toured with England B to Spain (1989), scoring 25-yard try in 32–15 defeat of Spanish Select. Helped England B draw 15–15 with France B (1990)

Hodgkinson, S.D.   England

Full Name: Simon David
Hodgkinson
International category: England
Full
Club: Nottingham
Position: Full-back
Height: 5'10" **Weight:** 12st
Occupation: Schoolmaster
Born: Bristol, 15.12.62
Family: Single
Family links with rugby: Father
played for Thornbury (Bristol)
International debut: Romania 3,
England 58, 1989
Five Nations' debut: England 23,
Ireland 0, 1990
Best moment in rugby: Winning
first England cap in Bucharest
Worst moments in rugby:
Performance for England XV in
7-13 defeat by England B XV,
1988 England final trial
Most embarrassing moment: As
above
Most respected opponent:
French full-back Serge Blanco –
brilliant, resilient all-round player
Other sporting achievements:
Midlands U-15 cricket
Best memory last season: Five
Nations debut v Ireland (scored 7
points)

	apps.	pts.
England B (1988)		
Last Season	0 caps	0
England (1989)		
Last Season	8 caps	103
Career	8 caps	103
1990	Tour to Argentina	
1991	World Cup squad	
England XV 1989/90	1 app	14

Most improved International player last season: England centre Will
Carling
Suggestions to improve rugby: Allow sponsorship payments to players
Other notable landmarks in rugby career: Leading scorer in the 1989/90
Five Nations' Championship with 42 points (10 pens and 6 cons). Only 15th
player ever to score more than 40 points in Championship season. Hold
English record for most conversions

127

Hogg, C.D.   Scotland

Full Name: Carl David Hogg
International category: Scotland U-21
Club: Melrose
Positions: No.8, lock, flanker
Height: 6'4" **Weight:** 15st 4lb
Occupation: Civil engineering student
Born: Galashiels
Family: Single
Family links with rugby: Uncle Jim Telfer played for Scotland and Lions
International debut (U-21): Scotland 10, Wales 24, 1990
Best moment in rugby: Melrose clinching Scottish First Division against Jed-Forest last season
Worst moment in rugby: Being well beaten by Randwick in 1990 Melrose Sevens
Most respected opponent: Kelso's Scotland flanker John Jeffrey
Serious injuries: Back operation to remove disc

	apps.	pts.
Scotland U-21 (1990)		
Last Season	1 cap	0

Best memory last season: Captaining Scotland U-21s
Most improved International player last season: Scotland lock Chris Gray
Other notable landmarks in rugby career: Represented Scottish Schools and U-19s

Hooks, K.J.   Ireland

Full Name: Kenneth John Hooks
International category: Ireland
Full
Club: Ards
Position: Right wing
Height: 5'11" **Weight:** 13st 11lb
Occupation: Mathematics teacher
Born: Markethill, 1.1.60
Family: Married with son
Former clubs: Queen's University
Belfast, Bangor
International debut: Scotland 10,
Ireland 9, 1981
Five Nations' debut: As above
Best moment in rugby: Captain
of Bangor Grammar School when
winning the Ulster School Cup in
front of 20,000 people
Worst moment in rugby: Having
to leave the field with concussion
during the Ireland/New Zealand
game last season – especially after
having had to wait so long to make
second appearance
Most embarrassing moment:
Being asked for my autograph by a
schoolboy before my first cap.
When he realised I was not Tony
Ward he snatched his book away
before I had the chance to sign

	apps.	pts.
Ireland B **(1979)**		
Last Season	0 caps	0
Ireland **(1981)**		
Last Season	3 caps	0
Career	4 caps	0

Most respected opponent: Ireland wing Keith Crossan – tremendous change
of pace and deceptively strong
Other sporting achievements: Represented Irish Schools at athletics
Best memory last season: Playing for Ireland against the All Blacks –
especially the pre-match atmosphere and 'Haka incident' when we advanced
on the tourists' Maori ritual
Most improved International player last season: England captain Will
Carling – from a wing's point of view he is now the best centre in the world
Suggestions to improve rugby: Stop forwards touching or kicking the ball,
except at set pieces – and then only for a maximum 10 seconds!

Other notable landmarks in rugby career: Replacement for Irish Schools aged 16 (won 4 caps). Played for Ulster and Ireland B aged 19. First capped for Ireland aged 21, second cap aged 29 – Irish record for the longest break between first and second caps. Ards' captain
Touchlines: Member of Christians in Sport organisation

Hopkins, D.S.   Wales

Full Name: David Spencer Hopkins
International category: Wales B
Club: Pontypridd
Positions: No.8, flanker
Height: 6'5" **Weight:** 15st
Occupation: Insurance consultant
Born: Cardiff, 6.3.64
Family: Single
Former clubs: Cowbridge, Penarth
International debut: Ontario 10, Wales B 23, 1989 (non-cap)
Best moment in rugby: Being selected for 1988 Wales B squad
Worst moment in rugby: Missing two years of rugby after cracking a vertebra
Most embarrassing moment: Twice dropping ball over try-line in Wales B's 47–0 defeat of Saskatchewan (1989)
Most respected opponent: Wales' Clive Burgess – quite simply the best

Wales B 1989   Tour to Canada

Serious injuries: Cracked vertebra in middle back
Other sporting achievements: County pool player
Most improved International player last season: Welsh prop Laurance Delaney
Suggestions to improve rugby: Improve fitness coaching – concentrating more on individuals rather than groups
Other notable landmarks in rugby career: Joining Pontypridd from Penarth
Touchlines: Golf

Horrobin, J.K.   England

Full Name: Julian Keith Horrobin
International category: England U-21 (squad)
Club: Bristol
Positions: Lock, flanker
Height: 6'3" **Weight:** 15st 2lb
Occupation: Apprentice electrical engineer
Born: Lydney, 17.4.69
Family: Single
Former club: Berry Hill
Best moments in rugby: Beating London Welsh in national knock-out with Berry Hill, and winning Gloucestershire Cup
Worst moment in rugby: Breaking collarbone and having to withdraw from England U-18 team for International season
Most embarrassing moment: Having Julian Davis run rings around me in the Gloucestershire Cup final between Berry Hill and Lydney after I had come back from injury short of fitness

	apps.
England U-21 (1989/90)	Rep 1

Most respected opponent: Leicester's Neil Back – his workrate never seems to falter
Serious injuries: Broken collarbone, four ribs
Other sporting achievements: Selected to county schools athletic team for discus
Best memory last season: After all my injuries, getting to end of season and being able to look forward to start of 1990/91
Most improved International player last season: Scotland flanker John Jeffrey
Suggestions to improve rugby: Raise my fitness to a level where I can keep working and giving 100 per cent for 80 minutes
Other notable landmarks in rugby career: England selection at 16 and 18 age-group. Captaining Gloucestershire U-21s to semi-finals of County Championship. Captaining South West v Leinster. England U-21 replacement v Romania in Bucharest (1989)

Hull, P.A. England

Full Name: Paul Anthony Hull
International category: England B
Club: Bristol
Positions: Fly-half, centre
Height: 5'10" **Weight:** 11st 7lb
Occupation: RAF PTI
Born: London, 17.5.68
Family: Single
Former club: Milton Keynes
International debut: England B
12, Fiji 20, 1990
Best moment in rugby: Being
selected for England tour to
Argentina (1990)
Worst moment in rugby: Missing
Bristol v Harlequins 1988 Cup
final through injury
Most embarrassing moment:
Being kicked in the privates the
first time my girlfriend watched me
play
Serious injuries sustained: Torn
ankle ligaments
Other sporting achievements:
Soccer trials with Southampton
Youth
Best memory last season:
Playing for England U-21 in
Romania
Most improved International

	apps.	pts.
England U-21 (1989)		
Last Season	1 cap	0
England B (1989)		
Last Season	1 cap	0
England 1990	Tour to Argentina	
1995	Development squad	

player last season: England fly-half Rob Andrew
Suggestions to improve rugby: Make game more professional, bring
youngsters on with aid of fitness advisors and private medical insurance
Touchlines: Soul music, nightlife

132

Hynes, M.P. — England

Full Name: Martin Peter Hynes
International category: England U-21
Club: Orrell
Position: Prop
Height: 5'9" **Weight:** 15st
Occupation: Electrician
Born: Wigan, Lancs, 23.8.68
Family: Single
Family links with rugby: Father played Rugby league for Wigan Colts
International debut (U-21): Romania 13, England 54, 1989
Best moment in rugby: Making England debut in Bucharest
Worst moment in rugby: Orrell losing to Gloucester last season in English First Division
Most embarrassing moment: Being sent off for punching v Bedford
Most respected opponent: England prop Jeff Probyn
Serious injuries: Broken coccyx
Other sporting achievements: Swam butterfly for Wigan Wasps in National Championships
Best memory last season: Helping Lancashire win County Championship
Most improved International player last season: England flanker Peter Winterbottom
Other notable landmarks in rugby career: Played for Lancashire Colts and was reserve for Northumberland Colts. Played for Lancashire and North of England U-21s and, after Lancashire's 1989/90 County Championship success, toured with county to Zimbabwe last summer

	apps.	pts.
England U-21 (1989)		
Last Season	1 cap	0

Irwin, D.G.   Ireland

Full Name: David George Irwin
International category: Ireland
Full
Club: Instonians
Position: Centre
Height: 6'1½" **Weight:** 13st 10lb
Occupation: General practitioner
Born: Belfast, 1.2.59
Family: Married with son
Family links with rugby: Brother
Alan represented Ireland B and
toured with me in South Africa
Former club: Queen's University
Belfast
International debut: France 19,
Ireland 18, 1980
Five Nations' debut: As above
Best moments in rugby: Scoring
against Wales in Dublin (1980).
Being picked for 1983 Lions
Worst moment in rugby: 1983
Lions losing first Test to New
Zealand
Most respected opponent:
French centre Philippe Sella
Serious injuries: Broken right tibia
(1982), torn cruciate ligaments in
right knee (1985)
Other sporting achievements:
Northern Ireland pole vault and
triple jump International

	apps.	pts.
Ireland B (1979)		
Last Season	0 caps	0
Ireland (1980)		
Last Season	3 caps	0
Career	25 caps	8
Lions 1983	3 Tests	0

Best memory last season: Leading Ulster against All Blacks and confronting
their 'Haka' for Ireland
Most improved International player last season: England fly-half Rob
Andrew
Suggestions to improve rugby: No loss of earnings when training and
playing
Other notable landmarks in rugby career: Toured Australia with Ireland
aged 20 (1979). Played for combined Ireland/Scotland team in Welsh
Centenary match (1981). Helped Ireland win Triple Crown but broke leg
against Wales (1982). Second top try-scorer for 1983 Lions. Involved in 1987

World Cup. Caught in terrorist bomb explosion (Newry, 1987). Picked to captain Ireland in France (1988) and North America (1989) and missed both through injury. Longest serving International in 1990 Five Nations' Championship

Touchlines: Sports medicine, drawing, painting. Very fortunate to be able to play rugby and achieve in medicine

Jackson, D.A.   Scotland

Full Name: David Alexander Jackson
International category: Scotland U-21
Club: Hillhead/Jordanhill
Position: Lock
Height: 6'5" **Weight:** 15st 2lb
Occupation: Public relations administrator
Born: Elderslie, 16.3.69
Family: Single
Former club: Hillhead
International debut (U-21): Scotland 10, Wales 24, 1990
Best moment in rugby: Helping Glasgow beat Anglo-Scots to win 1989/90 Inter-District Championship
Most respected opponent: Scotland lock Chris Gray
Serious injuries: Knee (1988)
Other sporting achievements: Won 200m Inverclyde Sports Schoolboys final

	apps.	pts.
Scotland U-21 (1990)		
Last Season	1 cap	0

Best memories last season: Hillhead/Jordanhill beating Langholm. Glasgow winning I-D Championship
Suggestions to improve rugby: Neutral touch judges at all games so referees can be informed of foul play
Notable landmarks in rugby career: Joined H/J when school rugby ceased because of school strikes and made debut in senior XV aged 18. Graduated

from Glasgow U-21s to full team and national U-21s. Scored try in Scotland
U-21s' 21–4 defeat of Combined Services, March 1990
Touchlines: Officer in Boys Brigade, enjoy music

Jardine, I.C.   Scotland

Full Name: Ian Carrick Jardine
International category: Scotland B
Club: Stirling County
Position: Centre
Height: 6'1" **Weight:** 13st 7lb
Occupation: Civil engineer
Born: Dunfermline, 20.10.64
Family: Married
Family links with rugby: Four
brothers play at Stirling
International debut (B): Scotland
22, Ireland 22, 1990
Best moments in rugby: Winning
promotion with Stirling from
Scottish Second to First Division
(1988/89). Winning Inter-District
Championship with Glasgow
(1989/90)
Worst moment in rugby: Losing
any match
Most respected opponent:
Former Scotland wing Keith
Robertson
Best memory last season:
Winning first Scotland B cap v
Ireland

	apps.	pts.
Scotland B (**1989**)		
Last Season	1 cap	0

Most improved International player last season: Scotland wing Tony
Stanger
Suggestions to improve rugby: Players compensated for earnings lost due
to rugby
Other notable landmarks in rugby career: Warmed bench for Scotland
U-21s (1986) and again for Scotland B in Italy (1988/89)
Touchlines: Hill walking, cycling

Jardine, S.   Scotland

Full Name: Stewart Jardine
International category: Scotland B (squad)
Club: South Glamorgan Institute
Position: Scrum-half
Height: 5'10" **Weight:** 12st
Occupation: PE student
Born: Edinburgh, 24.12.65
Family: Single
Family links with rugby: Father played for Edinburgh Academicals and Scotland B
Former clubs: Edinburgh Academicals, Glamorgan Wanderers
Best moment in rugby: Touring Japan with Scotland (1989)
Worst moment in rugby: Requiring 17 stitches after being head-butted 10 minutes into match against Kyushu on above tour
Most respected opponent: Wales scrum-half Robert Jones
Other sporting achievements: Cricket for Shropshire 2nd XI. Ran half-marathon

	apps.
Scotland B (**1989/90**)	Rep 2

Best memory last season: Playing (for Reds) in Scotland Trial at Murrayfield, despite 4–45 defeat
Most improved International player last season: Scotland wing Tony Stanger
Other notable landmarks in rugby career: Attended school in South Africa
Touchlines: Windsurfing, waterskiing, canoeing

Jeffrey, J.   Scotland

Full Name: John Jeffrey
International category: Scotland Full
Club: Kelso
Positions: Flanker, No.8
Height: 6'4" **Weight:** 14st 5lb
Occupation: Farmer
Birthplace: Kelso, 25.3.59
Family: Single
International debut: Scotland 12, Australia 37, 1984
Five Nations' debut: Scotland 15, Ireland 18, 1985
Best moment in rugby: Winning 1990 Five Nations' Grand Slam with Scotland
Worst moment in rugby: Scotland losing 12–21 to England (April 1988) when playing for Triple Crown
Most embarrassing moment: Being 'wound-up' by Fin Calder the day before the 1990 Grand Slam decider against England
Most respected opponent: Ireland flanker Phil Matthews
Serious injuries: Cartilage operation whilst at school
Best memory last season: Winning Grand Slam

	apps.	pts.
Scotland B (1983)		
Last Season	0 caps	0
Scotland (**1984**)		
Last Season	8 caps	0
Career	30 caps	36
Lions 1986		
1989		

Most improved International player last season: Scotland prop Paul Burnell
Suggestions to improve rugby: Work harder on fitness
Other notable landmarks in rugby career: Hold Scottish record for a forward of 9 tries in cap Internationals. Member of both the British Lions and Five Nations teams in the 1986 IRB celebration matches. Captained Kelso to Scottish Division One title in 1988/89 . Most capped Kelso International, with 29. Played five times for 1989 British Lions' midweek team in Australia. Last season represented Home Unions against Europe

Jenkins, G.R.   Wales

Full Name: Garin Richard Jenkins
International category: Wales
Full (squad)
Club: Pontypool
Position: Hooker
Height: 5'10" **Weight:** 15st 7lb
Occupation: Builder
Born: Ynysybwl, 18.8.67
Family: Single
Family links with rugby: Father's
uncle played for Wales. Mother's
cousin propped for Wales and
Lions
Former clubs: Ynysybwl,
Pontypridd, King Country (NZ)
Best moment in rugby: Welsh
replacement against France (1990)
Worst moment in rugby: Being
dropped as replacement when Ian
Watkins returned from suspension
Most respected opponent: All of
them
Best memory last season:
Playing for Pontypool against All
Blacks
**Most improved International
player last season:** Wales scrum-half Robert Jones
Other notable landmarks in rugby career: Represented Boys Clubs of
Wales U-18s and Glamorgan U-23s. Toured Kenya with Pontypool (1990)
Touchlines: Soccer, cricket, weightlifting

	apps.
Wales B (**1989/90**)	Rep 1
Wales (**1989/90**)	Rep 1

John, P.   Wales

Full Name: Paul John
International category: Wales U-21
Club: Cardiff
Position: Scrum-half
Height: 5'10" **Weight:** 12st 10lb
Occupation: Student
Born: Pontypridd, 25.1.70
Family: Single
Family links with rugby: Father played for Pontypool, Penarth, Pontypridd and Barbarians
Former club: Pontypridd (youth)
International debut (U-21): Scotland 10, Wales 24, 1990
Best moment in rugby: Helping Cardiff beat Llanelli in 1989/90 Welsh Cup
Worst moment in rugby: Dislocating shoulder in Wales U-18 Trial and requiring operation
Most respected opponent: Swansea's Wales scrum-half Robert Jones
Serious injuries: Broken arm, dislocated shoulder and elbow

	apps.	pts.
Wales U-21 **(1990)**		
Last Season	1 cap	0

Best memory last season: Beating Scotland with Wales U-21s
Most improved International player last season: Wales fly-half David Evans
Other notable landmarks in rugby career: Represented Wales at U-15, U-18, U-20 and U-21 levels. Also played for Welsh Students last season
Touchlines: Golf, squash

Johns, P.S.   Ireland

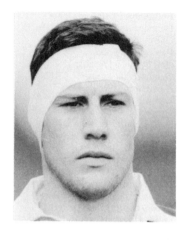

Full Name: Patrick Stephen Johns
International category: Ireland B
Club: Dublin University
Position: Lock
Height: 6'6" **Weight:** 16st
Occupation: Dental student
Born: Portadown, 19.2.68
Family: Single
Former clubs: Dungannon, Newcastle University, Gosforth
International debut (B): Scotland 22, Ireland 22, 1989
Best moment in rugby: First match for Ireland (Schools v Australia, 1988)
Most embarrassing moment: Getting my shorts ripped off aged 13
Most respected opponent: New Zealand lock Alan Whetton – the best about
Serious injuries: Neck injury, broken wrist
Best memory last season: Winning record sixth Inter-Pro Championship with Ulster
Most improved International player last season: Ireland full-back Kenny Murphy

	apps.	pts.
Ireland B (1989)		
Last Season	1 cap	0

Suggestions to improve rugby: Less emphasis on set-play. Encourage more open rugby
Other notable landmarks in rugby career: Ulster v 1989 All Blacks. Toured Canada with Dungannon (1989). Played for Ireland at U-25, U-21 and Schools level
Touchlines: Cycling

Jones, C.J. Wales

Full Name: Ceri John Jones
International category: Wales B
Club: Pontypridd
Position: Centre
Height: 6'1" **Weight:** 15st
Occupation: Fitter
Born: Ynysybwl, 30.7.65
Family: Single
Former clubs: Ynysybwl, Cardiff, King Country Province (NZ)
International debut: Canada 29, Wales B 31, 1989
Best moment in rugby: Being picked for B Test v Canada
Worst moment in rugby: Knee injury sustained during 1989 Canadian tour
Most embarrassing moment: Jumping in the air in celebration after a Cup final, only to find we had lost by a point, not won
Most respected opponent: Ynysybwl's Phil Humphreys
Serious injuries: Knee, ligaments and cartilage

	apps.	pts.
Wales B (**1989**)		
Last Season	1 cap	4
1989	Tour to Canada	

Other sporting achievements: Ynysybwl Boys Club five-a-side soccer champions, District champions (1976)
Best memory last season: Scoring try v Canada at Edmonton
Most improved International player last season: Wales centre Mark Ring
Suggestions to improve rugby: Involve more ex-players in administration
Other notable landmarks in rugby career: Captain of Pontypridd. Vice-captain of King Country Province

Jones, G.   Wales

Full Name: Gary Jones
International category: Wales Full
Club: Llanelli
Position: Flanker
Height: 6'3" **Weight:** 15st 4lb
Occupation: Fitter
Born: Porth, 17.7.60
Family: Married with two sons
Family links with rugby: Brother
plays
Former clubs: Pontypridd, Ystrad
Rhondda
International debut: New
Zealand 54, Wales 9, 1988
Five Nations' debut: France 31,
Wales 12, 1989
Best moment in rugby: Beating
England at Cardiff (1989)
Worst moment in rugby: Llanelli
losing 1989/90 Schweppes Cup
final to Neath
Most embarrassing moment:
First game for Wales (v North
Auckland, 1988 NZ tour).
Opposition penalty hit bar, I
turned, ball bounced back over my
head and they scored
Most respected opponent:
England No.8 Mike Teague
Serious injuries: Broken shoulder,
twice dislocated

	apps.	pts.
Wales B (1986)		
Last Season	0 caps	0
Wales (1988)		
Last Season	2 caps	0
Career	5 caps	0

Best memory last season: Playing for Llanelli v New Zealand (lost 0-11)
Most improved International player last season: England centre Will
Carling
Suggestions to improve rugby: Broken time payments
Other notable landmarks in rugby career: One of few players not to have
picked up representative honours at Schools' or Youth level. Joined Llanelli
(1985) after six seasons with Pontypridd and within year had played for Wales
B and toured Italy. Made full debut in second Test of 1988 New Zealand
tour. Have represented Barbarians
Touchlines: Golf

Jones, M.A.   Wales

Full Name: Mark Alun Jones
International category: Wales Full
Club: Neath
Positions: No.8, lock, flanker
Height: 6'5" **Weight:** 16st 6lb
Occupation: Fitness officer
Born: Tredegar, 22.6.65
Family: Single
Former club: Tredegar
International debut: Scotland 21,
Wales 15, 1987
Five Nations' debut: As above
Best moment in rugby: Wales
beating England at Cardiff (1989)
Worst moment in rugby: Being
left out of Neath's 1988 Cup final
team
Most respected opponent: New
Zealand No.8 Wayne Shelford
Best memory last season: Neath
playing All Blacks at The Gnoll
**Most improved International
player last season:** Scotland
fly-half Craig Chalmers
Suggestions to improve rugby:
More consideration towards
players. At present we are putting
in all the effort and not receiving
any benefits

	apps.	pts.
Wales B (1985)		
Last Season	1 cap	0
Wales (1987)		
Last Season	7 caps	0
Career	13 caps	8

Other notable landmarks in rugby career: Won 4 caps for Wales Youth
in 1983. Played three times for Wales B before moving up a grade and scoring
try on full Welsh debut. Joined Neath (1985/86)
Touchlines: Watching Clint Eastwood films

Jones, R.N.   Wales

Full Name: Robert Nicholas Jones
International category: Wales Full
Club: Swansea
Position: Scrum-half
Height: 5'7" **Weight:** 11st 3lb
Occupation: Marketing executive
Born: Trebanos, 10.11.65
Family: Married
Family links with rugby:
Father-in-law Clive Rowlands
played for Wales and Lions.
Brother has played for Llanelli and
Aberavon
International debut: England 21,
Wales 18, 1986
Five Nations' debut: As above
Best moments in rugby:
Captaining Wales. 1989 Lions
winning decisive third Test against
Australia

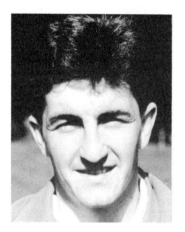

Worst moments in rugby:
Captaining Wales in whitewash –
very, very despondent. Defeat by
New Zealand in 1987 World Cup
Most embarrassing moment:
Attempted dropped goal for Wales
against Ireland, hit ground before
ball and sent it 3 yards. Paul Dean
collected and initiated move which
led to Irish try

	apps.	pts.
Wales B (**1985**)		
Last Season	0 caps	0
Wales (**1986**)		
Last Season	5 caps	0
Career	32 caps	4
Lions 1986		
1989	3 Tests	0

Most respected opponents:
Scrum-halves Pierre Berbizier and Gary Armstrong
Serious injuries: None
Other sporting achievements: Represented Wales at cricket at three
age-group levels
Best memory last season: Lions' success
Most improved International player last season: England centre Will
Carling
Suggestions to improve rugby: Greater depth of consideration for players.
Re-consider amateur issue so that players can benefit away from play. Look
after players' employers with tickets etc

Other notable landmarks in rugby career: Wales and Swansea captain. First represented All Whites while still at Cwmtawe School, having already played for West Wales U-11s and Wales 12-group. Enjoyed outstanding World Cup (1987) and toured New Zealand (1988). Partnered Jonathan Davies in twenty-two Internationals. A member of the 1989 Lions' series win in Australia. Missed Welsh tour of Namibia last summer through injury
Touchlines: Golf (24-handicap)

Jones, S.N.   Wales

Full Name: Spencer Nathan Jones
International category: Wales U-21
Club: Taffs Well
Position: No.8
Height: 6'5" **Weight:** 16st 4lb
Occupation: Technician
Born: Cardiff, 7.11.68
Family: Single
International debut (U-21): Scotland 10, Wales 24, 1990
Best moment in rugby: Scoring winning try in Schweppes Cup-tie v Maesteg
Worst moment in rugby: Being forced, by strained groin, to leave field early while playing Wales U-21s v Combined Services U-21s
Most embarrassing moment: Trying, and failing, to kick ball in semi-finals of East District Cup v Llanharan

	apps.	pts.
Wales U-21 (**1990**)		
Last Season	1 Cap	0

Best memory last season: Coming on as replacement for Wales U-21 v Scotland at Ayr, 1990
Most improved International player last season: Wales fly-half David Evans
Suggestions to improve rugby: Make game more attractive to youngsters
Touchlines: Swimming, weight training

Jones, S.T.   Wales

Full Name: Stephen (Staff)
Thomas Jones
International category: Wales B
Club: Pontypool
Position: Prop
Height: 5'11" **Weight:** 16st 7lb
Occupation: Blacksmith's striker
Born: Pontypridd, 4.1.59
Family: Married with child
Family links with rugby: Father
played
Former club: Ynysybwl
International debut: Scotland 15,
Wales 19, 1983
Five Nations' debut: As above
Best moment in rugby: Playing
for 1983 British Lions v New
Zealand

Worst moments in rugby:
Playing in Pontypool teams beaten
by New Zealand and Australia
Most embarrassing moment:
Running line at Cardiff
Most respected opponent:
Scotland prop Iain Milne
Serious injuries: Damaged knee
ligaments
Best memory last season:
Pontypool finishing third in Merit
Table

	apps.	pts.
Wales B (1981)		
Last Season	1 cap	0
Wales (1983)		
Last Season	0 caps	0
Career	10 caps	4
Lions 1983	3 Tests	0

Most improved International player last season: England lock Paul
Ackford
Suggestions to improve rugby: Scrap 90-degree scrum wheel law
Other notable landmarks in rugby career: First selected for Wales squad
in 1979 for Romania game, having previously played for Wales Youth and B.
Scored try on full debut at Murrayfield. Made nearly 400 appearances for
Pontypool
Touchlines: Gardening (allotment), badminton, swimming

Full Name: Wayne Patrick Paul
Kearns
International category: Ireland
U-21
Club: London Irish
Position: Wing
Height: 5'11" **Weight:** 13st
Occupation: Car mechanic
Born: Newmarket, England,
15.4.69
Family: Single
Former club: Harlow
International debut (U-21): Italy
9, Ireland 10, 1989
Best moment in rugby: Being
picked for Ireland U-21s
Worst moment in rugby: Not
being picked the year before
Most respected opponent:
England B wing Tony Underwood
Best memory last season:
Playing New Zealand U-21s
**Most improved International
player last season:** Ireland flanker
Paul Collins
**Other notable landmarks in
rugby career:** Represented London Division Colts (1987/88)

	apps.	pts.
Ireland U-21 (**1989**)		
Last Season	2 caps	0

Kenny, P.   Ireland

Full Name: Paddy Kenny
International category: Ireland B
Club: Wanderers
Positions: Flanker, No.8
Height: 6'3" **Weight:** 15st 2lb
Occupation: Investment banker
Born: Philippines, 28.4.60
Family: Married with one child
Family links with rugby:
Son-in-law of former Ireland
International Jim McCarthy
(1948–55)
Former club: University College
Dublin
International debut (B): Scotland
22, Ireland 22, 1989
Best moment in rugby: Taking
part in 1988 Hong Kong Sevens
Worst moment in rugby: Missing
selection for Ireland v Fiji (1985)
Most respected opponent: New
Zealand back row Zinzan Brooke
Serious injuries: Damaged
shoulder

	apps.	pts.
Ireland B (1989)		
Last Season	1 cap	4

Best memory last season:
Playing for Leinster v New Zealand
Most improved International player last season: Former New Zealand
full-back John Gallagher
Other notable landmarks in rugby career: UCD tour to USA (1981).
Ireland tour to Japan (1985). Scored one of Ireland B's two tries in 22–22
draw with Scotland B last season

Keyes, R.P.   Ireland

Full Name: Ralph Patrick Keyes
International category: Ireland
Full
Club: Constitution
Position: Fly-half
Height: 5'9" **Weight:** 12st 7lb
Occupation: Pension and
investment broker
Born: Cork, 1.8.61
Family: Married with son and
daughter
Family links with rugby: Father
played for Cork and Munster
International debut: England 25,
Ireland 20, 1986
Five Nations' debut: As above
Best moment in rugby: Being
capped v England at Twickenham
Worst moment in rugby: Injury
in a club game seven days after
Ireland debut, which forced me out
of next game v Scotland
Most respected opponent:
Former Ireland fly-half Paul Dean
Serious injuries: Ripped hamstring
Best memory last season:
Representing Munster v All Blacks
**Most improved International
player last season:** England wing
Rory Underwood

	apps.	pts.
Ireland B (1984)		
Last Season	0 caps	0
Ireland (1986)		
Last Season	Rep 2	0
Career	1 cap	0

Suggestions to improve rugby: Re-structure present archaic amateur laws
Other notable landmarks in rugby career: Member of 1983 and 1985
Munster Cup-winning Cork teams. Captained club in 1989/90 season. Made
Ireland B debut in 23–20 defeat of Scotland at Galway in 1984. Bench reserve
for Ireland in 1985 and toured Japan that same year. Replaced Paul Dean at
half-time of second Test in Tokyo (won 38–15) and again replaced
unfortunate Dean when winning first full cap (1986)
Touchlines: Golf

Kiernan, M.J.   Ireland

Full Name: Michael J. Kiernan
International category: Ireland Full
Club: Dolphin
Positions: Centre, wing
Height: 6' **Weight:** 14st
Occupation: Company director
Born: Cork, 17.1.61
Family: Married with daughter
Family links with rugby: Several
Former club: Lansdowne
International debut: Ireland 20, Wales 12, 1982
Five Nations' debut: As above
Best moment in rugby: Winning Triple Crown in 1985
Worst moment in rugby: British Lions losing 6-38 to New Zealand in fourth Test (1983)
Most respected opponent: All Black centre Joe Stanley
Serious injuries: Depressed cheekbone (1988)
Other sporting achievements: National 200m sprint champion (1981)
Best memory last season: Beating Wales in Dublin in Wooden Spoon decider

	apps.	pts.
Ireland (1982)		
Last Season	4 caps	20
Career	41 caps	283
Lions 1983	3 Tests	0
1986		

Most improved International players last season: Ireland's Terry Kingston and Michael Bradley
Suggestions to improve rugby: Increase try worth to 5 points
Other notable landmarks in rugby career: Record points scorer for Ireland, having taken tally to 283 since winning first cap in 1982 as a replacement against Wales. Set Irish record for overseas tour with 65 on 1985 tour of Japan. Began representative career with Schools cap in 1979 and toured South Africa with Ireland in 1981 and North America (scoring 61 points) in 1989
Touchlines: Golf, tennis, athletics

Kilford, W.A.   England

Full Name: Wayne Ashley Kilford
International category: England U-21
Club: Nottingham
Position: Full-back
Height: 5'11" **Weight:** 13st
Occupation: Sales engineer
Born: Malvern, 25.1.69
Family: Single
Family links with rugby: Father played for Nottingham. Brother plays for Notts, Lincs & Derby
Former club: Mansfield
International debut: Netherlands 3, England U-21 24, 1990
Best moment in rugby: Nottingham beating Bath and Gloucester in English First Division last season
Worst moment in rugby: England Colts losing to French Juniors 15–24 at Bristol in 1988 after dominating
Most respected opponent: Former England fly-half Les Cusworth – for his awareness

	apps.	pts.
England U-21 (**1990**)		
Last Season	2 caps	8

Other sporting achievements: Played cricket for Nottinghamshire 2nd XI
Best memory last season: Scoring 2 of England U-21's 3 tries in 23–16 defeat of French Armed Forces
Most improved International player last season: England fly-half Rob Andrew
Suggestions to improve rugby: Give more points for a try and less for kicks
Other notable landmarks in rugby career: Played for Notts, Lincs & Derby in English County Championship. Represented Midlands U-21s last season against New Zealand U-21s
Touchlines: Golf

Killick, N.J.   England

Full Name: Nicholas James Killick
International category: England U-21
Club: Harlequins
Position: Hooker
Height: 5'7" **Weight:** 13st 7lb
Occupation: Chemical salesman
Born: Haywards Heath, 27.9.67
Family: Single
Family links with rugby: Father played for Streatham/Croydon
Former club: Haywards Heath
International debut (U-21):
Romania 13, England 54, 1989
Best moment in rugby: England debut in Bucharest
Worst moment in rugby:
Harlequins v Headingley (1988/89) – travelled to Yorkshire only to find game was called off
Most embarrassing moment: Performing an after-dinner speech
Most respected opponent: England hooker Brian Moore
Other sporting achievements: Captain of school volleyball team

	apps.	pts.
England U-21 (**1989**)		
Last Season	1 cap	4

Best memory last season: Helping an inexperienced Harlequins team beat Cardiff 43–31
Most improved International player last season: England prop Jeff Probyn
Suggestions to improve rugby: Give touch judges more authority to help stamp out foul play
Other notable landmarks in rugby career: Moved to Harlequins in 1986/87. Toured Kenya with Penguins

Kimmins, R.   England

Full Name: Robert Kimmins
International category: England B
Club: Orrell
Position: Lock
Height: 6'8" **Weight:** 18st 5lb
Occupation: Bricklayer
Born: Wigan, 28.1.62
Family: Married with child
International debut: Spain v
England U-23s, 1984
Best moment in rugby: Being
selected by England to tour
Argentina (1990)
Most respected opponent: None.
I let them respect me
Best memory last season:
Playing for England XV in 33–15
defeat of Italian XV
**Other notable landmarks in
rugby career:** Made seven
appearances for England B
(scoring 1 try), including caps
against Spain and Fiji last season

	apps.	pts.
England B (1985)		
Last Season	2 caps	0
England 1990	Tour to Argentina	
England XV 1989/90	1 app	0

Kingston, T.J.   Ireland

Full Name: Terence John Kingston
International category: Ireland
Full
Club: Dolphin
Position: Hooker
Height: 5'10" **Weight:** 14st 6lb
Occupation: Computer consultant
Born: Cork, 19.9.63
Family: Single
Former club: Lansdowne
International debut: Ireland 6,
Wales 13, 1987 World Cup
Five Nations' debut: Ireland 22,
Scotland 18, 1988
Best moment in rugby: Selection
for 1987 World Cup and gaining
first cap v Wales during the
tournament
Worst moment in rugby: Being
dropped from Irish team and
Dolphin's failure to qualify for
National League in play-off match
last season
Most respected opponent: All of
them
Best memory last season:
Scoring winning try v Wales,
having been called up as a late replacement

	apps.	pts.
Ireland (1987)		
Last Season	2 caps	4
Career	9 caps	8

Most improved International player last season: Ireland prop John
Fitzgerald
Suggestions to improve rugby: An extra 5 metres should be added to all
penalties as an increased deterrent and to encourage team benefiting to take
fast, running ball while opposition is retreating

Knight, P. Wales

Full Name: Paul Knight
International category: Wales Full
Club: Pontypridd
Position: Prop
Height: 6' **Weight:** 16st
Occupation: Production controller
Born: Tonypandy, 30.4.61
Family: Married with a daughter
Former clubs: Treorchy, Aberavon
International debut: Namibia 9,
Wales 18, 1990
Best moment in rugby: Winning
first full cap in first Test at
Windhoek
**Other notable landmarks in
rugby career:** Selected for Wales
tour of Namibia (1990) and played
in both Tests

	apps.	pts.
Wales (**1990**)		
Last Season	2 caps	0
Career	2 caps	0

Laity, C.   Wales

Full Name: Colin Laity
International category: Wales B
Club: Neath
Position: Centre
Height: 5'10" **Weight:** 13st 7lb
Occupation: Bank clerk
Born: Helston, Cornwall, 19.6.65
Family: Single
Former clubs: Helston, Redruth, Penarth, Llanelli, South Glamorgan Institute
Best moment in rugby: Representing Barbarians v 1988 Australians
Worst moment in rugby: Neath losing to Llanelli in 1989 Schweppes Cup final and suffering concussion during game
Most respected opponent: Neath flanker Lyn Jones
Serious injuries: Damaged knee and ankle ligaments, concussion
Best memory last season: Arriving back at The Gnoll to 6,000 fans after winning Cup

Wales B (1988)
  Last Season   Tour to Canada

Most improved International player last season: England scrum-half Richard Hill
Suggestions to improve rugby: Adequate reimbursment to players for loss of earnings due to rugby
Other notable landmarks in rugby career: Represented Cornwall, South and South West Division, Crawshays and Barbarians. Educated at Helston Comprehensive School, Cornish College of Further and Higher Education and South Glamorgan Institute where I was rugby captain. Played for England Students in inaugural Students World Cup, scoring 2 tries in 16–9 defeat of Scotland. Eligible for England or Wales but chose latter
Touchlines: Cycling, sea-fishing (best is 6lb bass)

Lamerton, A.E.   Wales

Full Name: Andrew Edwin
Lamerton
International category: Wales
U-21
Club: Llanelli
Position: Hooker
Height: 6' **Weight:** 14st 2lb
Occupation: Student
Born: Pontypridd, 28.5.70
Family: Single
Former club: Beddau
International debut (U-21):
Scotland 10, Wales 24, 1990
Best moment in rugby: Playing
for Llanelli v 1989 All Blacks
Most embarrassing moment:
Attempted to touch loose ball down
behind own try-line at Newport last
season but it bounced over my
hands and Newport wing scored
Most respected opponent:
Former England hooker Graham
Dawe
Best memory last season:
Llanelli beating Neath at Stradey
Park

	apps.	pts.
Wales U-21 (1990)		
Last Season	1 cap	0

Most improved International player last season: Wales prop Brian
Williams
Other notable landmarks in rugby career: Played four times for Wales
U-18s and four times for Wales Youth
Touchlines: Golf

158

Langford, S.R.   England

Full Name: Simon Robert
Langford
International category: England B
Club: Orrell
Position: Full-back
Height: 6'1" **Weight:** 13st 10lb
Occupation: Graphic designer
Born: Wigan, Lancs, 18.12.61
Family: Single
Family links with rugby: None.
But grandfather (Manchester
United and Manchester City) and
father (Manchester United) played
professional soccer
International debut: England B
18, Soviet Union 10, 1989
Best moments in rugby: Debut
for Lancashire aged 19, alongside
Cotton, Neary and Beaumont.
North beating 1988 Wallabies
Worst moment in rugby: Not
being selected for England training
trip to Lanzarote last season
Most embarrassing moment:
Missing 5 kicks at goal for Lancashire
in defeat by Northumberland

	apps.	pts.
England B (1989)		
Last Season	1 cap	0

Most respected opponents: England trio of Peter Winterbottom, Fran
Clough and Rob Andrew
Serious injuries: Dislocated shoulder (five times), cartilage operation
Other sporting achievements: Soccer for Manchester United Schoolboys
and Preston Reserves
Best memory last season: Making debut for England B
Most improved International player last season: England fly-half Rob
Andrew
Suggestions to improve rugby: Introduce home and away structure to
English Leagues to make it more competitive
Other notable landmarks in rugby career: Played for England Schools (16
Group) and toured Australia with England U-19s. Also played for England
U-23s. Represented Northern Division for last five years, and helped
Lancashire win 1989/90 County Championship
Touchlines: Golf, soccer

159

Leckie, D.E.W.   Scotland

Full Name: David Eric William
Leckie
International category: Scotland B
Club: Edinburgh Academicals
Position: No.8
Height: 6'3" **Weight:** 15st 7lb
Occupation: Solicitor
Born: Edinburgh, 20.10.62
Family: Single
Family links with rugby: Father's
uncle, Ross Logan, played
scrum-half for Scotland (1931–37)
International debut (B): Scotland
9, France 15, 1987
Best moment in rugby: Scoring 5
tries for Scotland in 48–6 defeat of
Goshawks on 1988 tour of
Zimbabwe
Worst moment in rugby: Missing
tackle for Scotland in B
International against Ireland last
season which led to try
Most respected opponent:
Former Scotland flanker Finlay
Calder
Serious injuries: Broken
cheekbone, damaged medial knee ligaments

	apps.	pts.
Scotland B (1987)		
Last Season	1 cap	0

Best memory last season: Watching Scotland win Grand Slam
Most improved International player last season: Scotland wing Tony
Stanger
Suggestions to improve rugby: Unions must reimburse employers for time
players take off work for rugby
Other notable landmarks in rugby career: Captained Scottish Universities
on tour to France. Captained North and Midlands in Inter-District
Championship
Touchlines: Tennis, squash

Lee, A.J.   England

Full Name: Andrew John Lee
International category: England U-21
Club: Saracens
Position: Fly-half
Height: 5'9" **Weight:** 13st
Occupation: Settlements clerk
Born: Wanstead, 10.11.68
Family: Single
Family links with rugby: Father coaches Woodford U-8s
Former club: Woodford
International debut: French Armed Forces 16, England U-21 23, 1990
Best moment in rugby: Scoring winning try for Saracens against Bath in English First Division last season

Worst moment in rugby: Missing simple first kick at goal on England U-21 debut
Most embarrassing moment: As above

	apps.	pts.
England U-21 (1990)		
Last Season	1 cap	11

Most respected opponent: England fly-half Rob Andrew
Serious injuries: Torn Achilles tendon aged 16 (out for six months). Osgood Schlatter's disease in knees
Other sporting achievements: Professional cricketer for two years. Played with Essex CCC between U-12 and Colts level. Played for Haringey Cricket College
Best memory last season: First-team debut for Saracens against Rosslyn Park in First Division – kicked last-minute penalty to win match
Most improved International player last season: England full-back Simon Hodgkinson
Suggestions to improve rugby: Bring closet payments of players out into open. Very strange for me, having come from sport where I was paid to play, to put in same hours of commitment for an amateur game
Other notable landmarks in rugby career: Never played rugby seriously until last season when plucked out of Saracens' U-21 team and given first-team place. Had to pull out of England U-21 squad to play Netherlands because

of club commitments. Captained Eastern Counties to U-21 County Championship last season and played in team which won previous final
Touchlines: Cricket for Woodford Wells. Coach over 100 U-13s every Sunday

Lenihan, D.G.   Ireland

Full Name: Donal Gerald Lenihan
International category: Ireland Full
Club: Constitution
Position: Lock
Height: 6'4" **Weight:** 17st
Occupation: Building Society manager
Born: Cork, 12.9.59
Family: Married with son
Former club: University College, Cork
International debut: Ireland 12, Australia 16, 1981
Five Nations' debut: Ireland 20, Wales 12, 1982
Best moments in rugby: Winning two Triple Crowns with Ireland
Most respected opponent: Former England lock Maurice Colclough
Serious injuries: Broken nose, finger
Best memory last season: Regaining captaincy of Ireland
Most improved International player last season: Ireland full-back Kenny Murphy, and entire Scotland team
Suggestions to improve rugby: Standardise refereeing interpretations in southern and northern hemispheres

	apps.	pts.
Ireland B (1980)		
Last Season	0 caps	0
Ireland (1981)		
Last Season	4 caps	0
Career	46 caps	4
Lions 1983		
1986		
1989		

Other notable landmarks in rugby career: Made Ireland debut for Schools (1977) and within four years had graduated through U-23s (1979) and Ireland B (1980) to full status (1981)

Leonard, J. England

Full Name: Jason Leonard
International category: England B
Club: Harlequins
Position: Loose-head prop
Height: 5'10" **Weight:** 16st 7lb
Occupation: Builder
Born: Barking, London, 14.8.68
Family: Single
Former clubs: Barking, Saracens
International debut: Argentina 12, England 25, 1990
Best moments in rugby: Playing against Fiji for England B. Saracens beating Bath in English First Division
Worst moments in rugby: Two seasons of Cup defeats with Saracens
Most embarrassing moment: Ball landing on my head during B match in France last season
Most respected opponent: England prop Jeff Probyn – technique and physical abilities
Best memory last season: Saracens' League success
Most improved International players last season: England props Paul Rendall and Probyn

	apps.	pts.
England B (1989)		
Last Season	2 caps	0
England (1990)	2 caps	0
1990	Tour to Argentina	
1991	World Cup squad	
1995	Development squad	

Suggestions to improve rugby: Improve grass roots part of game
Other notable landmarks in rugby career: Helped Barking win Essex Colts Cup before tasting success at Twickenham with Eastern Counties winning U-21 County Championship. Won English Second Division title with Saracens (1988/89) and sat on England U-21 bench in Romania (1989). Broke into

England B ranks last season, winning caps v Fiji and France and warming bench v USSR. Moved to Harlequins at start of season

Liley, J.G.   England

Full Name: John Garin Liley
International category: England (squad)
Club: Leicester
Position: Full-back
Height: 5'11" **Weight:** 12st 10lb
Occupation: Trainee accountant
Born: Wakefield, 21.8.67
Family: Single
Family links with rugby: Father and grandfather played for Wakefield
Former clubs: Sandal, Wakefield
International debut: Banco Nacion (Arg.) 29, England 21, 1990
Best moment in rugby: Scoring 15 points against Bath in final game of last season to beat Dusty Hare's season-scoring record at Leicester (438) by 1 point
Worst moment in rugby: Wakefield losing to Headingley in 1987/88 Yorkshire Cup final
Most respected opponent: Scotland full-back Gavin Hastings
Serious injuries: Pulled hamstrings

| England 1990 | Tour to Argentina |
| 1995 | Development squad |

Other sporting achievements: Represented Yorkshire U-14s at basketball. Played for 1986/87 England Colleges Rugby League team v Welsh Colleges
Best memory last season: Beating Dusty's record and being selected for England's tour of Argentina
Most improved International player last season: England fly-half Rob Andrew
Other notable landmarks in rugby career: 1989/90 total of 439 points put me top of Tandem Computers English scoring charts: 1. Liley 439 (18t, 89c, 63p); 2. A. Green (Exeter) 333; 3. S. Burnage (Fylde) 326. Also topped

goal-kicking table: 1. Liley 367; 2. Burnage 310; 3. Green 309. Played for North of England U-21s v Midlands (1987/88). Selected for England's summer tour to Argentina
Touchlines: Cricket, golf, driving

Lineen, S.R.P.   Scotland

Full Name: Sean Raymond Patrick Lineen
International category: Scotland Full
Club: Boroughmuir
Position: Centre
Height: 6'1" **Weight:** 13st 9lb
Occupation: Property manager
Born: Auckland, New Zealand, 25.12.61
Family: Single
Family links with rugby: Terry (father) played twelve times for New Zealand
Former club: Counties (NZ)
International debut: Scotland 23, Wales 7, Murrayfield, 1989
Five Nations' debut: As above
Best moment in rugby: Winning first Scotland cap against Wales and winning 1990 Grand Slam
Touchlines: Qualified for Scotland through grandfather who came from the Hebrides. Returned to New Zealand on tour with Scotland last summer

	apps.	pts.
Scotland (1989)		
Last Season	8 caps	4
Career	12 caps	4

165

Linnett, M.S.   England

Full Name: Mark Stuart Linnett
International category: England Full
Club: Moseley
Position: Loose-head prop
Height: 5'11" **Weight:** 17st
Occupation: Policeman
Born: Rugby, 17.2.63
Family: Married with son
Former club: Rugby
International debut: England 58, Fiji 23, 1989
Best moment in rugby: Scoring try on England debut
Worst moments in rugby: Losing to Bristol and Bath in Cup semi-finals
Most respected opponent: England tight-head prop Jeff Probyn – extremely awkward scrummager
Other sporting achievements: Qualified PTI
Best memory last season: Scoring try v Fiji
Most improved International player last season: England centre Jeremy Guscott
Suggestions to improve rugby: English Leagues should operate on home and away. Improve standards of refereeing
Other notable landmarks in rugby career: England Colts (1981), England U-23 (1984), England B (1988), England and Barbarians (1989)

	apps.	pts.
England B (1988)		
Last Season	1 cap	0
England (1989)		
Last Season	1 cap	4
Career	1 cap	4
England XV 1990	1 app	0
1990	Tour to Argentina	
1995	Development squad	

Llewellyn, G.   Wales

Full Name: Gareth Llewellyn
International category: Wales Full
Club: Neath
Position: Lock
Height: 6'6" **Weight:** 18st
Occupation: Fitter and turner
Born: Cardiff, 27.2.69
Family: Single
Family links with rugby: Brother
(Glyn) plays for Neath and toured
Namibia with Wales (1990)
Former club: Llanharan
International debut: Wales 9,
New Zealand 34, 1989
Five Nations' debut: England 34,
Wales 6, 1990
Best moment in rugby: Winning
first Wales cap
Most embarrassing moment:
Almost tripping over when running
out at Cardiff for first cap
Most respected opponent: Wales
lock Bob Norster
Serious injuries: Dislocated
collarbone, damaged pelvis
Best memory last season:
Playing for Neath v All Blacks
**Most improved International
player last season:** Ireland lock
Neil Francis

	apps.	pts.
Wales B (**1989**)		
Last Season	1 cap	0
Wales (**1989**)		
Last Season	4 caps	4
Career	4 caps	4

Other notable landmarks in rugby career: Capped three times by Wales
Youth. Toured New Zealand with Welsh U-19 team. Also played for
Crawshays and Barbarians
Touchlines: Motocross, golf, squash

Llewellyn, G.D.   Wales

Full Name: Glyn David Llewellyn
International category: Wales Full
Club: Neath
Position: Lock
Height: 6'6" **Weight:** 17st 7lb
Occupation: Architect
Born: Bradford on Avon, Wilts,
9.8.65
Family: Single
Family links with rugby: Brother
(Gareth) plays for Neath and
Wales. Father, who was in Army
with Will Carling's dad, is qualified
WRU coach
Former clubs: Llanharan,
Bridgend, London Welsh
International debut: Namibia 9,
Wales 18, 1990
Best moment in rugby: Wales
winning second Test in Namibia
(1990)
Worst moment in rugby: Welsh
Schools defeat by British Columbia
during 1983 Canadian tour – only
time ever on losing Welsh national
team

	apps.	pts.
Wales (1990)		
Last Season	2 caps	0
Career	2 caps	0

Most embarrassing moment:
Having shorts ripped off when jockstrap-less
Most respected opponent: England B lock John Morrison
Serious injuries: Torn knee ligaments (1987)
Other sporting achievements: Schoolboy basketball International
Best memory last season: Winning Welsh Cup final with Neath and
afterwards returning to The Gnoll for barbeque with 6,000 fans
Most improved International player last season: England centre Will
Carling
Suggestions to improve rugby: Unification of laws. Present interpretations
differ widely between northern and southern hemispheres
Other notable landmarks in rugby career: Spent five years with London
Welsh before returning to Wales on obtaining a post in Barry. Won 6 Schools
caps
Touchlines: Windsurfing, cricket

168

Lloyd, M.J.   Wales

Full Name: Matthew John Lloyd
International category: Wales
U-21
Club: Cardiff
Position: Flanker
Height: 6' **Weight:** 14st 7lb
Occupation: Student
Born: Cardiff, 14.8.70
Family: Single with son
Family links with rugby: Father
referees on Cardiff District Panel
Former clubs: St Alban's, South
Glamorgan Institute
International debut (U-21):
Scotland 10, Wales 24, 1990
Best moment in rugby: Scoring 2
tries for Wales U-21s against
Scotland last season
Worst moment in rugby: Leaving
field injured in above game
Most respected opponent:
Neath's Welsh flanker Martyn
Morris
Serious injuries: Damaged
cruciate knee ligaments (1990)

	apps.	pts.
Wales U-21 (**1990**)		
Last Season	1 cap	8

Other sporting achievements:
Baseball for Wales B (squad). Soccer for Glamorgan U-16s
Best memory last season: Cardiff beating Llanelli in Welsh Cup
Most improved International player last season: Wales centre Allan
Bateman
Suggestions to improve rugby: Relax laws on amateurism
Other notable landmarks in rugby career: Represented Wales at U-18 and
U-20 level prior to U-21s
Touchlines: Weight training, keep-fit

Lloyd, S.J. Wales

Full Name: Stephen John Lloyd
International category: Wales
(World Cup squad)
Club: Moseley
Position: Lock
Height: 6'6" **Weight:** 17st 7lb
Occupation: Computer operator
Born: Montevideo, Uruguay,
11.7.68
Family: Single
Family links with rugby: Father
played lock
Former club: Kidderminster
Carolians
International debut (non-cap):
Wales U-21 v Combined Services,
1990
Best moment in rugby: Selection
to Welsh U-21 squad
Worst moment in rugby: Being
dropped from England Colts squad
Most embarrassing moment:
Moseley losing to Aspatria in third
round of English Cup (1988/89)

Wales 1991   World Cup squad

Most respected opponent: Wales lock Robert Norster
Other sporting achievements: County basketball
Best memory last season: Crawshays tour to Toulouse
Most improved International player last season: England wing Rory
Underwood
Suggestions to improve rugby: Slacken amateur rules to allow players to be
paid for activities outside rugby
Other notable landmarks in rugby career: Picked for Wales 1991 World
Cup squad
Touchlines: Golf, shooting, tennis, theatre

Lozowski, R.   England

Full Name: Robert Lozowski
International category: England B
Club: Wasps
Position: Centre
Height: 6'2" **Weight:** 14st 4lb
Occupation: Sales manager
Born: London, 18.11.60
Family: Married
Family links with rugby: Steve
Moriarty (brother-in-law) plays for
Harlequins and Surrey
Former club: Old Gaytonians
International debut: England 3,
Australia 19, 1984
Best moment in rugby: Final
whistle London v 1988 Wallabies
(won 21–10)
Worst moment in rugby: Being
told I had to room with Mark
Williams on US club tour
Most embarrassing moment:
Explaining to wife that Harlequins
prop John Kingston was going to
Antigua on his honeymoon at same
time as us – same flight, same
hotel, next door room
Most respected opponent:
England centre Fran Clough –
most outstanding pair of hands in
modern game

	apps.	pts.
England B (1989)		
Last Season	1 cap	0
England (1984)		
Last Season	0 caps	0
Career	1 cap	0

Serious injuries: Broken leg (three times)
Other sporting achievements: Taking former England full-back Huw
Davies to cleaners on golf course
Most improved International player last season: England centre Jeremy
Guscott
Suggestions to improve rugby: Keep alickadoos out of changing rooms after
winning performances
Other notable landmarks in rugby career: Meeting Lisa at Northampton
RFC in 1988 and marrying her following summer

Luxton, C.T.   England

Full Name: Craig Thomas Luxton
International category: England B
Club: Harlequins
Position: Scrum-half
Height: 5'10" **Weight:** 12st
Occupations: International head hunter and part-time tennis coach
Born: Opotiki, New Zealand, 11.3.64
Family: Single
Family links with rugby: Father played for Bay of Plenty (NZ)
Former clubs: Leamington, Cambridge United (NZ)
International debut (non-cap): Spanish Select 15, England B 32, 1989
Best moment in rugby: Being a Kiwi wearing the red rose of England (B)
Worst moment in rugby: Harlequins losing to Leicester in 1989 Cup semi-final

England B **(1989/90)**   Tour to Spain

Most embarrassing moment: Doing a big dive for try-line with no-one in sight and dropping ball
Most respected opponents: Waikato's Stephen Putt, England's Richard Hill and Wales' Robert Jones
Serious injuries: Broken knee cartilage, damaged medial ligaments
Other sporting achievements: NZ age-group tennis champion. NZ national development tennis squad. Waikato Schools softball team
Best memories last season: Harlequins winning National Sevens. Touring Spain with England B
Most improved International player last season: England centre Jeremy Guscott
Suggestions to improve rugby: Make training as enjoyable and constructive as possible. Don't place heavy demands on players (i.e. not too many games)
Other notable landmarks in rugby career: Spent two seasons with Waikato. Co-coaching local club in NZ to Second Division Grand Final
Touchlines: Surviving drinking sessions with England flanker Mick 'Munch' Skinner, body surfing, golf

Lyman, N.M.   England

Full Name: Neil Michael Lyman
International category: England U-21
Club: Moseley
Position: Tight-head prop
Height: 6'1" **Weight:** 17st
Occupation: Carpenter
Born: Bedford, 6.5.70
Family: Single
Family links with rugby: Father played for Bedford
Former club: Kidderminster Carolians
International debut: Netherlands 3, England U-21 24, 1990
Best moment in rugby: Pulling on England shirt
Worst moment in rugby: Not coming off bench when England U-21s played French Armed Forces (1990)
Most respected opponent: England U-21 flanker Neil Back
Serious injuries: Torn bicep (1990)

	apps.	pts.
England U-21 (**1990**)		
Last Season	1 cap	0

Other sporting achievements: County soccer for Hereford & Worcestershire
Best memory last season: England U-21 beating Netherlands in front of 4,000 spectators
Most improved International player last season: Neil Back
Suggestions to improve rugby: Players should stay on feet more to keep game moving quicker
Other notable landmarks in rugby career: Only started playing rugby four years ago. Joined Moseley from junior club Kidderminster last summer

Lynagh, D.J.   Ireland

Full Name: David James Lynagh
International category: Ireland
U-21
Club: Terenure College
Position: Centre
Height: 6' **Weight:** 13st 4lb
Occupation: Insurance official
Born: Dublin, 17.3.69
Family: Single
International debut (U-21):
Ireland 22, Italy 13, 1988
Best moment in rugby: Putting
on Irish jersey for first time, for
Irish Schools
Worst moment in rugby: Being
run around four times by same
player (who scored 2 tries and
made a 3rd) in match selectors
were watching
Most embarrassing moment: As
above
Most respected opponent:
Ireland centre Brendan Mullin –
such is his speed and reading of
game that he allows you no time to
think when you have ball

	apps.	pts.
Ireland U-21 (1988)		
Last Season	1 cap	10

Serious injuries: Broken collarbone (four times), nose (twice)
Best memory last season: Helping Dublin University beat Clontarf
Most improved International player last season: England centre Jeremy
Guscott
Suggestions to improve rugby: Draft more younger players into squads to
give them experience
Other notable landmarks in rugby career: Irish Schools to Australia (1987).
Played in first ever Irish U-21 team (1988). Playing for only team (Leinster)
to beat a New Zealand International team on tour in British Isles last season

McBride, W.D.   Ireland

Full Name: William **Denis** McBride
International category: Ireland Full
Club: Malone
Position: Flanker
Height: 5'11" **Weight:** 14st
Occupation: Mechanical engineer
Born: Belfast, 9.9.64
Family: Married
Family links with rugby: Brother also plays
Former club: Queen's University Belfast
International debut: Ireland 9, Wales 12, 1988
Five Nations' debut: As above
Best moment in rugby: Ireland XV beating France XV 19–18 at Auch (1988) in non-cap tour match
Worst moment in rugby: Second half of Ireland's 3-35 defeat by England in 1988 when we conceded 35 points without reply
Most embarrassing moment: Ireland v England (1988)
Most respected opponents:

	apps.	pts.
Ireland (1988)		
Last Season	2 caps	4
Career	7 caps	8

No.8s Wayne Shelford (New Zealand) and Laurent Rodriguez (France)
Other sporting achievements: Completed the 1982 Belfast City Marathon
Best memory last season: Beating Wales to avoid Wooden Spoon
Most improved International player last season: England centre Jeremy Guscott
Suggestions to improve rugby: Better marketing of the sport. All countries should send official teams to Hong Kong Sevens
Other notable landmarks in rugby career: Ulster v 1989 All Blacks (lost 21–3). 1989 Hong Kong Sevens with Irish Wolfhounds

McCoy, J.J.   Ireland

Full Name: James Joseph McCoy
International category: Ireland
Full
Club: Bangor
Position: Tight-head prop
Height: 6'1½" **Weight:** 17st
Occupation: Civil servant
Born: Enniskillen, 28.6.58
Family: Married (Fiona) with one
daughter (Nicola)
Former clubs: Enniskillen,
Dungannon
International debut: Ireland 9,
Wales 18, 1984
Five Nations' debut: As above
Best moment in rugby: Winning
Triple Crown in 1985
Worst moment in rugby: Getting
injured in stupid Irish Trial match
last season
Most respected opponent: All of
them at International level
Serious injuries: Ruptured
tendons in thumb (1989/90)
Best memory last season: Playing
twice against All Blacks in four
days and living to tell the tale
**Most improved International
player last season:** Ireland flanker Denis McBride
Suggestions to improve rugby: Broken time payments
Other notable landmarks in rugby career: Every game is another landmark
due to Irish selection. Played Irish Schools (1975–76). Won U-23 and B caps
(1979). Became one of only seven players capped at four levels when made
full debut. Toured with Ireland to 1987 World Cup, Japan and France (1988)
and North America (1989)

	apps.	pts.
Ireland B (1979)		
Last Season	0 caps	0
Ireland (1984)		
Last Season	1 cap	0
Career	16 caps	0

MacDonald, A.E.D.   Scotland

Full Name: Andrew Edward
Douglas MacDonald
International category: Scotland B
Clubs: London Scottish,
Cambridge University
Positions: No.8, lock
Height: 6'8" **Weight:** 17st 12lb
Occupation: Student
Born: Nairn, 17.1.66
Family: Single
Former club: Loughborough
University
International debut (B): France
31, Scotland 9, 1989
Best moment in rugby: Winning
1989 Varsity match
Worst moments in rugby:
Missing 1988 Varsity match after
being injured 5 minutes from end
of preceding match. Being sent off
and breaking hand simultaneously
in UAU semi-final
Most embarrassing moment:
Being headlined as a 'villain' in
Times report after above dismissal
Most respected opponent: Wales
lock Robert Norster – constantly outjumps taller opponents

	apps.	pts.
Scotland B (1990)		
Last Season	2 caps	0

Serious injuries sustained: Broken hand, ankle ligaments
Other sporting achievements: Bowling Steve James (future cricket star with Glamorgan) in net practice
Best memory last season: Final whistle against Oxford University
Most improved International player last season: Scotland centre Sean Lineen
Suggestions to improve rugby: Eliminate 90-degree scrum wheel law
Other notable landmarks in rugby career: Capped by Scotland once at U-21 and twice at B level. Scotland trial (1990)
Touchlines: Keen ukelele player

McDonald, J.P.   Ireland

Full Name: John Parker McDonald
International category: Ireland Full
Club: Malone
Position: Hooker
Height: 5'10" **Weight:** 13st 4lb
Occupation: Civil Servant
Born: Banbridge, Co Down, 9.4.60
Family: Married with two children
Former club: Dungannon
International debut: Ireland 46, Canada 19, 1987 World Cup
Five Nations' debut: England 23, Ireland 0, 1990
Best moment in rugby: Making full Ireland debut in Dunedin
Worst moment in rugby: Having to pull out of Ireland's 1990 game with Wales 15 minutes before kick-off after tearing a calf muscle warming up. Had even been included in pre-match team photo!
Most embarrassing moment: Looking at above photograph
Most respected opponent: Former Scotland hooker Colin Deans – more a rugby player than an athlete, proved size isn't everything

	apps.	pts.
Ireland B (1984)		
Last Season	1 cap	0
Ireland (1987)		
Last Season	2 caps	0
Career	3 caps	0

Serious injuries: Torn calf muscle, ankle ligaments (on debut against Canada) and rib cartilage
Best memory last season: Home debut for Ireland against Scotland
Most improved International player last season: Scotland hooker Kenny Milne
Suggestions to improve rugby: Universal uniformity. Why should only some countries' players be afforded luxuries?
Other notable landmarks in rugby career: Influence of former Irish coach Jimmy Davidson, with whom I played at Dungannon and was coached by with Ulster and Ireland. Made B debut against Scotland (1984/85) and played for Ulster v Fiji (1985/86). Toured with Ulster to Italy (1986). Called out to 1987 World Cup as second replacement hooker. Toured with Ireland to

France (1988) and North America (1989). Involved in perennial battle with Steve Smith for right to play for Ulster and Ireland
Touchlines: Weight training, soccer

McKee, G.T. Scotland

Full Name: Graham Thomas McKee
International category: Scotland U-21
Club: Glasgow High/Kelvinside
Position: Tight-head prop
Height: 5'9" **Weight:** 15st
Occupation: Student
Born: Motherwell, 23.10.69
Family: Single
Former club: Hutchesons
International debut (U-21): Scotland 10, Wales 24, 1990
Best moment in rugby: Being selected for U-21s
Worst moment in rugby: Playing in Scotland Schools side that failed to score with last-minute penalty (run) and, as a result, lost 9-13 to Ireland Schools
Most respected opponent: Scotland loose-head prop David Sole
Best memory last season: GHK winning at Selkirk in Scottish First Division

	apps.	pts.
Scotland U-21 (1990)		
Last Season	1 cap	0

Most improved International player last season: Scotland tight-head prop Paul Burnell
Suggestions to improve rugby: Alter rucking laws so that man obstructing ball on ground should be penalised rather than man trying to get ball (providing no foul is being committed)
Other notable landmarks in rugby career: Moved up Scottish representative ladder from Schools (U-18s), Youth, U-19s, Students and Colleges, to U-21s
Touchlines: Golf

McKeen, A.J.W.   Ireland

Full Name: Angus John William McKeen
International category: Ireland U-21
Club: Lansdowne
Position: Tight-head prop
Height: 5'11" **Weight:** 15st 9lb
Occupation: Farmer
Born: Drogheda, 13.2.69
Family: Single
Former club: Ballymena
International debut (U-21): Italy 9, Ireland 10, 1989
Best moment in rugby: Helping Leinster beat touring New Zealand U-21s last season (only team to do so)
Serious injuries: Broken leg (aged 16)
Most improved International player last season: Ireland flanker Pat O'Hara
Other notable landmarks in rugby career: Represented Irish Schools U-18s and toured Australia with them (1987). Also played for Ireland U-21s against New Zealand U-21s last season

	apps.	pts.
Ireland U-21 (**1989**)		
Last Season	1 cap	0

McKenzie, K.D.   Scotland

Full Name: Kevin Duncan McKenzie
International category: Scotland B
Club: Stirling County
Position: Hooker
Height: 5'6" **Weight:** 14st 3lb
Occupation: Sales representative
Born: Stirling, 22.1.68
Family: Single
Family links with rugby: Brother Mark played two seasons for Scotland U-18s
International debut (B): Scotland 22, Ireland 22, 1989
Best moment in rugby: Winning 1989/90 Inter-District Championship with Glasgow
Worst moment in rugby: Not being selected for Scotland's 1989 tour of Japan
Most embarrassing moment: Conceding 3 penalties playing for Scotland in Schools International against Australia at Murrayfield

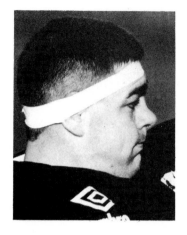

	apps.	pts.
Scotland B (1989)		
Last Season	1 cap	0

Most respected opponent: Former Scotland flanker Finlay Calder
Serious injuries: Head wound (required 13 stitches) playing for Scotland against Wales in U-21 International in 1988/89
Other sporting achievements: Soccer for Central Region Schools
Best memory last season: Taking two heels off Scotland hooker Kenny Milne during Stirling's defeat of centenary club Heriot's, who were then leading Scottish First Division
Most improved International player last season: Scotland wing Tony Stanger
Suggestions to improve rugby: Provide players with kit rather than them having to incur extra expenditure
Other notable landmarks in rugby career: Joined Stirling aged 8, when club was in Scottish Seventh Division. Played for Glasgow for past three seasons. Represented Scotland at U-15, Schools (three seasons), U-19, U-21 (three seasons) and B levels
Touchlines: Badminton, weight-lifting, jogging

McKenzie, L.   England

Full Name: Leroy McKenzie
International category: England U-21
Club: Coventry
Position: Wing
Height: 5'9" **Weight:** 12st 7lb
Occupation: Estimator (joinery)
Born: Birmingham, 2.9.69
Family: Single
Former clubs: Five Ways, Old Edwardians
International debut: Netherlands 3, England U-21 24, 1990
Best moment in rugby: Playing opposite Rory Underwood and scoring try – only third ever senior game
Worst moment in rugby: Pulling both hamstrings in one game
Most respected opponent: England wing Rory Underwood
Best memory last season: Scoring winning try for Coventry v Moseley (1990)
Most improved International player last season: England fly-half Rob Andrew
Suggestions to improve rugby: Less kicking

	apps.	pts.
England U-21 (**1990**)		
Last Season	2 caps	0

McKibbin, B.M.   Ireland

Full Name: Brian Martin McKibbin
International category: Ireland B
Club: Instonians
Position: Prop
Height: 6' **Weight:** 16st 4lb
Occupation: Bank official
Born: Belfast, 13.3.61
Family: Married
Family links with rugby: Father and two cousins played for Ireland. Uncle played for Ireland and Lions
International debut (B): Scotland 22, Ireland 22, 1989
Best moment in rugby: Making Ireland B debut in Scotland
Worst moment in rugby: Ulster losing final 'Test' v Zimbabwe (Harare 1987)
Most respected opponent: Former Ireland prop Phil Orr
Other sporting achievements: Completed Belfast City marathon
Best memory last season: Playing for Ireland B
Most improved International player last season: Ireland full-back Kenny Murphy

	apps.	pts.
Ireland B (1989)		
Last Season	1 cap	0

Other notable landmarks in rugby career: Won 2 Irish Schools caps prior to B recognition. Played part in Ulster's domination of Inter-Provincial Championship. Replacement when Ulster lost 3-21 to 1989 All Blacks

Mackay, G.T.   Scotland

Full Name: George Thomas Mackay
International category: Scotland U-21
Club: Glasgow Academicals
Position: Lock
Height: 6'4" **Weight:** 15st
Occupation: Banker
Born: Glasgow, 9.4.69
Family: Single
International debut (U-21): Scotland 10, Wales 24, 1990
Best moment in rugby: 'Coasting' round Matt Duncan for 40-yard winning try v West of Scotland (1989)
Worst moment in rugby: Relegation with Glasgow Accies to Scottish Second Division (1988/89)
Most respected opponent: Scotland flanker John Jeffrey – fantastic ball skills, game sense, strength and rugby mentality
Serious injuries sustained: Broken shoulder, nose (ten times)
Other sporting achievements: West District cricket XI

	apps.	pts.
Scotland U-21 (**1990**)		
Last Season	1 cap	0

Best memory last season: Beating Blackheath on pre-season tour of Portugal
Most improved International player last season: Scotland wing Tony Stanger
Suggestions to improve rugby: Increased selectorial notice of performances in lower divisions. More money made available for youth development

184

Macklin, A.J.   Scotland

Full Name: Alastair Jeremy Macklin
International category: Scotland B
Club: London Scottish
Positions: Flanker, No.8
Height: 6'3" **Weight:** 14st 7lb
Occupation: Area manager Latin America/Asia for ICI agrochemicals
Born: Leamington, 16.2.61
Family: Deborah (wife)
Family links with rugby: Alastair MacNaughton Smallwood (grandfather) played on wing for England (1920–25)
Former clubs: Cambridge University, Exeter
International debut (B): Scotland 21, France 12, 1985
Best moments in rugby: Beating France B 12–10 in Villefranche (1986). Beating France with Anglo-Scots at Cupar (1987)
Worst moment in rugby: Captaining Scotland B in 31–9 loss to France B at Oyonnax (Jan 1990)
Most respected opponent: Scotland flanker John Jeffrey

	apps.	pts.
Scotland B (1985)		
Last Season	2 caps	0
Career	10 caps	4

Serious injuries sustained: Torn knee ligaments
Most improved International player last season: Scotland prop Paul Burnell
Other notable landmarks in rugby career: English Schoolboys tour to Australia. Won three Blues at Cambridge University (1979,80,82). Represented Scotland B seven times and captained them twice last season

Maclean, R.R.W. — Scotland

Full Name: Richard **Ruari** Willard Maclean
International category: Scotland (Japan squad)
Club: Moseley
Positions: Centre, full-back
Height: 5'11" **Weight:** 13st 7lb
Occupation: PE teacher
Born: London, 27.9.61
Family: Married with son and daughter
Family links with rugby: Uncle coached Llanelli and is on WRU committee
Former clubs: Old Alleynians, South Glamorgan Institute, Gloucester, Llanelli, Newport
International debut (B): Scotland 37, Italy 0, 1987
Best moment in rugby: Helping Anglo-Scots beat France XV 19–16 at Cupar in 1987 (playing opposite Denis Charvet) and being called into Scotland squad for first time afterwards
Worst moment in rugby: Scotland losing 24–28 to Japan (Tokyo 1989)

	apps.	pts.
Scotland B (1987)		
Last Season	0 caps	0
Scotland XV 1989	Tour to Japan	

Most embarrassing moment: Making debut for Moseley against Gloucester – first game since leaving Kingsholm
Most respected opponent: Former Wales centre Ray Gravell
Serious injuries: Broken arm, shoulder, leg. Arthritis in back (missed three complete seasons through injuries)
Other sporting achievements: Soccer for Chelsea until aged 15. Qualified tennis coach. Rugby league for Welsh Students
Best memory last season: Watching Tony Stanger score decisive Scotland try against England in Grand Slam decider
Most improved International player last season: England fly-half Rob Andrew
Suggestions to improve rugby: Clear up pro-am wrangle and improve sportsmanship in game – it's supposed to be played for enjoyment

Other notable landmarks in rugby career: Injured throughout Schools. Played for Welsh Colleges and captained Welsh Students Rugby League team which beat English counterparts in 1984 for first time. Represented Scotland B three times and, while at Gloucester, Anglo-Scots. Toured with Scotland to Zimbabwe (1988) and Japan (1989)

Macrae, D.   Scotland

Full Name: Duncan Macrae
International category: Scotland U-21
Club: Cambridge University
Position: Wing
Height: 6' **Weight:** 13st 7lb
Occupation: Chemistry student
Born: Bida, Nigeria, 24.12.69
Family: Single
International debut: Wales 26, Scotland 18, 1989
Best moment in rugby: Scoring first try at Murrayfield, for Anglo-Scots U-21s against Glasgow (1988/89)
Worst moment in rugby: Being knocked-out playing (aged 14)
Most respected opponent: Wales U-21 fly-half Adrian Davies
Serious injuries: Concussion
Other sporting achievements: County soccer for Northumberland (until 13)
Best memory last season: Scoring try for Scotland U-21s against Wales in 10–24 defeat

	apps.	pts.
Scotland U-21 (**1990**)		
Last Season	1 cap	4

Most improved International player last season: Scotland prop David Sole
Suggestions to improve rugby: Keep it as amateur as possible
Other notable landmarks in rugby career: Did not start playing until aged 11. Represented Northumberland U-18s (year young) and Scotland U-18s (two seasons), U-19s and U-21s (two seasons)
Touchlines: Computing

Mannion, N.P.S.   Ireland

Full Name: Noel Patrick Stephen Mannion
International category: Ireland Full
Club: Corinthians
Positions: No.8, flanker
Height: 6'5" **Weight:** 17st
Occupation: Sales representative
Born: Ballinasloe, 12.1.63
Family: Single
Family links with rugby: Brother plays for Galwegians and Connacht
Former clubs: Ballinasloe, Drumoyne (Aus)
International debut: Ireland 49, Western Samoa 22, 1988
Five Nations' debut: Ireland 21, France 26, 1989
Best moment in rugby: Intercepting Welsh kick on own 22 and running ball back for Ireland try in 19–13 win (Cardiff 1989)
Worst moment in rugby: Running a quick penalty for Connacht against Ulster, tripping for no apparent reason, and knocking ball forwards

	apps.	pts.
Ireland (1988)		
Last Season	5 caps	0
Career	11 caps	4

Most embarrassing moment: As above
Most respected opponent: New Zealand No.8 Wayne Shelford
Serious injuries: Broken collarbone, wrist. Twisted knee
Other sporting achievements: Played one season of Gaelic football for Galway. Came on as replacement in 1987 All-Ireland semi-final replay against Cork
Best memory last season: Ireland scoring early try in Wooden Spoon decider against Wales. Such a relief – took so much pressure off us
Most improved International player last season: Ireland flanker Pat O'Hara
Suggestions to improve rugby: Standardise refereeing in southern and northern hemispheres. Presently too many different interpretations
Other notable landmarks in rugby career: Represented Connacht at Schools and U-20 level before making senior Provincial debut in 1985. Played

for Ireland U-25s against Canada following season. Scored famous try in second full appearance. Toured with Ireland to Canada (1989) and was an ever-present. Made Barbarians bow against Newport last season
Touchlines: Music, reading

Marshall, G.R.   Scotland

Full Name: Graham Robert Marshall
International category: Scotland Full
Club: Selkirk
Position: Flanker
Height: 6'3½" **Weight:** 15st 7lb
Occupation: PE teacher
Born: Glasgow, 23.5.60
Family: Married with one daughter
Former clubs: Jordanhill, Wakefield
International debut: Scotland 13, Australia 32, 1988
Best moment in rugby: Coming on as replacement for Derek White against Wallabies to win first cap
Worst moment in rugby: Losing 28–24 to Japan (Tokyo 1989)
Most respected opponent: Whoever playing against next
Serious injuries: Knee (1983)
Best memory last season: Watching Scotland win Grand Slam
Most improved International player last season: Scotland lock Chris Gray
Notable landmarks in rugby career: Toured with Scotland to Japan (1989) and New Zealand (1990). Played in 38–17 win v Fiji (Oct 1989). Twice represented Scottish XVs

	apps.	pts.
Scotland B (1987)		
Last Season	0 caps	0
Scotland (1988)		
Last Season	1 cap	0
Career	2 caps	0

Mason, J.   Wales

Full Name: Jonathan Mason
International category: Wales
Full (squad)
Club: Pontypridd
Position: Full-back
Height: 6'1" **Weight:** 14st
Occupation: Furniture design
technician
Born: Aberdare, 13.6.65
Family: Married with a son
Family links with rugby:
Grandfather played five times for
Welsh Schools in 1930s
Former club: Mountain Ash
International debut: New
Zealand 54, Wales 9, 1988
Best moment in rugby: Making
Welsh debut as replacement in
second Test v NZ
Worst moment in rugby:
Breaking ankle prior to 1989/90
season
Most embarrassing moment:
Being called a 'pretty boy' by New
Zealand commentator (1988)
Most respected opponent:
Former Wales fly-half Jonathan
Davies – a cocky little devil
Serious injuries: Broken ankle (twice)
Other sporting achievements: County footballer, 2-handicap golfer

	apps.	pts.
Wales (1988)		
Last Season	0 caps	0
Career	1 cap	0
1991	World Cup squad	

Matchett, W.D.A.   Ireland

Full Name: William David **Andrew** Matchett
International category: Ireland U-21
Club: Portadown
Position: Scrum-half
Height: 6' **Weight:** 12st 6lb
Occupation: Student
Born: Portadown, 25.5.69
Family: Single
Family links with rugby: Father played for Portadown. Brother plays for Bangor and Ulster
International debut (U-21): Ireland 13, New Zealand 13, 1989
Best moment in rugby: Scoring try for Ulster U-21s against New Zealand U-21s
Worst moment in rugby: Dislocating collarbone against CIYMS last season
Most respected opponent: Brother Stephen (Bangor scrum-half)
Serious injuries: Dislocated collarbone

	apps.	pts.
Ireland U-21 (1989)		
Last Season	1 cap	0

Other sporting achievements: Cricket for Portadown
Best memory last season: Playing for Ireland U-21s
Most improved International player last season: England scrum-half Richard Hill
Other notable landmarks in rugby career: Educated at Portadown College. Played for Irish Schools, and Ulster at U-20 and U-21 level
Touchlines: Enjoy music

Matthews, P.M.   Ireland

Full Name: Phillip Michael
Matthews
International category: Ireland
Full
Club: Wanderers
Position: Flanker
Height: 6'3" **Weight:** 16st
Occupation: Marketing manager
Born: Gloucester, 24.1.60
Family: Married
Family links with rugby:
Father-in-law is former Ireland
International Kevin Flynn
(1959–73)
Former clubs: Queen's University
Belfast, Ards
International debut: Ireland 9,
Australia 16, 1984
Five Nations' debut: Scotland 18,
Ireland 15, 1985
Best moment in rugby: Scoring
for Barbarians against 1989 All
Blacks at Twickenham
Worst moment in rugby: 1987
World Cup – injured in first game
Most respected opponent: None
in particular

	apps.	pts.
Ireland (**1984**)		
Last Season	3 caps	0
Career	27 caps	16

Serious injuries sustained: Dislocated elbow
Best memory last season: Wanderers winning League and Cup double
Most improved International player last season: Ireland full-back Kenny
Murphy
Suggestions to improve rugby: Pay players
Other notable landmarks in rugby career: The Bull & Bear in Hong Kong.
Won 5 Schools caps (1977–78), captaining team three times. Became Ards'
first International when capped in 1984. Captained Ireland six times. Irish
rugby writers' choice as 'Player of Year' in 1988. Represented Barbarians and
Home Unions (against France) last season

Milne, I.G.   Scotland

Full Name: Iain Gordon Milne
International category: Scotland
Full
Club: Heriot's FP
Position: Tight-head prop
Height: 6' **Weight:** 17st 9lb
Occupation: Sales manager of
printing firm
Born: Edinburgh, 17.6.58
Family: Marian (wife)
Family links with rugby: Kenny
(brother) plays for Heriot's and
Scotland. David (brother) played
for Scotland B
Former club: Harlequins
International debut: Scotland 11,
Ireland 11, 1979
Five Nations' debut: As above
Best moments in rugby: Winning
1979 Scottish Championship with
Heriot's and 1984 Grand Slam
with Scotland
Worst moment in rugby:
Damaging bones in a foot against
Wales in 1989 and missing game
against England
Most embarrassing moment:

	apps.	pts.
Scotland (**1979**)		
Last Season	2 caps	0
Career	44 caps	0
Lions 1983		
1986		

Putting on too much Deep Heat
before first match as Heriot's captain and having to leave for a shower
midway through my first pre-match team talk
Most respected opponent: Any French front row forward
Best memory last season: Captaining Heriot's to River Series victory and
runner-up spot in Championship in centenary season
Most improved International player last season: Scotland lock Chris Gray
Notable landmarks in career: First called into national squad as 20-year old
in 1978. Toured New Zealand with 1983 British Lions. With Scotland, toured
New Zealand (1981 and 1990), Australia (1982) and North America (1985),
and played in 1987 World Cup
Suggestions to improve rugby: Play Internationals later in season. 90-degree
wheels: put-in should go to team going forwards
Touchlines: Keen angler (salmon and trout)

Milne, K.S.   Scotland

Full Name: Kenneth Stuart Milne
International category: Scotland
Full
Club: Heriot's FP
Position: Hooker
Height: 6' **Weight:** 14st 3lb
Occupation: Sales rep for printing
firm
Born: Edinburgh, 1.12.61
Family: Eleanor (wife)
Family links with rugby: Iain
(brother) plays for Heriot's,
Scotland and British Lions. David
(brother) played for Scotland B
International debut: Scotland 23,
Wales 7, 1989
Five Nations' debut: As above
Best moment in rugby: 1990
Grand Slam
Worst moment in rugby: Being
dropped at any level
Most embarrassing moment:
Accidentally flooring the referee
when the front rows of Heriot's
and Jed-Forest squared up. He let
me off
Most respected opponents:
Scotland's Gary Callender and
England's Brian Moore

	apps.	pts.
Scotland B (1985)		
Last Season	0 caps	0
Scotland (1989)		
Last Season	7 caps	4
Career	11 caps	4

Best memory last season: Winning Grand Slam with Scotland
Most improved International player last season: Scotland lock Chris Gray
Other notable landmarks in rugby career: Ever-present in last season's
Championship team. Scored first International try against Fiji (Oct 1989)

Milward, A.W.   England

Full Name: Alexander William Milward
International category: England U-21
Club: Rosslyn Park
Position: Lock
Height: 6'9" **Weight:** 16st 9lb
Occupation: Student electronic engineer
Born: Croydon, 23.10.68
Family: Single
Former clubs: Warlingham, Loughborough Students
International debut: Netherlands 3, England U-21 24, 1990
Best moment in rugby: Loughborough winning 1989 UAU final at Twickenham
Worst moment in rugby: Losing to France at 18-Group level
Most embarrassing moment: Atempting a 'chip' kick over Oxford University's Ireland fly-half Brian Smith

	apps.	pts.
England U-21 **(1990)**		
Last Season	2 caps	0

Most respected opponent: England flanker Peter Winterbottom – combination of speed, skill and strength
Other sporting achievements: National age-group finals for swimming, basketball for Crystal Palace juniors
Best memory last season: Rosslyn Park winning away at Bristol in English First Division
Most improved International player last season: England lock Wade Dooley
Suggestions to improve rugby: Maintain interest in fitness levels but not place too much emphasis on track results – they don't always reflect a player's ability when actually playing. Encourage players to coach when careers are over
Other notable landmarks in rugby career: England Schools (U-18s), English Universities
Touchlines: Swimming, basketball

Moloney, R.J. — Ireland

Full Name: Rory John Moloney
International category: Ireland U-21
Club: University College Cork
Position: Centre
Height: 6' **Weight:** 13st 9lb
Occupation: Student
Born: Cork, 24.4.69
Family: Single
Family links with rugby: Three uncles played for Munster
International debut (U-21): Ireland 13, New Zealand 13, 1989
Best moment in rugby: Winning 1987 Munster Schools' Senior Cup
Worst moment in rugby: Being injured for Ireland U-21s 1989 tour to Italy
Most respected opponent: Ireland centre Michael Kiernan – instinctive player who can turn game in split-second
Other sporting achievements: U-14 and U-16 Cork County Championship Gaelic Football medals

	apps.	pts.
Ireland U-21 (**1989**)		
Last Season	1 cap	0

Best memory last season: Being part of a UCC team that did not win a single Munster Senior League match, but who made it to Senior Cup final
Most improved International player last season: Ireland full-back Kenny Murphy
Suggestions to improve rugby: Improved facilities and more competition within and between clubs is key to improving standards
Other notable landmarks in rugby career: Constitution winning Munster U-12 Cup. Capped by Irish Schools and touring Australia with them (1987). Capped at Irish Universities and U-21 level. Munster against Italy (1989)
Touchlines: Tae-kwon-do

Moncrieff, M.   Scotland

Full Name: Mark Moncrieff
International category: Scotland U-21 (squad)
Club: Gala
Position: Wing
Height: 5'10" **Weight:** 11st 10lb
Occupation: Textile finisher
Born: Edinburgh, 19.12.68
Family: Single
Best moment in rugby: Scoring only try 1985/86 Australian Schools conceded during tour, for Scotland Schools (U-18s) at Murrayfield **Worst moment in rugby:** Injury preventing participation in Scotland U-19s v West Germany
Most embarrassing moment: Missing eight weeks rugby after injuring an ankle whilst trying to rescue a neighbour's cat
Best memory last season: Inclusion on Scottish U-21 bench v Wales
Other notable landmarks in rugby career: Won 4 caps for Scottish Schools (U-18s) and 1 for U-19s (against Italy). Spent last summer playing in New Zealand

	apps.
Scotland U-21 (**1989/90**)	Rep 1

Moon, R.H.StJ.B.   England

Full Name: Rupert Henry St.John
Barker Moon
International category: England
U-21
Club: Neath
Position: Scrum-half
Height: 6' **Weight:** 13st
Occupation: Student
Born: Birmingham, 1.2.68
Family: Single
Family links with rugby: Brother
Richard plays scrum-half for
Rosslyn Park. Sister plays
scrum-half for Wasps Ladies
Former clubs: Walsall, Abertillery
International debut (U-21):
Romania 13, England 54, 1989
Best moment in rugby: Scoring
first try in above match in Bucharest
Worst moment in rugby:
Captaining England Students to
defeat by Welsh Students at
Cardiff (1988/89) after popping rib
cartilage in first minute
Most respected opponent:
Former Wales scrum-half David
Bishop

	apps.	pts.
England U-21 (**1989**)		
Last Season	1 cap	4
England 1995	Development squad	

Serious injuries sustained: Popped rib cartilage
Other sporting achievements: Cricket for Walsall. Soccer for Midlands
Schools
Best memory last season: Captaining England Students to 'Grand Slam'
Most improved International player last season: England full-back Simon
Hodgkinson
Suggestions to improve rugby: Scrap farcical 90-degree scrum wheel law
Other notable landmarks in rugby career: Sat on bench for England
Schools, stood on wing for England Students (twice) and Colts. Represented
England in 1988 Student World Cup. Included in Neath's squad for
Schweppes Cup final defeat of Bridgend

Moore, A.   Scotland

Full Name: Alexander Moore
International category: Scotland
Full
Club: Edinburgh Academicals
Position: Wing
Height: 5'7" **Weight:** 13st
Occupation: Sales representative
Born: Queensland, Australia,
19.8.63
Family: Single with two sons
Former clubs: Livingston, Gala
International debut: New
Zealand 21, Scotland 18, 1990
Best moment in rugby: Winning
first cap in second Test at Auckland
Worst moment in rugby: Being
left out of Edinburgh side to play
1988 Australians
Most respected opponent:
Scotland wing Iwan Tukalo
Serious injuries: Dislocated collar-
bone
Best memory last season:
Scoring try on Scotland debut
**Most improved International
player last season:** Scotland wing
Tony Stanger
**Other notable landmarks in
rugby career:** Won 3 Scotland B
caps (against Italy, Ireland and France). Toured with Scotland to
Zimbabwe in 1988 and to New Zealand in 1990
Touchlines: High jump, power weightlifting

	apps.	pts.
Scotland B (**1986**)		
Last Season	2 caps	4
Scotland (**1990**)		
Last Season	1 cap	4
Career	1 cap	4

Moore, B.C.   England

Full Name: Brian Christopher Moore
International category: England Full
Club: Harlequins
Position: Hooker
Height: 5'9" **Weight:** 14st 2lb
Occupation: Corporate financier
Born: Birmingham, 11.1.62
Family: Single
Former clubs: Old Crossleyans, Nottingham
International debut: England 21, Scotland 12, 1987
Five Nations' debut: As above
Best moment in rugby: 1989 Lions beating Australia in third Test to clinch series
Worst moment in rugby: Wales 16, England 3, 1987 World Cup quarter-final
Most embarrassing moment: Being forced to watch pre-match team talks on video
Most respected opponent: England lock Wade Dooley's wallet – I have never managed to open it!
Serious injuries: Fractured ego v Scotland, Murrayfield 1990
Other sporting achievements: Intermediate swimming certificate
Best memory last season: First scrum – England 34, Wales 6

	apps.	pts.
England B (1985)		
Last Season	0 caps	0
England (1987)		
Last Season	8 caps	0
Career	25 caps	4
1990	Tour to Argentina	
1991	World Cup squad	
England XV 1989/90	1 app	0
Lions 1989	3 Tests	0

Most improved International player last season: England centre Will Carling
Suggestions to improve rugby: Automatic retirement from RFU Committee at 55. Player representation on all major decision and law-making committees. Major revision of amateurism laws, along with those concerning foul play, line-outs and kickable penalties. Southern Hemisphere referees to be prevented from officiating Grand Slam deciders

Other notable landmarks in rugby career: Beneficiary of Mark Bailey's understating and self-deprecating wit. Missed only one of England's last 24 matches. Have captained England B and Nottingham. Voted Whitbread/Rugby World 'Player of Year' last season. Joined Harlequins at start of season

Touchlines: Not allowed life outside rugby in these amateur days

Morgan, M.   Wales

Full Name: Michael Morgan
International category: Wales B (squad)
Club: Swansea
Position: Prop
Height: 6' **Weight:** 16st 7lb
Occupation: Lecturer
Born: Southampton, 31.3.65
Family: Single with daughter
Former club: Mumbles
Best moment in rugby: Playing for Swansea against 1989 All Blacks
Most respected opponent: All of them
Other sporting achievements: Cricket for Mumbles
Best memory last season: The atmosphere at Swansea
Most improved International player last season: Wales prop Brian Williams
Suggestions to improve rugby: Greater understanding of players' needs
Other notable landmarks in rugby career: Replacement for Wales B against France (lost 15–28) last season

	apps.
Wales B (1989/90)	Rep 1

Morris, C.D.   England

Full Name: Colin **Dewi** Morris
International category: England B
Club: Orrell
Position: Scrum-half
Height: 6' **Weight:** 13st 7lb
Occupation: Distillery production controller
Born: Crickhowell, Wales, 9.2.64
Family: Single
Former clubs: Brecon, Crewe & Alsager College, Winnington Park, Liverpool St Helens
International debut: England 28, Australia 19, 1988
Five Nations' debut: England 12, Scotland 12, 1989
Best moments in rugby: Scoring try on England debut and winning. Scoring winning try for North in 15–9 defeat of Australia (Oct 1988)
Worst moment in rugby: Losing 9-12 to Wales at Cardiff (March 1989)
Most embarrassing moment: Being dropped by North for match v US Eagles after 5 consecutive International caps and 5 consecutive Divisional caps
Most respected opponent: Wales scrum-half Robert Jones – possesses perfect pass and kick

	apps.	pts.
England B (1988)		
Last Season	2 caps	0
England (1988)		
Last Season	0 caps	0
Career	5 caps	4
1990	Tour to Argentina	
1995	Development squad	

Serious injuries: Broken nose (three times), serious ligament damage to left shoulder, both knees and right ankle
Other sporting achievements: Gwent Schools U-19 County cricket finalists
Best memory last season: LSH promoted to English First Division. Selection for England tour to Argentina
Most improved International player last season: England centre Will Carling
Suggestions to improve rugby: More consistency among referees. Immediate action for serious offences. Reduce points-worth of penalties. Scrap 90-degree scrummaging law

Other notable landmarks in rugby career: Progressing from junior rugby to International level in six months (Winnington Park-LSH-Lancashire-North-England B-England)
Touchlines: Holidays spent on lazy beaches
Rugby hates: Reporters who have never played game to any notable standard, let alone on International stage, talking as if they could do better and know all the answers

Morris, M.S.   Wales

Full Name: Martyn Stuart Morris
International category: Wales Full
Club: Neath
Position: Flanker
Height: 6'3" **Weight:** 15st
Occupation: Police officer
Born: Neath, 23.8.62
Family: Married with daughter
Former clubs: Neath Athletic, South Wales Police
International debut: Scotland 21, Wales 25, 1985
Five Nations' debut: As above
Best moment in rugby: Being recalled to Welsh team against Ireland last season after five years away
Worst moment in rugby: Being dropped in first place
Most respected opponent: 1989 All Blacks
Serious injuries: Broken nose
Other sporting achievements: Cricket for Neath
Best memory last season: Returning to The Gnoll after winning Welsh Cup – like an FA Cup victory parade
Most improved International players last season: Welsh trio Glyn Llewellyn, Alan Reynolds and Owain Williams

	apps.	pts.
Wales B (1983)		
Last Season	0 caps	0
Wales (1985)		
Last Season	3 caps	0
Career	6 caps	0

Suggestions to improve rugby: Better standard of refereeing in Wales and improved treatment of players
Other notable landmarks in rugby career: Former vice-captain of Wales Youth (played No.8) and also represented Wales B before making his full debut in 1985. Rejoined Neath last season from SWP
Touchlines: Road running for training

Morrison, J.S.C.   England

Full Name: John Stewart Charles Morrison
International category: England B
Club: Bath
Position: Lock
Height: 6'5" **Weight:** 16st 7lb
Occupation: Insurance inspector
Born: Bexley, Kent, 6.4.63
Family: Single
Family links with rugby: Father played soccer for Tottenham Hotspur
Former club: Loughborough Students
International debut: England B v Italy, 1986
Best moment in rugby: Bath beating Leicester in final minute of 1988/89 English Cup final in front of packed house at Twickenham
Worst moment in rugby: Missing 1989/90 Cup final v Gloucester
Most respected opponents: England B lock Bob Kimmins and Harlequins' Neil Edwards
Serious injuries: Lost front tooth playing v Pontypool
Other sporting achievements: Soccer for Bristol Juniors. Discus at National Schools' Championship
Best memory last season: Being Best Man at England flanker Andy Robinson's wedding

	apps.	pts.
England B (1986)		
Last Season	1 cap	4

Most improved International player last season: England lock Paul Ackford

Other notable landmarks in rugby career: Began life in Bath Colts, alongside Jeremy Guscott. Won two UAU titles with Loughborough. Played in three Cup finals for Bath and helped South West beat 1988 touring Australians. Have represented England at schools, Colts, Universities, Students, U-23 and B levels

Touchlines: Public 'after dinner' speaking

Moseley, K.   Wales

Full Name: Kevin Moseley
International category: Wales Full
Club: Pontypool
Position: Lock
Height: 6'7" **Weight:** 17st 6lb
Occupation: Printer
Born: Blackwood, 2.7.63
Former clubs: Blackwood, Bay of Plenty (NZ)
International debut: New Zealand 54, Wales 9, 1988
Five Nations' debut: Scotland 23, Wales 7, 1989
Worst moment in rugby: Being sent off playing for Wales against France at Cardiff last season
Most embarrassing moment: As above
Serious injuries: Damaged foot (1988)
Other notable landmarks in rugby career: Began career with home-club Blackwood, before moving to Pontypool in 1984. Spent a season playing with Bay of Plenty in New Zealand's Inter-Provincial Championship. Has played for Wales B and toured New Zealand (1988) with Wales

	apps.	pts.
Wales B (1984)		
Last Season	0 caps	0
Wales (1988)		
Last Season	1 cap	0
Career	5 caps	0

Mosses, G.B.   England

Full Name: Glyn Barry Mosses
International category: England
B (squad)
Club: Nottingham
Position: Tight-head prop
Height: 5'10" **Weight:** 16st 7lb
Occupation: General manager
(Pressed Drums Ltd)
Born: Birmingham, 2.1.61
Family: Single
Former clubs: Stourbridge,
Bromsgrove
Best moment in rugby: Being
selected for England squad at start
of 1989/90
Worst moment in rugby: Missing
England's game against Fiji
through injury
Most embarrassing moment:
Turning up for training with dyed
red hair
Most respected opponent:
England prop Paul Rendall –
impossible to relax against because
so strong

	apps.
England B (1989/90)	Rep 1
England 1995	Development squad

Serious injuries: Torn hamstring,
calf muscle
Best memory last season: Helping Nottingham beat Bath and Gloucester
in English First Division
Most improved International player last season: England lock Paul
Ackford
Suggestions to improve rugby: Reduce number of games played in season
Other notable landmarks in rugby career: Replacement for England B
against Fiji last season

Mulcahy, W.J.M.   Ireland

Full Name: William Joseph
Michael Mulcahy
International category: Ireland
U-25 (squad)
Club: Skerries
Position: Hooker
Height: 6' **Weight:** 14st
Occupation: Chartered accountant
Born: Dublin, 15.8.64
Family: Single
Family links with rugby: Father
(Bill) former Ireland captain (35
caps, 1958–65) who toured with
1959 and 1962 Lions
Best moment in rugby: Ireland
U-21 internal tour (1985)
Worst moment in rugby: Sitting
it out as replacement for Ireland
U-25s v US Eagles (1989)
Best memory last season:
Inter-Provincial debut for Leinster
v Munster
**Most improved International
player last season:** Ireland
full-back Kenny Murphy

	apps.
Ireland U-25 (**1989/90**)	Rep 1

Suggestions to improve rugby: Operate season from March to October
rather than September to April in order to play in better conditions
Other notable landmarks in rugby career: Leinster U-20s won 1984
Inter-Pro's. Ireland U-21 squad (1985). Captained Skerries (1987/88).
Thirteen times a replacement for Leinster. Twice a replacement for Ireland
U-25s (1988–90)

Mullin, B.J.   Ireland

Full Name: Brendan John Mullin
International category: Ireland Full
Club: Blackrock College
Position: Centre
Height: 6'1" **Weight:** 13st
Occupation: Stockbroker
Born: Israel, 31.10.63
Family: Single
Former clubs: Trinity College Dublin, Oxford University, London Irish
International debut: Ireland 9, Australia 16, 1984
Five Nations' debut: Scotland 15, Ireland 18, 1985
Best moment in rugby: Selection for 1989 Lions
Worst moment in rugby: Ireland's dreadful campaign at 1987 World Cup
Most respected opponent: Former Australian centre Brett Papworth
Serious injuries: Operation on knee cartilage (1989/90)
Other sporting achievements: International hurdling for Ireland
Best memory last season: Beating Wales to avoid Five Nations' Wooden Spoon

	apps.	pts.
Ireland B (1983)		
Last Season	0 caps	0
Ireland (1984)		
Last Season	4 caps	0
Career	32 caps	52
Lions 1986		
1989	1 Test	0

Most improved International player last season: England scrum-half Richard Hill
Suggestions to improve rugby: International Rugby Board must give sport some direction and leadership. Rugby has outgrown what archaic IRB was set up to administer
Other notable landmarks in rugby career: Jim Burns, hurdles coach at school and still, has been major influence on career which began, in representative terms, when played six times for Irish Schools (1981–82), three as captain. Made B debut against Scotland in 1983 and following season broke into full team. Played for 1986 Lions against The Rest in Cardiff to mark

centenary of IRB. Scored 3 tries against Tonga in 1987 World Cup. Won two Oxford Blues (1986,87). 1988/89 Irish Player of Year. Leading try-scorer for 1989 Lions with 7. Played for Lions in first Test against Australia, and against Anzacs, and for 1989 Home Unions in 29–27 defeat of France
Touchlines: Tennis

Mullins, A.R.   England

Full Name: Andrew Richard Mullins
International category: England Full
Club: Harlequins
Position: Tight-head prop
Height: 5'11" **Weight:** 16st
Occupation: Accountant
Born: Eltham, London, 12.12.64
Family: Married
Former clubs: Old Alleynians, Durham University
International debut: England 58, Fiji 23, 1989
Best moment in rugby: Running out at Twickenham against Fiji
Worst moment in rugby: Not making London team immediately after Fiji game. Knew that would determine England selection as Jeff Probyn got nod instead
Most disappointing moment: Grounding ball inches short of try-line against Fijians
Biggest problem in rugby: Wasps' England tight-head Jeff Probyn
Most respected opponent: England loose-head Paul 'Judge' Rendall – good all-rounder...in bar
Serious injuries: Broken nose, bone in foot
Other sporting achievements: London Schools breaststroke swimming champion

	apps.	pts.
England B (1988)		
Last Season	3 caps	0
England (1989)		
Last Season	1 cap	0
Career	1 cap	0
1995	Development squad	

Best memory last season: Making full England debut
Most improved International player last season: England B wing Tony Underwood
Suggestions to improve rugby: Adopt a more professional (but realistic) approach over training. RFU send out training timetables which are not practical because of time involved. More helpful if they arranged memberships of local gyms and health clubs for players
Other notable landmarks in rugby career: Switched from flanker to prop aged 16 and immediately won selection to England Schools. Spent year in Army between school and Durham University. Represented England U-23s (1986) and joined Harlequins (1987/88). Share birthdate with fellow Quin Will Carling, who played in same University and England 18 Group Schools team. Played in English team at 1988 Student World Cap and same year made B debut against Australia
Touchlines: Enjoy black and white films, especially 'The Thirty-Nine Steps'

Munroe, D.S. Scotland

Full Name: Donald **Shade** Munroe
International category: Scotland B
Club: Glasgow High/Kelvinside
Position: Lock
Height: 6'6" **Weight:** 17st
Occupation: Civil engineer
Born: Paisley, 19.11.66
Family: Single
Family links with rugby:
Grandfather played for Scotland (1919–28)
International debut (B): France 12, Scotland 18, 1988
Best moment in rugby: Beating France at Chalon-sur-Saone on debut
Worst moment in rugby: Having to withdraw from Scotland's tour of New Zealand last summer after shattering knee playing for Scotland XV against West of Scotland in David Millar charity game

	apps.	pts.
Scotland B (1988)		
Last Season	1 cap	0

Most respected opponent: Hawick's former Scotland lock Alan Tomes
Serious injuries: Shattered knee (required bone graft and pins). Popped shoulder (missed 1989/90 Inter-District Championship)
Other sporting achievements: Junior captain of golf club
Best memory last season: GHK retaining Scottish First Division status
Most improved International player last season: Scotland scrum-half Gary Armstrong
Suggestions to improve rugby: Stricter refereeing of line-out. Set piece is a shambles at present
Other notable landmarks in rugby career: Capped once by Scotland at U-19 level, twice by U-21s, and three times by Scotland B (all against France)
Touchlines: Tennis, soccer

Murphy, K.J. Ireland

Full Name: Kenneth John Murphy
International category: Ireland Full
Club: Constitution
Position: Full-back
Height: 6' **Weight:** 12st 7lb
Occupation: Family garage business
Born: Cork, 31.7.66
Family: Single
Family links with rugby: Father and grandfather both played for Ireland
International debut: England 23, Ireland 0, 1990
Five Nations' debut: As above
Best moment in rugby: Winning first cap
Worst moment in rugby: Missing penalty which cost Christian Brothers College the Junior Schools Cup
Most respected opponents: Full-backs Gavin Hastings (Scotland) and Serge Blanco (France)

	apps.	pts.
Ireland B (1989)		
Last Season	1 cap	0
Ireland (1990)		
Last Season	4 caps	0
Career	4 caps	0

Best memory last season: Playing for Munster v All Blacks and helping Ireland beat Wales in Dublin
Most improved International player last season: England fly-half Rob Andrew
Other notable landmarks in rugby career: Unique family record – father and grandfather also played for country. Played Irish Schools against Junior All Blacks (1985). Represented Combined Provinces on internal tour and was a replacement for Ireland U-25s against Italy (1989)

Murray, P.V.   Ireland

Full Name: Patrick Vincent Murray
International category: Ireland B
Clubs: Shannon, Southland (NZ)
Position: Left wing
Height: 6' **Weight:** 13st 4lb
Occupation: Bank official
Born: Limerick, 12.10.63
Family: Single
Former club: Old Crescent
International debut (B): Scotland 22, Ireland 22, 1989
Best moment in rugby: Winning 1982 Munster Senior Schools Cup
Worst moment in rugby: Losing 1988/89 Senior Cup final to Constitution
Most embarrassing moment: Buying a dummy from a prop during a club game
Most respected opponent: All of them
Serious injuries sustained: Broken leg, thumb
Other sporting achievements: Played with Limerick football team in Munster Championship

	apps.	pts.
Ireland B **(1989)**		
Last Season	1 cap	4

Best memory last season: Playing against the All Blacks at Musgrave Park
Most improved International player last season: Ireland full-back Kenny Murphy

Suggestions to improve rugby: All penalties must be run – no kicking for touch

---

Mustoe, L.   Wales

Full Name: Lyndon Mustoe
International category: Wales U-21
Club: Pontypool
Position: Prop
Height: 6'1" **Weight:** 15st 7lb
Occupation: Bricklayer
Born: Newport, 30.1.69
Family: Single with son
Former club: Chepstow
International debut (U-21): Scotland 10, Wales 24, 1990
Best moment in rugby: Beating Scotland at Ayr on U-21 debut
Worst moment in rugby: Only replacement for Wales Youth (four times)
Most respected player: Pontypool's former Wales prop Staff Jones
Serious injuries: Damaged back, strained neck
Best memory last season: Beating Scotland U-21s
Other notable landmarks in rugby career: Played flanker for East Gwent, Gwent, and Newport Schools. Propped for Wales U-20s
Touchlines: Cross country running, weight training

	apps.	pts.
Wales U-21 (1990)		
Last Season	1 cap	0

Nichol, S.A.   Scotland

Full Name: Scott Alan Nichol
International category: Scotland U-21
Club: Selkirk
Positions: Fly-half (U-21), left wing (Schools)
Height: 5'10" **Weight:** 11st 7lb
Occupation: Postman
Born: Selkirk, 18.6.70
Family: Single
Family links with rugby: Alan Reid (grandfather) played for Watsonians and Edinburgh in late 1930s and 1940s
International debut (U-21): Scotland 10, Wales 24, 1990
Best moment in rugby: Being chosen to tour with Scottish Schools in New Zealand (1987/88)
Worst moment in rugby: Getting injured at first training session in New Zealand and missing first three games
Most embarrassing moment: Mistaking centre line at kick-off
Most respected opponent: John Jeffrey – always gives 100 per cent effort

	apps.	pts.
Scotland U-21 (**1990**)		
Last season	1 cap	0

Other sporting achievements: Under-15 Border tennis champion
Best memory last season: Beating Stirling County in Scottish First Division to avoid relegation
Most improved International player last season: Scotland wing Tony Stanger
Suggestions to improve rugby: Scotland having parity with England and Wales in sponsorship deals
Other notable landmarks in rugby career: Touring Canada with Selkirk High School. Selection for South U-21s, Scotland U-19s and U-21s
Touchlines: Non-competitive golf

Norster, R.L.   Wales

Full Name: Robert Leonard Norster
International category: Wales Full
Club: Cardiff
Position: Lock
Height: 6'5" **Weight:** 16st 4lb
Occupation: Marketing manager
Born: Ebbw Vale, 23.6.57
Family: Married
Family links with rugby: Since turn of century everyone played at various levels except mother
Former club: Abertillery
International debut: Wales v Romania, 1979 (non-cap)
Five Nations' debut: Wales 18, Scotland 34, 1982
Best moment in rugby: Any International victory
Worst moment in rugby: Any International defeat
Most embarrassing moment: Nearly ruining a 25-yard try v Ireland in 1986 by waving to crowd
Most respected opponent: All respected – as most over 6'6" and 17st, wouldn't you?
Serious injuries:
Broken/dislocated – back, knees, shoulder, jaw, nose (four times)

	apps.	pts.
Wales B (1979)		
Last Season	0 caps	0
Wales (1982)		
Last Season	0 caps	0
Career	34 caps	8
Lions 1983	2 Tests	0
1989	1 Test	0

Other sporting achievements: Ex-Sunday cricketer, current Sunday golfer
Best memory last season: To a Welshman there wasn't one
Most improved International player last season: England lock Paul Ackford
Suggestions to improve rugby: Provide a more attractive image to youngsters
Other notable landmarks in rugby career: Captain of Cardiff and Wales. Toured with 1983 and 1989 Lions. Most-capped Welsh lock (34) with Allan Martin. Played for World XV v South Africa (1989) where damaged shoulder which side-lined me throughout last season

O'Connell, K. Ireland

Full Name: Ken O'Connell
International category: Ireland
U-25
Club: Sunday's Well
Position: Lock
Height: 6'2" **Weight:** 15st 7lb
Occupation: Sales manager
Born: Cork
Family: Single
Former club: Lansdowne
International debut: Ireland
Schools v Australia, 1986
Best moment in rugby: Playing
for Munster against 1989 All Blacks
Worst moment in rugby: Being
taken off in above match
Most embarrassing moment:
Having shorts ripped off in Cup
final
Most respected opponent: New
Zealand No.8 Wayne Shelford –
like hitting a brick wall
Serious injuries: Dislocated
collarbone
Best memory last season:
Running out against New Zealand
**Most improved International
player last season:** Myself
Suggestions to improve rugby: Players should be looked after better

	apps.	pts.
Ireland U-21 (1989)		
Last Season	2 caps	0

O'Hara, P.T.   Ireland

Full Name: Patrick Thomas O'Hara
International category: Ireland Full
Club: Sunday's Well
Position: Flanker
Height: 6'2" **Weight:** 15st
Occupation: Sales director
Born: Essex, England, 4.8.61
Family: Married with two sons
International debut: Ireland 49, Western Samoa 22, 1988
Five Nations' debut: Ireland 21, France 26, 1989
Best moment in rugby: First full cap against France
Worst moment in rugby: Getting concussed against England 1989 (lost 3-16)

Most embarrassing moment: Playing in front of provincial selectors in 1984/85, ended up in centre and attempted long pass to wing that was intercepted for try
Most respected opponent: Scotland flanker Finlay Calder – great reader of the game, very street wise, and always willing to advise

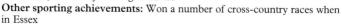

	apps.	pts.
Ireland (1988)		
Last Season	5 caps	0
Career	9 caps	0

Other sporting achievements: Won a number of cross-country races when in Essex
Best memory last season: Sunday's Well beating Dolphin to qualify for All-Ireland League
Most improved International player last season: England centre Will Carling
Suggestions to improve rugby: Play ball on ground, within reason
Other notable landmarks in rugby career: Munster against 1984 Wallabies and 1989 All Blacks. Cork Charity Cup (1981), Irish tours to France (1988) and North America (1989). Irish debut 15 minutes from end v Western Samoa, replacing Phil Matthews
Touchlines: Built garden shed all by myself

O'Leary, S.T.   England

Full Name: Sean Thomas O'Leary
International category: England B
Club: Wasps
Position: Lock
Height: 6'8" **Weight:** 17st 4in
Occupation: Doctor
Born: Plymouth, 25.9.64
Family: Single
Former clubs: Plymouth Albion,
Cambridge University
International debut (B): France
6, England 18, 1989
Best moment in rugby: Beating
France B in Paris on debut
Worst moment in rugby: Because
of injury, not playing in Wasps'
defeat of Saracens which clinched
English First Division title
Most embarrassing moment:
The Lawson Obscene Publications
Act prevents reference to an
incident related to London Division
Most respected opponent:
England lock Nigel Redman
Other sporting achievements:
National League basketball
Best memory last season: Wasps
and London winning respective
championships

	apps.	pts.
England B (1988)		
Last Season	2 caps	0
England 1991	World Cup squad	
1995	Development squad	

Most improved International player last season: England lock Paul
Ackford
Suggestions to improve rugby: More consistent refereeing of line-outs
Other notable landmarks in rugby career: Cambridge Blues (1984,85).
Selection for England tour to Argentina last summer but had to cry off through
injury. Capped three times by England Students
Touchlines: If you are a doctor and play first-class rugby, there is hardly
sufficient time to do either properly and certainly no time for hobbies

O'Sullivan, E.T.   Ireland

Full Name: Eoin Thomas O'Sullivan
International category: Ireland U-21
Club: Old Crescent
Position: Lock
Height: 6'4" **Weight:** 16st 7lb
Occupation: Sales representative
Born: Limerick, 20.3.70
Family: Single
International debut (U-21): Italy 9, Ireland 10, 1989
Best moment in rugby: Irish Schools tour to Australia (1987)
Worst moment in rugby: Missing large part of season after chipping ankle playing for Munster
Most respected opponent: Ireland B lock Michael Galwey – tough but fair
Serious injuries sustained: Chipped ankle
Other sporting achievements: Gaelic football for Limerick
Best memory last season: Scoring try for Ireland U-21s in 13–13 draw with New Zealand U-21s

	apps.	pts.
Ireland U-21 (**1989**)		
Last Season	2 caps	4

Most improved International player last season: Scotland wing Tony Stanger
Suggestions to improve rugby: Improved refereeing and de-powering of scrum
Other notable landmarks in rugby career: Played rugby in New Zealand last summer. Scored try for Munster U-21s in 10–13 defeat by New Zealand U-21s last season
Touchlines: Parachuting, swimming

Oliver, G.H.   Scotland

Full Name: Greig Hunter Oliver
International category: Scotland Full
Club: Hawick
Position: Scrum-half
Height: 5'8½" **Weight:** 12st 6lb
Occupation: Computer operator
Born: Hawick, 12.9.64
Family: Single
Family links with rugby: Derek (brother) plays for Hawick Linden, as did father
Former clubs: Hawick PSA, Hawick Trades
International debut: Scotland 60, Zimbabwe 21, 1987 (World Cup)
Best moment in rugby: Winning first cap
Worst moment in rugby: Having to sit and watch on the Scotland bench
Most embarrassing moment: Not being able to walk for a week because of a skin burn on my behind
Most respected opponent: Former Scotland scrum-half Roy Laidlaw – for his dedication to the game and assistance to younger players

	apps.	pts.
Scotland B (1986)		
Last Season	0 caps	0
Scotland (1987)		
Last Season	1 cap	0
Career	2 caps	4

Other sporting achievements: Won the 1986 St Ronan's Sprint. Broke 100 at Minto Golf Club
Best memory last season: Enjoying a good International Trial
Most improved International player last season: Scotland lock Chris Gray
Suggestions to improve rugby: Make the scrum a way of starting the game, and not a means of spoiling it
Other notable landmarks in rugby career: Being a small part of the 1990 Grand Slam squad. Member of Scotland's 1987 World cup squad. Scored try on Scotland debut v Zimbabwe. Toured with Scotland to Zimbabwe (1988), Japan (1989) and New Zealand (1990), coming on as replacement for Gary Armstrong in second Test at Auckland
Touchlines: Tennis and golf

Olver, C.J.   England

Full Name: Christopher John Olver
International category: England
Full (squad)
Club: Northampton
Position: Hooker
Height: 5'9" **Weight:** 13st 8lb
Occupation: Teacher
Born: Manchester, 23.4.62
Family: Married with a daughter
Former clubs: Sandbach,
Harlequins
International debut: Italian XV
15, England XV 33, 1990
Best moment in rugby: Lifting
John Player Cup after captaining
Harlequins to 1988 final win v
Bristol
Worst moment in rugby: Losing
two JP Cup semi-finals with Quins
Most embarrassing moment:
Every time I lose a strike against
head
Most respected opponents:
Former England hookers Phil
Keith-Roach and Peter Wheeler
Serious injuries: Achilles tendon
(operation). Dislocated shoulder (twice)

	apps.	pts.
England B (1988)		
Last Season	1 cap	0
England (1989/90)	Rep 5	0
1990	Tour to Argentina	
1991	World Cup squad	
England XV 1989/90	1 app	0

Other sporting achievements:
Hit Australian cricket captain Allan
Border for three consecutive sixes. 7-handicap golfer
Best memory last season: Winning Divisional Championship with London
Most improved International player last season: England fly-half Rob
Andrew
Suggestions to improve rugby: Structure season so that all League rugby is
conducted on consecutive Saturdays (Sept-Nov). Then play divisionals (Dec)
and then, after Christmas, Internationals. This would remove present ludicrous
dilemma of players having to play major league games seven days before
Internationals
Other notable landmarks in rugby career: Being invited to Mark Bailey's
for dinner – this means, above all else, that I've made it in rugby
Touchlines: Fly fishing and shooting

Orrell, T.   Wales

Full Name: Tony Orrell
International category: Wales
U-21
Club: Cardiff
Position: Loose-head prop
Height: 6'1" **Weight:** 18st 2lb
Occupation: Quantity surveyor
Born: Church Village, 17.12.70
Family: Single
Family links with rugby: Two
brothers play
International debut (U-21):
Scotland 10, Wales 24, 1990
Best moment in rugby: Cardiff
beating Llanelli in quarter-finals of
1989/90 Welsh Cup
Worst moment in rugby: Being
dropped for 1989/90 semi-final tie
against Neath
Most embarrassing moment:
Having shorts ripped open after 10
minutes, playing against Neath,
and waiting 30 minutes for new
pair to be brought on
Most respected opponent: Wales
prop Laurance Delaney

	apps.	pts.
Wales U-21 (**1990**)		
Last Season	1 cap	0

Best memory last season: Winning place in Cardiff team in first season and
earning Cardiff cap for playing 20 games
Most improved International player last season: Neath's Wales scrum-half
Chris Bridges
Other notable landmarks in rugby career: Represented Welsh Senior
Schools (two seasons) and Youth prior to Wales U-21s last season
Touchlines: Weight training

Oti, C.   England

Full Name: Christopher Oti
International category: England
Full
Club: Wasps
Position: Wing
Height: 5'11" **Weight:** 13st 2lb
Occupation: Chartered surveyer
Born: London, 16.6.65
Family: Single
Former clubs: Nottingham,
Cambridge University
International debut: Scotland 6,
England 9, March 1988
Five Nations' debut: As above
Best moment in rugby: Three
tries on England home debut in
35–3 defeat of Ireland (March
1988)

Worst moment in rugby:
Returning home early due to injury
from 1989 Lions' tour to Australia
Most embarrassing moment:
Not scoring hat-trick in every
subsequent International after
Ireland 1988
Most respected opponent:
Scotland flanker Finlay Calder –
superb captain and leader
Serious injuries sustained: Knee
ligament damage (operated on
successfully in 1989)

	apps.	pts.
England B (1987)		
Last Season	0 caps	0
England (1988)		
Last Season	3 caps	20
Career	9 caps	32
1990	Tour to Argentina	
1991	World Cup squad	
England XV 1989/90	1 app	4
Lions 1989		

Other sporting achievements:
Hold Millfield School 100m sprint record – 10.8sec, achieved aged 17
Best memory last season: Scoring try in comeback match for England in
33–15 non-cap win v Italy
Most improved International player last season: England centre Will
Carling
Suggestions to improve rugby: Allow players to be financially rewarded for
non-playing matters – advertising, speeches etc.

Other notable landmarks in rugby career: Cambridge Blues (1986,87). Four tries on Barbarians debut (1988). Celebrated third cap with 4 tries for England v Romania in Bucharest (May 1989). Selected for 1989 Lions

Packman, F.   England

Full Name: Frank Packman
International category: England B
Club: Northampton
Position: Wing
Height: 5'11" **Weight:** 13st 2lb
Occupation: Police constable
Born: Dortmund, West Germany, 29.2.64
Family: Married
Former club: Towcestrians
International debut: England B 18, USSR 10, 1989
Best moment in rugby: Scoring 6 tries v Cheltenham to equal Northampton try-scoring record of 33 in a season set by Barry Oldham
Worst moment in rugby: Not taking record outright in final game of 1988/89 season when failing to score v Rugby
Most embarrassing moment: Missing a tackle in front of selectors
Most respected opponent: Former England scrum-half Richard Harding
Serious injuries sustained: Broken cheekbone

	apps.	pts.
England B (1989)		
Last Season	1 cap	0

Other sporting achievements: Winning Plessey golf competition
Most improved International player last season: England fly-half Rob Andrew
Suggestions to improve rugby: Increase standard of referees and their understanding of laws
Other notable landmarks in rugby career: Three England Colts caps. Completed 100 tries for Northampton (1988). Helped Saints gain promotion to English First Division in 1989/90

Parfitt, S.A.   Wales

Full Name: Stuart Ashley Parfitt
International category: Wales Full
Club: Swansea
Position: Centre
Height: 5'11½" **Weight:** 13st
Occupation: Financial consultant
Born: Usk, 4.3.66
Family: Single
Former club: Bridgend
International debut: Namibia 9,
Wales 18, 1990
Best moment in rugby: Swansea
against 1989 All Blacks – we
played very well
Worst moment in rugby: Sitting
on bench through 1987 Welsh Cup
final which Swansea lost 15–16 to
Cardiff
Most respected opponent:
Cardiff's Welsh centre Mark Ring
Serious injuries: Broke collarbone
at school
Best memory last season:
Winning first cap in Namibia
**Most improved International
player last season:** England centre
Will Carling

	apps.	pts.
Wales (1990)		
Last Season	1 cap	0
Career	1 cap	0

Other notable landmarks in rugby career: Won 8 caps for Welsh Schools
before joining Bridgend, aged 18. Also represented Wales at U-20 and U-21
level before making full bow on tour to Namibia last summer
Touchlines: Golf (28-handicap)

Paul, S.W.   Scotland

Full Name: Stuart Watson Paul
International category: Scotland
U-21 (squad)
Club: Heriot's FP
Position: Prop
Height: 6' **Weight:** 16st 2lb
Occupation: Law student
Born: Haddington, 7.3.70
Family: Single
Best moment in rugby: Playing
for Scotland Schools at Eden Park
against New Zealand on 1988 tour
Most respected player: Heriot's
Scotland prop Iain Milne
Other sporting achievements:
Swam for Haddington District
U-12s
Best memory last season:
Hearing of Scotland U-21 call-up
**Most improved International
player last season:** Scotland wing
Tony Stanger
**Other notable landmarks in rugby
career:** Represented Scottish Schools
for two years. Also Scotland U-19s,

	apps.
Scotland U-21 (**1989/90**)	Rep 1

Edinburgh U-21s (two seasons), and Scottish Students. Replacement for
Scotland U-21s against Wales last season
Touchlines: Golf (10-handicap)

Paxton, I.A.M.   Scotland

Full Name: Iain Angus MacLeod Paxton
International category: Scotland Full (New Zealand squad)
Club: Selkirk
Positions: No.8, lock
Height: 6'4" **Weight:** 16st
Occupation: Insurance consultant
Born: Dunfermline, 29.12.57
Family: Married
Former club: Glenrothes
International debut: New Zealand 11, Scotland 4, 1981
Five Nations' debut: Scotland 9, England 9, 1982
Best moments in rugby: Winning Grand Slam (1984). Beating England 33–6 (1986)
Worst moment in rugby: Losing 24–28 to Japan (Tokyo 1989)
Most embarrassing moment: Tripping when running onto pitch at Murrayfield in 1985 as a replacement for John Beattie against Ireland
Most respected opponent: Former New Zealand No.8 Murray Mexted – tremendous athlete as well as rugby player

	apps.	pts.
Scotland (1981)		
Last Season	0 caps	0
Career	36 caps	20
Lions 1983	4 Tests	0
1986		

Serious injuries sustained: Ligament damage in both knees
Other sporting achievements: Scottish Schoolboy cap at basketball
Best memory last season: Watching Scotland win the Grand Slam
Most improved International player last season: Scotland wing Tony Stanger
Other notable landmarks in rugby career: Scotland's most capped No.8 (27 caps). Played all four Tests on British Lions' 1983 tour of New Zealand, playing in 9 of the 18 games and scoring 4 tries to be joint leading forward try-scorer. Toured with Scotland to New Zealand (1981), Australia (1982), North America (1985), Spain and France (1986), Japan (1989) and New Zealand (1990)

Pears, D.   England

Full Name: David Pears
International category: England B
Club: Harlequins
Position: Fly-half
Height: 5'10" **Weight:** 12st 6lb
Occupation: Trainee project
manager
Born: Workington, 6.12.67
Family: Single
Family links with rugby: Father
played rugby league for Cumbria
Former clubs: Aspatria, Sale
International debut: Argentina
12, England 25, 1990
Best moment in rugby: Scoring
all 15 points when England B drew
with France in Paris last season
Worst moment in rugby: Missing
penalty kick which would have
earned Sale promotion to English
First Division (1988/89)
Most embarrassing moment:
Asking Gary Pearce (England's
most capped prop with 35 to his
credit), on England B trip to Italy
in 1989, whether it was his first
International
Most respected opponent: Bath's
former England fly-half Stuart
Barnes – dictates games so well
Serious injuries: Torn knee
ligaments (out twelve weeks)

	apps.	pts.
England U-21 (1989)		
Last Season	1 cap	2
England B (1988)		
Last Season	2 caps	25
England (1990)		
Last Season	2 caps	0
1990	Tour to Argentina	
1995	Development squad	

Other sporting achievements: Cumbria Schools soccer captain
Best memory last season: Being told of England selection for tour to
Argentina
Most improved International player last season: England fly-half Rob
Andrew
Suggestions to improve rugby: Make game professional to raise standards
even higher

Other notable landmarks in rugby career: Capped six times by England B and was a replacement when an England XV beat an Italy XV 33–15 in Rovigo last season. Scored well over 500 points in two seasons of English League rugby

---

Pegler, D.J.   England

Full Name: David James Pegler
International category: England B
Club: Wasps
Position: Flanker
Height: 6'1" **Weight:** 14st
Occupation: Publisher
Born: Bristol, 24.11.61
Family: Single
Family links with rugby: Father played prop for Bristol
Former clubs: Bristol, Loughborough University
International debut: England B 9, Australia 37, 1988
Best moment in rugby: Winning 1987 Monte Carlo Sevens
Worst moment in rugby: Wasps losing two successive Cup finals to Bath
Most embarrassing moment: Being run around by Harlequins in 1989 National Sevens final live on TV
Most respected opponent: Anyone who gets around the field in a No.7 shirt quicker than me

	apps.	pts.
England B (1988)		
Last Season	4 caps	4

Other sporting achievements: Represented Somerset at triple jump
Best memory last season: Winning English First Division title with Wasps
Suggestions to improve rugby: Allow broken time payments
Other notable landmarks in rugby career: Winning Middlesex Sevens with Wasps (1985). John Player Cup final appearances (1986–87). Divisional Championship with London (1988–89). Captaining London to 21–10 defeat of 1988 Wallabies and scoring try

Perego, M.A.   Wales

Full Name: Mark Angelo Perego
International category: Wales Full
Club: Llanelli
Position: Flanker
Height: 6' **Weight:** 14st 7lb
Occupation: Fireman
Born: Winchester, Hants, 8.2.64
Family: Married
Family links with rugby: Father
played for Llanelli, Army and
Wales Youth
Former club: South Wales Police
International debut: Wales 9,
Scotland 13, 1990
Five Nations' debut: As above
Best moment in rugby: Llanelli
beating Neath 28–13 in 1988
Schweppes Cup final
Worst moment in rugby: Llanelli
losing to Cardiff in 1989/90 Cup
(first Cup-tie defeat with club)
Most respected opponent:
Former Wales scrum-half Jonathan
Griffiths (in training)
Serious injuries: Torn neck
muscles, concussion (twice)
Other sporting achievements:
Golf (8-handicap)

	apps.	pts.
Wales (1990)		
Last Season	1 cap	0
Career	1 cap	0

Best memory last season: Running out for Wales on debut at Cardiff Arms
Park
Most improved International player last season: Wales wing Arthur Emyr
Suggestions to improve rugby: Increase emphasis on schoolboy rugby
Other notable landmarks in rugby career: Represented Wales at U-15,
U-16, U-18, Youth and B level. Started career at Llanelli and returned to
Stradey Park after two-year spell at South Wales Police
Touchlines: River and mountain running, golf

Peters, E.W.   England

Full Name: Eric William Peters
International category: England
U-21
Club: Saracens
Position: No.8
Height: 6'5" **Weight:** 15st 7lb
Occupation: Student
Born: Glasgow, 28.1.69
Family: Single
Former club: Old Brentwoods
International debut: Netherlands
3, England U-21 24, 1990
Best moment in rugby: Putting
on England shirt for first time
Most respected team mate:
Argentine fly-half Hugo Porta
(Major Stanley's XV)
Serious injuries: Broken finger
Best memory last season:
Winning twice at Twickenham,
with Loughborough Students
(UAU final) and Eastern Counties
(U-21 County final)
**Most improved International
player last season:** England
fly-half Rob Andrew

	apps.	pts.
England U-21 (**1990**)		
Last Season	2 caps	0

Other notable landmarks in rugby career: Eligible for Scotland but chose
England. Had U-18 final Trial a year young and then played three seasons
with London (U-18,19,21). Member of Eastern Counties team which won
U-21 County Championship in 1989 and 1990. In final year at Loughborough,
with whom won UAU Championship last season. Played for England Students
against Soviet Union last season and have also represented English Univs and
Combined English/Welsh Univs

Peterson, G.L.   Scotland

Full Name: Gordon Laurence Peterson
International category: Scotland U-21 (squad)
Club: Glasgow High/Kelvinside
Position: Hooker
Height: 5'10" **Weight:** 13st 6lb
Occupation: Student
Born: Glasgow, 19.2.70
Family: Single
Former club: Glasgow University
Best moment in rugby: My best ever performance, for Dollar Academy v Kelvinside Academy
Worst moment in rugby: Withdrawing from Scotland v Wales U-21 match because of injury
Most embarrassing moment: Playing beside ugly props
Most respected opponent: Scotland hooker Kenny Milne – such a gentleman
Serious injuries sustained: Torn ligaments in both ankles
Best memory last season: Selection to U-21 squad for Wales match

	apps.
Scotland U-21 (1989/90)	Rep 1

Most improved International player last season: Scotland wing Tony Stanger
Other notable landmarks in rugby career: Captained Scotland 18 (1987–88) and 19 (1988–89) Groups and Students (1989–90). Captained Glasgow U-21s (1989–90)
Touchlines: Enjoy debating at Glasgow University

Phillips, K.H.   Wales

Full Name: Kevin Huw Phillips
International category: Wales Full
Club: Neath
Position: Hooker
Height: 5'11" **Weight:** 13st 7lb
Occupation: Farmer
Born: Hebron, 15.6.61
Family: Married
Former club: Cardigan
International debut: France 16,
Wales 9, 1987
Five Nations' debut: As above
Best moment in rugby: Winning
1988 Welsh Cup with Neath
Worst moment in rugby:
Dislocating shoulder against
Swansea at The Gnoll (1987/88)
and being out for three months
Most embarrassing moment:
Whenever I lose strike against head
Most respected opponent:
England hooker Brian Moore
Serious injuries: Dislocated
shoulder
Other sporting achievements:
Tug-of-war at international level

	apps.	pts.
Wales (1987)		
Last Season	7 caps	0
Career	14 caps	0

Best memory last season:
Captaining Neath and beating Swansea at St Helen's
Most improved International player last season: Wales centre Allan
Bateman
Suggestions to improve rugby: Improve education of younger players to
ensure future of game
Other notable landmarks in rugby career: Neath captain (for past three
years). First represented Wales in national seven at New South Wales
tournament in Australia (1986). Following year was selected to senior XV.
Played in 1987 World Cup and toured with Wales to New Zealand (1988)
and Namibia, as captain (1990)
Touchlines: Swimming

Phillips, R.D.   Wales

Full Name: Rowland David Phillips
International category: Wales
Full (squad)
Club: Neath
Position: Flanker
Height: 6'1½" **Weight:** 15st 7lb
Occupation: Police officer
Born: St David's, Pembrokeshire,
28.7.65
Family: Married with son
Former club: St David's Youth
International debut: Wales 46,
US Eagles 0, 1987
Five Nations' debut: England 3,
Wales 11, 1988
Best moment in rugby:
Reception from 6,000 fans at The
Gnoll on return from winning 1990
Welsh Cup
Worst moment in rugby: Being
dropped by Wales after win over
Western Samoa when I thought I
had not played badly
Most disappointing memory:
Hospitality received from New
Zealanders on our 1988 tour – not
treated very well

	apps.	pts.
Wales (1987)		
Last Season	0 caps	0
Career	10 caps	0

Most respected opponent: Neath and Wales team mate Phil Pugh (in training)
Serious injuries: Broke ankle against Penarth, damaged shoulder ligaments against Bridgend
Other sporting achievements: Cross-country for Pembrokeshire Schools
Best memory last season: Winning Welsh Cup with Neath
Most improved International player last season: Wales lock Phil Davies
Suggestions to improve rugby: Leave game alone but pick me for Wales every time
Other notable landmarks in rugby career: Represented Wales U-16s and U-18s but never B. Played in Wales' 1988 Triple Crown team. Toured Namibia with Wales last summer playing three games
Touchlines: Squash, tennis

Pickering, D.F. — Wales

Full Name: David Francis Pickering
International category: Wales B (squad)
Club: Neath
Position: Flanker
Height: 6'1" **Weight:** 14st 7lb
Occupation: Company director
Born: Briton Ferry, 16.12.60
Family: Single
Family links with rugby: Father played for Royal Marines
Former club: Llanelli
International debut: Wales 13, England 13, 1983
Five Nations' debut: As above
Best moment in rugby: Scoring 2 tries for Wales in 25–21 defeat of Scotland (1985)
Most respected opponent: England flanker Peter Winterbottom
Serious injuries: Damaged head (1986 v Fiji)
Other sporting achievements: Junior County hurdler
Best memory last season: Winning Welsh Cup with Neath
Most improved International player last season: Wales lock Glyn Llewellyn

	apps.	pts.
Wales B (1982)		
Last Season	0 caps	0
Wales (1983)		
Last Season	0 caps	0
Career	23 caps	12
1991	World Cup squad	

Suggestions to improve rugby: Develop a more commercially-minded attitude towards game
Other notable landmarks in rugby career: Captained Wales on eight occasions. Also represented Wales U-15s, U-19s and B, and captained Barbarians, Crawshays and Penguins

Pilgrim, S.J.   England

Full Name: Stephen John Pilgrim
International category: England B
Club: Wasps
Position: Full-back
Height: 5'10" **Weight:** 13st
Occupation: Student
Born: Sidcup, 26.10.67
Family: Single
Former club: Old Reigatians
International debut: England B
12, Fiji 20, 1989
Best moment in rugby: Running
round Rory Underwood (pictured
in *Daily Telegraph*) – Wasps v
Leicester, 1989
Worst moment in rugby: Wasps
losing to Gloucester in 1990 Cup
competition
Most embarrassing moment:
Intended kick-ahead for fellow
Wasp Simon Smith squirted
sideways – Nottingham wing
caught it and scored
Most respected opponent:
Former England full-back Dusty
Hare – despite his age, he's always
in right place
Other sporting achievements:
Basketball for Crystal Palace and
Kingston

	apps.	pts.
England U-21 **(1989)**		
Last Season	1 cap	12
England B **(1989)**		
Last Season	1 cap	8
England 1995	Development squad	

Best memory last season: Winning English Championship. Last training
session before Mark Taylor arrived
Most improved International players last season: England's Rob Andrew
and Jeff Probyn
Suggestions to improve rugby: Better referees
Other notable landmarks in rugby career: Captained first ever England
U-21 team to 54–13 win against Romania in Bucharest, 1989. Seeing Dick
Best smile twice

Poole, M.D.   England

Full Name: Matthew David Poole
International category: England U-21
Club: Leicester
Position: Lock
Height: 6'7" **Weight:** 17st 7lb
Occupation: Office equipment machines manager
Born: Leicester, 6.2.69
Family: Single
Family links with rugby: Father played for British Police
Former club: Syston
International debut (U-21): Romania 13, England 54, 1989
Best moment in rugby: Playing in Bucharest in first ever England U-21 team

Worst moment in rugby: Tearing medial ligaments, whilst beating Bristol in 1988, and trying to play on. I eventually had to be stretchered off and we lost
Most embarrassing moment: Spending night walking streets of Colorado daubed in women's make-up as 'punishment' for being youngest player on my first senior tour with Leicester

	apps.	pts.
England U-21 (1989)		
Last Season	3 caps	0
England 1990	Tour to Argentina	
1995	Development squad	

Most respected opponent: Gloucester's lock John Brain
Serious injuries: Torn knee ligaments, broken nose
Other sporting achievements: Swam in National Schools' Championships
Best memory last season: Helping England U-21s beat French Armed Forces
Most improved International player last season: England fly-half Rob Andrew
Suggestions to improve rugby: Relax amateur laws to reimburse players for time away from work
Other notable landmarks in rugby career: Played fly-half until age of 14. Did not take sport seriously until aged 17. Represented England Colts (1988)

237

and invited to tour with full England squad to Argentina last summer in place of injured Sean O'Leary
Touchlines: Horse racing enthusiast

Popplewell, N.   Ireland

Full Name: Nicholas Popplewell
International category: Ireland Full
Club: Greystones
Position: Prop
Height: 5'11" **Weight:** 16st 7lb
Occupation: Furniture store manager
Born: Dublin, 6.4.64
Family: Single
Former club: Gorey
International debut: Ireland 6, New Zealand 23, 1989
Best moment in rugby: Winning first cap v All Blacks
Worst moment in rugby: Only lasting 20 minutes in above match before cracking a rib
Most respected opponent: Ireland prop Des Fitzgerald
Serious injuries: Broken ribs (twice)
Other sporting achievements: Played hockey for Irish Schools (3 caps)
Best memory last season: Playing v New Zealand at Lansdowne Road

	apps.	pts.
Ireland (1989)		
Last Season	1 cap	0
Career	1 cap	0

Most improved International player last season: Ireland full-back Kenny Murphy
Suggestions to improve rugby: Compensate players for time lost away from work – not payments, just reduced hassle in claiming legitimate expenses
Other notable landmarks in rugby career: Helping to train Presentation Juniors Bray U-15s to two Leinster Junior Cups in past three years. Toured with Ireland to North America, playing in 24–21 defeat of Canada (1989).

Represented Ireland U-25s v US Eagles (1990). Ireland reserve three times in 1990 Five Nations Championship

---

Povoas, S.J.   England

Full Name: Simon John Povoas
International category: England B (squad)
Club: Leicester
Positions: Lock, No.8
Height: 6'2" **Weight:** 15st 7lb
Occupation: Sales manager
Born: Leicester, 10.6.66
Family: Single
Family links with rugby: Father played for Oadby-Wyggestonian
Former club: Oadby-Wyggestonian
Best moment in rugby: Scoring 3 tries for Leicester v Ponsonby during tour of New Zealand
Worst moment in rugby: Breaking jaw playing for Leicestershire in Italy (1987)
Serious injuries: Broken hand, jaw. Damaged knee and ankle ligaments
Best memory last season: Playing for Barbarians v East Midlands in Mobbs Memorial Match
Most improved International player last season: Scotland prop Paul Burnell
Other notable landmarks in rugby career: Scored 25 tries for Leicester last season – club record for a forward. Selected to England development squad for 1995 World Cup
Touchlines: Golf

	apps.
England B (**1989/90**)	Rep 1
England 1995	Development squad

Probyn, J.A.   England

Full Name: Jeffrey Alan Probyn
International category: England
Full
Club: Wasps
Position: Tight-head prop
Height: 5'10½" **Weight:** 15st 7lb
Occupation: Furniture
manufacturer
Born: London, 27.4.56
Family: Married with three children
Family links with rugby: Brother
plays
Former clubs: Old Albanians,
Streatham/Croydon, Richmond
International debut: France 10,
England 9, 1988
Five Nations' debut: As above
Best moment in rugby: Scoring
for England v Ireland (1990)
Worst moment in rugby: Leaving
field concussed in Ireland (1989)
Most embarrassing moment:
Getting lifted by Welsh prop Staff
Jones for trying to be clever
(Twickenham, 1988)
Most respected opponent:
England loose-head prop Paul
Rendall
Serious injuries sustained:
Damaged ligaments in left knee.
Ear stitches

	apps.	pts.
England B (1986)		
Last Season	1 cap	0
England (1988)		
Last Season	7 caps	8
Career	17 caps	8
1990	Tour to Argentina	
1991	World Cup squad	
England XV 1989/90	1 app	0

Best memory last season: Scoring try (v Ireland) on return from injury
Most improved International player last season: Paul Rendall
Suggestions to improve rugby: Improved media (especially TV)
Other notable landmarks in rugby career: Moving to Wasps. First B cap
v France. England debut in Paris. World XV v South Africa, and Home Unions
v France (1989)
Touchlines: Sailing, shooting, fishing

Pugh, J.D.   Wales

Full Name: Jeremy David Pugh
International category: Wales Full
Club: Neath
Position: Prop
Height: 5'10" **Weight:** 16st 4lb
Occupation: Entrepreneur
Born: Builth Wells, 4.3.61
Family: Single with child
Family links with rugby: Brother
plays for Builth
Former clubs: Swansea Youth,
Pontypridd, Ebbw Vale
International debut: Wales 46,
US Eagles 0, 1987
Five Nations' debut: Wales 25,
Scotland 20, 1988
Best moment in rugby: Winning
second full cap to convince
doubters that I was a real
international

Worst moment in rugby: Tearing
knee ligaments two days after
second cap playing in Breconshire
final of Counties Cup
Most embarrassing moment:
Tripping in a pot hole while trying
to catch a high ball, while messing
around with friends, and ball
bouncing on my head

	apps.	pts.
Wales B (1987)		
Last Season	0 caps	0
Wales (1987)		
Last Season	1 cap	0
Career	3 caps	0

Most respected opponents: Wales props Brian Williams and Anthony
Buchanan
Serious injuries: Damaged back (falling off a roof last season), dislocated
knee, broken nose (many)
Other sporting achievements: Motorbike racing
Best memory last season: Selected for Scotland game after two years out
of Wales squad
Most improved International players last season: Wales' duo David Evans
and Brian Williams
Suggestions to improve rugby: Bring back sin-bins and use in tandem with
tougher refereeing

Other notable landmarks in rugby career: Moving from Pontypridd to Neath (1984). Started career as scrum-half. Played once for Wales B (1988). Captained Brecon for past five years. Also represented Crawshays
Touchlines: Socialising with locals in my pub (The White Hart, in Builth)

Pugh, P.   Wales

Full Name: Philip Pugh
International category: Wales Full
Club: Neath
Position: Flanker
Height: 6'4" **Weight:** 15st 4lb
Occupation: Coal miner
Born: Neath, 8.10.59
Family: Single
Former club: Seven Sisters
International debut: Wales 9, New Zealand 34, 1989
Best moment in rugby: Hearing of Wales selection to play against 1989 All Blacks on television
Most respected opponent: England No.8 Mike Teague
Serious injuries sustained: Fractured skull playing for Seven Sisters, dislocated hip
Best memory last season: Neath against New Zealand at The Gnoll
Most improved International player last season: Wales prop Brian Williams
Suggestions to improve rugby: Look after players better
Other notable landmarks in rugby career: Toured with Wales to Fiji, Tonga and Western Samoa (1986).

	apps.	pts.
Wales B (1986)		
Last Season	0 caps	0
Wales (1989)		
Last Season	1 cap	0
Career	1 cap	0

Helped Wales beat France 13–10 at Pontypridd on B debut (1986/87). Started out on representative trail with Neath Schools
Touchlines: Enjoy cross-country horse riding, greyhound and pigeon racing

Rainey, P.I.   Ireland

Full Name: Philip Ian Rainey
International category: Ireland Full
Club: Ballymena
Position: Full-back
Height: 6' **Weight:** 13st 7lb
Occupation: Quality systems manager
Born: Ballymena, 12.7.59
Family: Married with son and two daughters
Former clubs: Queen's University Belfast, Lansdowne
International debut: Ireland 6, New Zealand 23, 1989
Best moment in rugby: Atmosphere on Irish debut against All Blacks, and march on their pre-match Haka. We wanted to set down a challenge and show them we meant business
Worst moment in rugby: Being forced to withdraw from Ireland squad to play England with thigh injury three days before match

	apps.	pts.
Ireland (1989)		
Last Season	1 cap	0
Career	1 cap	0

Most respected opponent: Scotland full-back Gavin Hastings
Serious injuries: Strained Achilles tendons, pulled hamstrings
Other sporting achievements: Soccer for Ballymena United U-15s
Best memories last season: Phone call telling me I had been picked for Ireland against New Zealand after sixteen games as replacement. Feeling of pride as I looked up at parents in stand during pre-match national anthem
Most improved International player last season: My replacement as Ireland full-back Kenny Murphy
Suggestions to improve rugby: Hierarchy must look after those who help players get where they are. Wives and girlfriends should be given trips to certain games, while employers should be compensated for employee's lost time – either financially or by being offered hospitality at Internationals
Other notable landmarks in rugby career: Represented Ulster at Schools, U-19, U-23 and senior level (since 1981). Played for Irish and British

Universities. Toured with Ireland to Japan (1985). Kicked match-winning penalty for Ulster against 1984 Australians
Touchlines: Golf (16-handicap)

Rayer, M.A. Wales

Full Name: Michael Anthony Rayer
International category: Wales Full (squad)
Club: Cardiff
Position: Full-back
Height: 5'10" **Weight:** 13st 2lb
Occupation: Works manager for glazing/mirror company
Born: Cardiff, 21.7.65
Family: Married
Family links with rugby: Father played for Penarth, Cardiff Athletic and Llandudno
Former club: Llandudno
International debut (B): France 26, Wales 0, 1987
Best moment in rugby: Dropping goal v Swansea in extra-time of 1987 Schweppes Cup final to put Cardiff in winning position
Worst moment in rugby: Dislocating elbow v Pontypool in 1988 (out for ten weeks)
Most embarrassing moment:
Aqua-planing 20 feet with ball in sodden conditions at St Helen's playing for Cardiff against Swansea

	apps.	pts.
Wales B (1987)		
Last Season	1 cap	0

Most respected opponent: French full-back Jean-Baptiste Lafond
Serious injuries: Dislocated elbow, sprung shoulder joint, damaged ribs, torn hamstring, ankle and knee ligaments
Other sporting achievements: Captained Wales B baseball team last season
Best memory last season: Scoring 28 points for Wales against North Region on Namibian tour
Most improved International player last season: French wing Patrice Lagisquet

244

Suggestions to improve rugby: Develop more professional attitude. Disband 'old school tie' committees and stop living in past
Other notable landmarks in rugby career: Captained Wales Youth (1983–85). Played twice for Wales B. Replacement for Wales against New Zealand last season

Redman, N.C.   England

Full Name: Nigel Charles Redman
International category: England Full
Club: Bath
Position: Lock
Height: 6'4" **Weight:** 17st 2lb
Occupation: Electrician
Born: Cardiff, 16.8.64
Family: Married
Family links with rugby: Younger brother plays No.8 for Weston-super-Mare
Former club: Weston-super-Mare
International debut: England 3, Australia 19, 1984
Five Nations' debut: Scotland 33, England 6, 1986
Best moment in rugby: Bath beating Gloucester 48–6 in 1989 Pilkington Cup final
Worst moment in rugby: Being left out of Bath Cup final team in 1988/89 after playing in all other games
Most embarrassing moment: South Australia v England (1988) – only occasion in which English team was not on pitch while National Anthem was being played, because I was on the toilet

	apps.	pts.
England B **(1986)**		
Last Season	0 caps	0
England **(1984)**		
Last Season	2 caps	0
Career	10 caps	4
1990	Tour to Argentina	

Most respected opponent: Wales lock Robert Norster – considered short for middle jumper but is still one of best
Best memory last season: Cup final defeat of Gloucester

245

Most improved International player last season: England scrum-half Richard Hill
Suggestions to improve rugby: Scrap 90-degree wheel law. Bigger effort to improve fitness of players and standard of refereeing at all levels
Other notable landmarks in rugby career: Joining Bath and playing in Cup final (1983/84) – first of five. England debut (1984/85). Playing in first World Cup (1987)
Touchlines: Volleyball, golf, DIY

Redpath, A.C.   Scotland

Full Name: Alexander **Craig** Redpath
International category: Scotland Full (squad)
Club: Melrose
Position: Full-back
Height: 6' **Weight:** 13st 10lb
Occupation: Student
Born: Galashiels, 21.9.69
Family: Single
Family links with rugby: Brother Andrew played for Scotland U-18s and U-21s. Brother Bryan was replacement for Scotland U-18s and U-19s
International debut: Poverty Bay/East Coast (NZ) 0, Scotland 45, 1990
Best moment in rugby: Winning Scottish First Division with Melrose last season
Worst moment in rugby: Being injured at any time
Most respected player: Melrose's former Scotland wing Keith Robertson
Serious injuries: Broken neck (playing soccer)
Other sporting achievements: Cricket for South of Scotland U-16s

	apps.	pts.
Scotland U-21 (**1990**)		
Last Season	1 cap	0
Scotland (**1990**)	Rep 1	0
1990	Tour to New Zealand	

Best memory last season: Scoring against Jed-Forest in last minute of League decider
Other notable landmarks in rugby career: Represented Scotland at U-19 and U-21 level and warmed bench for Scotland B. Replacement also for Scotland when they beat England to clinch Grand Slam at Murrayfield last season. Toured with Scotland to New Zealand (1990)
Touchlines: Golf, cricket

Rees, G.W.   England

Full Name: Gary William Rees
International category: England Full
Club: Nottingham
Position: Flanker
Height: 6' **Weight:** 14st 7lb
Occupation: Financial advisor
Born: Long Eaton, 2.5.60
Family: Single
International debut: South Africa 35, England 9, 1984
Five Nations' debut: England 25, Ireland 20, 1986
Best moment in rugby: Making England debut as replacement in second Test at Ellis Park
Worst moment in rugby: England losing 3-16 to Wales in quarter-finals of 1987 World Cup
Most respected opponent: Australian back row Simon Poidevin
Other sporting achievements: County Schools hockey and cricket
Best memory last season: Playing for Barbarians v New Zealand (lost 10–21)
Suggestions to improve rugby: Reduce amount of scrums
Other notable landmarks in rugby career: Joined Nottingham in 1978 as full-back or scrum-half. Played for

	apps.	pts.
England B (1988)		
Last Season	0 caps	0
England (1984)		
Last Season	2 caps	0
Career	20 caps	8

England U-23s in Italy (1982). Helped Midlands beat 1983 All Blacks. Represented England in 1987 World Cup and on tour in Australia (1988)

Rendall, P.A.G.   England

Full Name: Paul Anthony George Rendall
International category: England Full
Club: Wasps
Position: Loose-head prop
Height: 5'11" **Weight:** 16st 7lb
Occupation: Self-employed engineer
Born: London, 18.2.54
Family: Married with two children
Former club: Slough (1970–75)
International debut: England 15, Wales 24, 1984
Five Nations' debut: As above
Best moment in rugby: England beating France 26–7 in Paris (1990)
Worst moment in rugby: Not being selected for 1989 British Lions
Most embarrassing moment: Being asked to pay for extra breakfast after England v France 1989 (ate three)
Most respected opponent: Jeff Probyn – a boring so and so!
Best memory last season: England win in Paris
Most improved International player last season: England fly-half Rob Andrew

	apps.	pts.
England B (**1981**)		
Last Season	0 caps	0
England (**1984**)		
Last Season	5 caps	0
Career	27 caps	0
1991	World Cup squad	

Suggestions to improve rugby: Pay for broken time
Other notable landmarks in rugby career: Completing Five Nations Championship in 1988 without being dropped or injured. Gained first cap aged 30. Played for World XV against New Zealand (Tokyo 1987). Played for World XV in South Africa (1989). Toured with England to Australia,

Argentina, USA, Canada, South Africa and Italy, as well as 1987 World Cup.
Only International points came from a try in non-cap match v USA (1982)
Touchlines: Reading Halsbury

Renwick, W.L. Scotland

Full Name: William Lindsay
Renwick
International category: Scotland
Full
Club: London Scottish
Position: Wing
Height: 5'11" **Weight:** 13st 8lb
Occupation: Sports Centre
manager
Born: Hawick, 24.12.60
Family: Married with two children
(Charlotte and Paul)
Family links with rugby: Father
played for Hawick (1950)
Former clubs: Stirling County,
Alsager College, Broughton Park,
Sale
International debut: Scotland 39,
Romania 0, 1989

Best moment in rugby: Winning
first full Scotland cap. Captaining
Scotland B to 18–12 away win v
France (March 1988). Gaining
promotion with London Scottish to
English Second Division (1989/90)
Worst moment in rugby: Losing
Inter-District Championship
decider v Glasgow (1989/90).
Relegation with London Scottish
(1988/89)

	apps.	pts.
Scotland B (**1987**)		
Last Season	0 caps	0
Scotland (**1989**)		
Last Season	1 cap	0
Career	1 cap	0

Other notable landmarks in rugby career: Withdrew from Scotland tour
to New Zealand last summer because wife was pregnant

Reynolds, A.D.   Wales

Full Name: Alan David Reynolds
International category: Wales Full
Club: Swansea
Position: Flanker
Height: 6'1" **Weight:** 15st
Occupation: Plasterer
Born: 24.1.66
Family: Single
Family links with rugby:
Brother-in-law David Jacobs played
for Neath and Wales B
Former clubs: Whitland,
Laugharne
International debut: Namibia 9,
Wales 18, 1990
Best moment in rugby: Making
Welsh debut in first Test last
summer
Worst moment in rugby: Being
dropped for second Test
Best memory last season:
Playing for Swansea against New
Zealand
**Most improved International
player last season:** Wales lock
Paul Arnold
**Other notable landmarks in
rugby career:** Represented Wales

	apps.	pts.
Wales (1990)		
Last Season	2 caps	0
Career	2 caps	0

at Youth level and Pembrokeshire against touring US Eagles. Had Wales
U-21 trials. In Sevens, played for Wales in Hong Kong and Crawshays in
Dubai

Richards, D.   England

Full Name: Dean Richards
International category: England Full
Club: Leicester
Position: No.8
Height: 6'3½" **Weight:** 17st 7lb
Occupation: Policeman
Born: Nuneaton, 11.7.63
Family: Married
Family links with rugby: Father played for Nuneaton
Former club: Roanne (France)
International debut: England 25, Ireland 20, 1986
Five Nations' debut: As above
Best moment in rugby: Winning decisive third Test with 1989 Lions
Worst moment in rugby: England losing to Wales in Cardiff (1989)
Most respected opponent: New Zealand No.8 Wayne Shelford
Serious injuries: Recurring dislocated shoulder (1989/90)
Best memory last season: Lions' success in Australia
Most improved International player last season: Scotland prop Paul Burnell

England (1986)	apps.	pts.
Last Season	1 cap	4
Career	20 caps	24
1991	World Cup squad	
Lions 1989	3 Tests	0

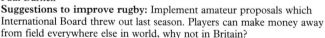

Suggestions to improve rugby: Implement amateur proposals which International Board threw out last season. Players can make money away from field everywhere else in world, why not in Britain?
Other notable landmarks in rugby career: Joined Leicester in 1982 after season playing in France. Played for England Schools at lock, before graduating to England U-23s (against Romania). Also represented Leicestershire (would like to play county rugby again after International career) and Midlands Division. Scored 2 tries on International debut against Ireland but it was one of my worst performances. Played in 1987 World Cup and returned to Australia with 1989 Lions. Shoulder injury ruled out last season
Touchlines: Squash, five-a-side soccer

Richards, D.G.   Wales

Full Name: David **Geraint** Richards
International category: Wales U-21 (squad)
Club: Haverford West
Position: Hooker
Height: 5'8" **Weight:** 14st
Occupation: Police constable
Born: Glanamman, 5.3.69
Family: Single
Former club: Ystradgynlais
International debut (U-18): Scotland 6, Wales 22, 1986/87
Best moment in rugby: Winning above match
Worst moment in rugby: Losing 12–32 to England Colts at Neath (April 1988)
Most respected hooker: Former Wales No.2 Alan Phillips
Serious injuries: Tearing top of hamstring off bone and taking piece of bone with it
Best memory last season: Winning the British Police Athletic Association Cup for the second successive year with the Dyfed-Powys Police XV

	apps.
Wales U-21 (**1989/90**)	Rep 1

Most improved International player last season: Wales fly-half David Evans
Suggestions to improve rugby: Make rugby more attractive for younger players to keep them in the game. Improve the administration
Other notable landmarks in rugby career: Changing from prop to hooker aged 14. Selection for Wales U-18 made me believe in my ability. Represented British Police v Public School Wanderers and Combined Services. Replacement for Wales U-21 in 1990 win v Scotland
Touchlines: Mountain walking, pot-holing

Richardson, J.F   Scotland

Full Name: Jeremy Francis Richardson
International category: Scotland B
Club: Edinburgh Academicals
Position: Second Row
Height: 6'5½" **Weight:** 16st
Occupation: Stockbroker
Born: Crawley, 7.9.63
Family: Single
Family links with rugby: Father played for Army, Edinburgh Academicals. Charlie (brother) captained Edinburgh Academicals, London Scottish, Scotland B. Guy (brother) played for Army
International debut (B): Scotland 9, France 15, 1987
Best moment in rugby: Beating France B 14–12 at Melrose in 1989 with brother Charlie captaining Scotland B
Worst moment in rugby: Not playing in 1987 World Cup
Most respected opponent: Scotland lock Chris Gray – never played with or against him when he has given less than 100 per cent

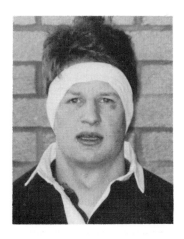

	apps.	pts.
Scotland B (1987)		
Last Season	2 caps	0
Scotland (1990)	Tour to New Zealand	

Best memory last season: Scotland's Grand Slam
Most improved International player last season: Chris Gray
Suggestions to improve rugby: Increase quality of referees
Other notable landmarks in rugby career: Played four times for Scotland U-21s. Scotland squad for 1987 World Cup. Toured with Scotland to Zimbabwe (1988) and New Zealand (1990), where played three games

Rigney, B.J.   Ireland

Full Name: Brian Joseph Rigney
International category: Ireland B
Club: Greystones
Position: Lock
Height: 6'4" **Weight:** 17st
Occupation: Brewers representative
Born: Portlaoise, 22.9.63
Family: Single
Former clubs: Portlaoise, Bective
Rangers
International debut (B): Scotland
22, Ireland 22, 1989
Best moment in rugby: Picked
for Ireland XV v Canada and US
Eagles during 1989 North
American tour. Although no caps
awarded to us, both opponents
received caps
Worst moment in rugby: Missed
1987 Munster Cup final after
breaking ankle in previous game
Most respected opponent:
Ireland lock Donal Lenihan –
tremendous dedication and
application
Serious injuries: Broken ankle

	apps.	pts.
Ireland B (1989)		
Last Season	1 cap	0

Other sporting achievements: Won honours for Gaelic football and
hurling with Portlaoise. Various swimming achievements as boy
Best memory last season: Leinster v New Zealand at Lansdowne Road
(lost 9-36)
Most improved International player last season: Ireland flanker Pat
O'Hara
Suggestions to improve rugby: Form a players committee at top level
Other notable landmarks in rugby career: Only played rugby for four
seasons at senior level, seven in all. Capped after two by Leinster

Full Name: Mark Gerard Ring
International category: Wales Full
Club: Cardiff
Positions: Centre, full-back
Height: 6' **Weight:** 13st 7lb
Occupation: Ask Ray Griffiths, Xell Sports Management!
Born: Cardiff, 15.10.62
Family: Single
Family links with rugby: Father played for Leicester, Maesteg, Glam Wdrs and Tredegar
Former club: Pontypool
International debut: Wales 13, England 13, 1983
Five Nations' debut: As above
Best moment in rugby: Welsh Rugby Player of Year 1985
Worst moment in rugby: Injury to left knee which meant two barren seasons
Most embarrassing moment: Showing off in Sevens. Ran to try-line with ball behind back. When placed ball over try line it slipped from my grasp
Most respected opponent: New Zealand centre Warwick Taylor – showed me a new dimension to centre play

	apps.	pts.
Wales B (1983)		
Last Season	1 cap	0
Wales (1983)		
Last Season	7 caps	0
Career	23 caps	12

Serious injuries sustained: Torn ligaments in both knees
Other sporting achievements: Welsh baseball international (3 caps)
Best memory last season: Captaining Cardiff to Q/F Cup defeat of Llanelli
Most improved International player last season: Wales flanker Martyn Morris
Suggestions to improve rugby: Relax and enjoy every game. Take advice from coaches and fellow players. Study videos of great players. Prepare well for every game
Other notable landmarks in rugby career: Played fly-half for Wales Youth before Cardiff (first spell) moved him to centre. Three Welsh Cup winners' medals. Cardiff's 1984 defeat of Australia. Barbarians v Australia (1988).

World XV v South Africa (1989). Toured with Wales to New Zealand (1988) and Namibia (1990)
Touchlines: Horse racing fanatic. Becoming a fan of Rugby League (esp. Wigan). Play Sunday soccer. Interested in Brazilian players who are given bad names because of off-field habits

Riordan, J.C.   Ireland

Full Name: James Cashel Riordan
International category: Ireland U-25 (squad)
Club: Wanderers
Position: Wing
Height: 6'2" **Weight:** 14st 7lb
Occupation: Investment banker
Born: Cork, 30.5.66
Family: Single
Family links with rugby: Cousins include Ireland Internationals Tom Kiernan, Michael Kiernan, Noel A. Murphy and Kenny Murphy
Former club: University College Cork
Best moment in rugby: Touring Japan with Irish Universities (1987)
Worst moment in rugby: Any injuries
Most embarrassing moment: Guesting in a Christmas 3rd XV match while a member of Munster team and playing absolute rubbish
Most respected opponent: Ireland wing John Sexton – sheer speed

	apps.
Ireland U-25 (**1989/90**)	Rep 1

Other sporting achievements: 1982 Irish under-age 400m champion. 1984 Irish Schools athletics team. Senior county champion four times
Best memory last season: Winning Leinster League and Cup double with Wanderers
Most improved International player last season: England fly-half Rob Andrew

Suggestions to improve rugby: Two referees per match. Stricter disciplinary measures
Touchline: School classmate of Ireland prop Gary Halpin. Played in same Munster Schools, Irish Schools and club side, as well as same athletics team at school, provincial and International schools level

Roberts, G.J.   Wales

Full Name: Gareth John Roberts
International category: Wales (World Cup squad)
Club: Llanelli
Position: Flanker
Height: 6'2½" **Weight:** 14st 10lb
Occupation: Pharmacist
Born: Pontlliw, 15.1.60
Family: Married with two daughters
Former clubs: Swansea, Cardiff
International debut: France 14, Wales 3, 1985
Five Nations' debut: As above
Best moment in rugby: Wales beating Australia 22–21 in third/fourth place play-off at 1987 World Cup
Worst moment in rugby: Being overlooked after World Cup
Most embarrassing moment: Losing contact lens playing for Swansea against Bridgend and having both sets of forwards on their knees looking for it (found it)
Most respected opponent: Former New Zealand flanker Graham Mourie
Serious injuries: Torn knee ligaments playing for Cardiff against Fiji
Other sporting achievements: Reached semi-finals of Langland Bay tennis championships

	apps.	pts.
Wales B (1983)		
Last Season	0 caps	0
Wales (1985)		
Last Season	0 caps	0
Career	7 caps	12
1991	World Cup squad	

Best memory last season: Llanelli beating Cardiff on my first return to Arms Park since leaving club
Most improved International player last season: Scotland wing Tony Stanger
Suggestions to improve rugby: Give more consideration to players and give them more freedom to do what they want when not playing
Other notable landmarks in rugby career: Made first-team debut for Swansea against Bristol aged 18. Represented Barbarians, Welsh Academicals, Penguins, Italian Barbarians and Wales B
Touchlines: Squash, golf

Robertson, G.B. Scotland

Full Name: George **Brian** Robertson
International category: Scotland B (squad)
Club: Stirling County
Position: Tight-head prop
Height: 6' **Weight:** 16st
Occupation: Potato merchant
Born: Falkirk, 9.8.59
Family: Married
Best moment in rugby: Winning 1989/90 Inter-District Championship with Glasgow
Worst moment in rugby: Damaging knee ligaments so badly on Glasgow's Irish tour (1989) that thought career was over
Most respected opponent: Scotland loose-head prop David Sole
Serious injuries: Knee ligaments

	apps.
Scotland B (**1989/90**)	Rep 2

Best memory last season: Stirling beating so many Border teams in first season in Scottish First Division
Most improved International player last season: Scotland wing Tony Stanger
Suggestions to improve rugby: Broken time payments

Other notable landmarks in rugby career: Only took up rugby at age of 22. Represented Glasgow since 1985 and toured with them to Holland and Belgium (1985), and Ireland (1989). Joined Stirling when in Scottish Third Division

Robinson, B.F.   Ireland

Full Name: Brian Francis Robinson
International category: Ireland B
Club: Ballymena
Position: No.8
Height: 6'4" **Weight:** 15st
Occupation: PE teacher
Born: Belfast, 20.3.66
Family: Single
International debut (B): Scotland 22, Ireland 22, 1989
Best moment in rugby: Playing for Ulster against 1989 All Blacks
Worst moment in rugby: Tearing cruciate and medial ligaments in first match after touring Zimbabwe with Ulster (1986/87) and missing next eighteen months
Most respected opponent: New Zealand back row Zinzan Brooke
Serious injuries: As above
Best memory last season: Ballymena winning Ulster League and Cup double for second consecutive season
Most improved International player last season: Ireland full-back Kenny Murphy

	apps.	pts.
Ireland B (**1989**)		
Last Season	1 cap	0

Suggestions to improve rugby: Relax amateur rules to allow players to earn money away from rugby. Reimburse employers for time lost
Other notable landmarks in rugby career: Played for Irish Wolfhounds Seven in Sicily last summer, and Ireland U-25s against US Eagles last season. Previously represented Combined Irish Provinces (aged 20)
Touchlines: Sub-aqua diving

Robinson, R.A.   England

Full Name: Richard **Andrew** Robinson
International category: England Full (squad)
Club: Bath
Position: Flanker
Height: 5'9" **Weight:** 13st 12lb
Occupation: Schoolmaster
Born: Taunton, Somerset, 3.4.64
Family: Married
Family links with rugby: Father captained Somerset and Royal Navy and coached Somerset. Brother Sean plays for Saracens. Brother Peter plays for Taunton
Former clubs: Loughborough Students, Taunton
International debut: Australia 28, England 8, 1988
Five Nations' debut: England 12, Scotland 12, 1989
Best moment in rugby: Being told of first ever England selection on beach in Wollongong
Worst moment in rugby: England losing to Wales at Cardiff (1989) – worse feeling than being dropped

	apps.	pts.
England B (1987)		
Last Season	0 caps	0
England (1988)		
Last Season	0 caps	0
Career	7 caps	4
1990	Tour to Argentina	
Lions 1989		

Most embarrassing moment: Welsh referee Clive Norling (wearing microphone for benefit of TV) telling me: 'British Lion or not, next time you're off'
Most respected opponents: England flankers Peter Winterbottom and Gary Rees
Serious injuries: Broken knee cap while at Loughborough
Other sporting achievements: Cricket for Somerset U-19s and West of England Schools
Best memory last season: Helping Bath beat Gloucester 48–6 in Pilkington Cup final
Most improved International player last season: Scotland flanker Finlay Calder

Suggestions to improve rugby: Retire all committee men at age of 40. Treat players better

Other notable landmarks in rugby career: Captained Loughborough to 1986 UAU title, having played in 1984 and 1985 winning teams. Played Debut for Bath at Pontypool where handed Pooler their first home defeat for twenty years. Won three Cup finals with Bath. Selected for 1989 Lions in first full International season. Toured Argentina with England last summer

Touchlines: Golf (24-handicap)

Rodber, T.A.K.   England

Full Name: Timothy Andrew Keith Rodber
International category: England B
Clubs: Northampton and Army
Position: No.8
Height: 6'6" **Weight:** 16st 7lb
Occupation: Student
Born: Richmond, Yorkshire, 2.7.69
Family: Single
Family links with rugby: Father played
Former clubs: Oxford Old Boys, Petersfield
International debut (U-21): Romania 13, England 54, 1989
Best moment in rugby: Being selected for England's tour to Argentina
Worst moment in rugby: Being injured by foul play v Plymouth Albion
Most respected opponent: England No.8 Dean Richards – awesome in every department
Serious injuries sustained: Popped ribs
Other sporting achievements: Hampshire Schools County hockey and cricket
Best memory last season: Scoring for Army v Navy at Twickenham

	apps.	pts.
England B (1990)		
Last Season	1 cap	0
England (1990)	Tour to Argentina	
1995	Development squad	

Most improved International player last season: England fly-half Rob Andrew
Suggestions to improve rugby: Anything to take away stagnant play (i.e. Gloucester scrums etc)
Other notable landmarks in rugby career: Leaving Oxford OBs for Northampton. Played for England at U-21 and B level.
Touchlines: Active interest in Army

Rolland, A.C.P.   Ireland

Full Name: Alain Colm Pierre Rolland
International category: Ireland B
Club: Blackrock College
Position: Scrum-half
Height: 5'10" **Weight:** 11st 9lb
Occupation: Bank official
Born: Dublin, 22.8.66
Family: Single
International debut (B): Scotland 22, Ireland 22, 1989
Best moment in rugby: Blackrock beating Trinity in 1988 Leinster Senior Cup final, having been given no chance
Worst moment in rugby: Blackrock losing Senior Schools Cup to De La Salle, aged 18
Most embarrassing moment: Concussed playing for Leinster U-20s and talking absolute nonsense while being helped off field
Most respected opponent: Ireland scrum-half Fergus Aherne
Best memory last season: Scoring 75-yard breakaway try for Blackrock against Trinity

	apps.	pts.
Ireland B (**1989**)		
Last Season	1 cap	0

Most improved International player last season: Ireland full-back Kenny Murphy
Suggestions to improve rugby: None. Very happy with game as it is

Other notable landmarks in rugby career: Played two seasons with Leinster U-20s. Three full caps for Leinster (1988/89). Replacement for Ireland U-25s last season against US Eagles
Touchlines: Half-French: speak language fluently and have dual nationality. Enjoy cycling and running

Rouse, P.R.   Scotland

Full Name: Paul Robert Rouse
International category: Scotland B
Club: Dundee High School Former Pupils
Position: Centre
Height: 6' **Weight:** 14st
Occupation: Student
Birthplace: Dundee, 13.3.66
Family: Single
Former club: Petone (NZ) (Summer 1988)
Best moment in rugby: Playing well in 1989/90 Scotland Trial
Worst moment in rugby: Dundee HSFP failing to beat Perthshire in match that would have clinched promotion to Scottish Second Division
Most respected opponent: Scotland centre Scott Hastings
Best memory last season: Winning first Scotland B cap against France
Most improved International player last season: England lock Paul Ackford

	apps.	pts.
Scotland B (**1990**)		
Last Season	1 cap	0

Biggest influence on rugby career: My coach at Sheffield Poly, Paul Barton
Other notable landmarks in rugby career: Played twice for Scotland U-21s before being capped by Scotland B

Rowlands, J.   Wales

Full Name: Jonathan Rowlands
International category: Wales B
Club: Newbridge
Position: Prop
Height: 5'11" **Weight:** 15st 6lb
Occupation: Operations manager
Born: 5.10.62
Family: Married
Family links with rugby: Father
played for Risca
Former clubs: Risca, Newport
International debut (B): France
28, Wales 15, 1989
Best moment in rugby: Ben
Francis Cup final when Man of
Match
Worst moment in rugby:
Newbridge losing 15–16 to
Western Samoa in 1988/89
centenary season
Most respected opponent: No-one
Other sporting achievements:
Kept wicket at school
Best memory last season:
Scoring against Wales for
Newbridge
Most improved International
player last season: Scotland prop David Sole
Suggestions to improve rugby: Give each player a ball
Other notable landmarks in rugby career: Represented Welsh Universities,
UAU and Wales B
Touchlines: Member of Christians in Sport. Youth club leader

	apps.	pts.
Wales B (1989)		
Last Season	1 cap	0

Russell, P.   Ireland

Full Name: Peter Russell
International category: Ireland
Full
Club: Instonians
Position: Fly-half
Height: 5'9" **Weight:** 12st
Occupation: Bank official
Born: Belfast, 22.2.62
Family: Married
Family links with rugby: Father
captained Instonians in 1950s
International debut: England 23,
Ireland 0, 1990
Five Nations' debut: As above
Best moment in rugby: Winning
first full cap at Twickenham
Worst moment in rugby: Being
left out after above game
Other sporting achievements:
Tennis for Ulster Schools. Cricket
for Instonians
Best memory last season:
Making full debut
**Other notable landmarks in
rugby career:** Came to light
playing for Ulster Schools. Won 2
Irish Schools caps v England and
Wales (1979/80) and toured with
them to Australia, playing four

	apps.	pts.
Ireland B (**1989**)		
Last Season	1 cap	14
Ireland (**1990**)		
Last Season	1 cap	0
Career	1 cap	0

games. Represented Ulster U-20s and won first full provincial cap in 1986
v International XV. Toured Zimbabwe with Ulster (1987), playing in three
games. Broke into Ireland team in Jan 1990, having scored 12 points for
Ireland B in 22–22 draw with Scotland, but after England game was
consigned to bench for game in France

Ryan, D.   England

Full Name: Dean Ryan
International category: England Full
Club: Wasps
Position: No.8
Height: 6'6" **Weight:** 17st
Occupation: Royal Engineers (Army)
Born: Tuxford, 22.6.66
Family: Single
Former club: Saracens
International debut: Argentina 12, England 25, 1990
Best moment in rugby: London 21, Australia 10, 1988
Worst moment in rugby: Fractured arm for second time in 1989 v Cardiff
Most embarrassing moment: Trying to stop Australian wing David Campese
Most respected opponent: England No.8 Dean Richards
Serious injuries sustained: Fractured left arm (twice)
Best memory last season: Wasps beating Gloucester 29–4 in English First Division on way to championship

	apps.	pts.
England B (1988)		
Last season	Rep 1	0
England (1990)		
Last season	2 caps	4
Career	2 caps	4
1990	Tour to Argentina	
1995	Development squad	

Disappointments in rugby career:
Had to withdraw from England B v France (1989) through injury. Left England for New Zealand before Wasps clinched title on final day of season v Saracens

Saunders, R.   Ireland

Full Name: Rob Saunders
International category: Ireland U-21
Club: Queen's University, Belfast
Position: Scrum-half
Height: 5'10" **Weight:** 13st
Occupation: Student
Born: Nottingham, 5.8.68
Family: Single
Family links with rugby: Father a Scottish trialist who played for Edinburgh and Leicester, and captained Glasgow
International debut (U-21): Italy 9, Ireland 10, 1989
Best moment in rugby: Being made captain of Irish tour to Italy
Worst moment in rugby: Being dropped for 13–13 draw v New Zealand (1990)
Other sporting achievements: Ireland U-16 squash team. Ulster Schools shot put champion
Best memory last season: QUB beating Trinity 42–13 – biggest win in history of fixture

	apps.	pts.
Ireland U-21 (**1989**)		
Last Season	1 cap	0

Most improved International player last season: Ireland full-back Kenny Murphy
Suggestions to improve rugby: Relax amateur status. Greater awareness of fitness
Other notable landmarks in rugby career: Captained Ulster Schools, Irish Schools (v Australia, 1987), Irish Universities and QUB

Sexton, J.F.   Ireland

Full Name: John Francis Sexton
International category: Ireland (North America squad)
Club: Lansdowne
Position: Wing
Height: 5'10" **Weight:** 12st 10lb
Occupation: Marketing representative
Born: Dublin, 27.6.63
Family: Single
Former club: Dublin University
International debut: Ireland 10, England 21, 1988
Five Nations' debut: Ireland 21, France 26, 1989
Best moment in rugby: Winning first cap in Millennium match
Worst moment in rugby: Underestimating Rory Underwood's pace when he ran past me for try in Millennium match
Most embarrassing moment: As above
Most respected opponent: French wing Patrice Lagisquet
Serious injuries: Broken shoulder, dislocated shoulder, torn cruciate ligaments (missed bulk of last season)

	apps.	pts.
Ireland (1988)		
Last Season	0 caps	0
Career	3 caps	7
1989	Tour to Canada	

Other sporting achievements: Captained Moyle Park College to Leinster Gaelic football championship. Sprinted in 100m final at National Championships
Best memory last season: Scoring try for Leinster against All Blacks
Most improved International player last season: Ireland full-back Kenny Murphy
Suggestions to improve rugby: Keep game as it is but identify players' employers in match programmes
Other notable landmarks in rugby career: Played soccer and Gaelic at school, but not rugby. Started game at 15 and went on to play for Irish Universities, Leinster and Ireland U-25s. Missed last season through injury, after returning from 1989 summer tour to North America
Touchlines: Golf, tennis

Sharp, A.V.   England

Full Name: Alan Victor Sharp
International category: England B
Club: Bristol
Position: Loose-head prop
Height: 5'10" **Weight:** 16st 7lb
Occupation: Builder
Born: Bristol, 17.10.69
Family: Single
Former club: St Brendan Old Boys
International debut: Spain 9,
England B 31, 1989
Best moment in rugby: Playing as
first-choice for England B in Spain
(1989)
Worst moment in rugby: Bristol
losing at Moseley in 1989/90
Pilkington Cup
Most embarrassing moment:
Charging down penalty kick playing
v Australian Schools at Twickenham
Most respected opponent:
Gloucester prop Richard Pascall
Other sporting achievements:
Avon Schools shot put and discus
champion
Best memory last season:
England B tour to Spain

	apps.	pts.
England B (1989)		
Last Season	1 cap	0
England 1995	Development squad	

Most improved International player last season: England scrum-half
Richard Hill
Suggestions to improve rugby: Inject more money into grass roots of game

Sheppeard, R.   Wales

Full Name: Richard Sheppeard
International category: Wales U-21
Club: Pontypridd
Position: Centre
Height: 5'9" **Weight:** 12st 8lb
Occupation: Workshop technician
Born: Pontypridd, 24.11.69
Family: Single
Family links with rugby: Brother
played No.8 for Pontypridd and
Wales U-15, U-16 and Youth
Former club: Cardiff
International debut (U-21):
Scotland 10, Wales 24, 1990
Best moment in rugby: Touring
New Zealand with Wales Youth
Worst moment in rugby: Being
dropped from Welsh Schools for
two matches
Most respected opponent:
Cilfynydd's Steve Smith
Serious injuries sustained:
Dislocated thumb
Other sporting achievements:
Took part in Welsh athletics
championships

	apps.	pts.
Wales U-21 (**1990**)		
Last Season	1 cap	0

Best memory last season: Scoring try for Pontypridd in defeat of former club, Cardiff
Most improved International player last season: Wales wing Arthur Emyr
Suggestions to improve rugby: Free training facilities (kit etc) throughout Wales
Other notable landmarks in rugby career: Represented Wales at U-15, U-18, U-19 and U-20 level. Toured NZ with Wales Youth. Captained U-21s v Combined Services (1990)
Touchlines: Swimming, weightlifting, golf

Shiel, A.G.   Scotland

Full Name: Andrew **Graham** Shiel
International category: Scotland
Full (NZ squad)
Club: Melrose
Positions: Fly-half, centre, full-back
Height: 5'10" **Weight:** 12st 8lb
Occupation: Apprentice
stonemason
Born: Galashiels, 13.8.70
Family: Single
Family links with rugby: Father
played for Melrose GS
International debut (U-21):
Scotland 10, Wales 24, 1990
Best moment in rugby: Being
selected to tour New Zealand
Worst moment in rugby: Not
making the Scottish Schools XV to
play New Zealand in 1988
Most embarrassing moment:
Ball toppled over in front of posts
before I kicked it during 1990
Hawick Sevens
Most respected opponent:
Scotland centre Sean Lineen –
always a great experience playing
against a national player in your
own position

	apps.	pts.
Scotland U-21 (**1990**)		
Last Season	1 cap	6
Scotland (**1990**)	Tour to New Zealand	

Serious injuries: Straining inner and exterior quadriceps and adductor muscle
(1988/89) and missing over four months rugby
Other sporting achievements: Athletics for Borders Schools and Borders
AAA
Best memory last season: Winning Scottish First Division with Melrose
Most improved International player last season: Scotland centre Tony
Stanger
Suggestions to improve rugby: Gain experience, and dedication to game
Other notable landmarks in rugby career: Represented Scottish Schools
three times, Scotland U-19s and U-21s. Made four appearances for Scotland
in New Zealand last summer
Touchlines: Golf, tennis, cricket

Shiel, D.K.   Scotland

Full Name: David Kevin Shiel
International category: Scotland B
Club: Jed-Forest
Position: Fly-half
Height: 5'9" **Weight:** 12st
Occupation: Plumber and slater
Born: Jedburgh, 30.7.69
Family: Single
Family links with rugby: Father played for Jed-Forest
Former clubs: Melrose, Waimatai (NZ)
International debut (B): Scotland 22, Ireland 22, 1989
Best moment in rugby: Setting World record by landing 5 dropped goals for Melrose against Langholm
Most respected opponent: Former Scotland wing Keith Robertson
Serious injuries: Damaged Achilles tendon
Other sporting achievements: Cricket for St Boswell's
Best memory last season:

	apps.	pts.
Scotland B (1989)		
Last Season	1 cap	11

Jed-Forest finishing third in Scottish First Division
Most improved International player last season: Scotland scrum-half Gary Armstrong
Other notable landmarks in rugby career: Captained Scottish Schools (U-18s), represented U-19s and U-21s. Kicked 11 points for Scotland B against Ireland last season. Spent summer in New Zealand playing for Waimatai
Touchlines: Soccer, Fives

Shortland, S.M.   England

Full Name: Stephen Michael Shortland
International category: England U-21
Club: Harlequins
Position: Lock
Height: 6'7" **Weight:** 17st
Occupation: PE student
Born: Sheffield, 12.1.68
Family: Single
Former clubs: Dinnington, Headingley
International debut (U-21): Romania 13, England 54, 1989
Best moment in rugby: Helping England Students beat the French 32–4 at Verdun
Worst moment in rugby: Headingley losing 10–0 to Gordon League in 1987/88 John Player Cup
Most embarrassing moment: As above
Most respected opponent: England flanker Peter Winterbottom
Best memory last season: Playing for England U-21s in Bucharest

	apps.	pts.
England U-21 (**1989**)		
Last Season	1 cap	0
England 1995	Development squad	

Most improved International player last season: England Students' flanker Martin Pepper
Suggestions to improve rugby: Bring more TV and sponsorship into game
Other notable landmarks in rugby career: Capped 4 times by England Students
Touchlines: Enjoy company of locals at father's pub. Keen fisherman

Silva, M.A.   Wales

Full Name: Matthew Alan Silva
International category: Wales B (squad)
Club: Cardiff
Position: Full-back
Height: 6'1" **Weight:** 13st 8lb
Occupation: Sales representative
Born: Cardiff, 15.3.70
Family: Single with two daughters
Former club: St Albans (Cardiff)
Best moment in rugby: Playing for Cardiff v 1989 All Blacks
Worst moment in rugby: Cardiff losing to Aberavon in quarter-finals of 1989/90 Schweppes Cup
Most respected opponent: New Zealand centre Joe Stanley
Other sporting achievements: Baseball for South Glamorgan
Best memory last season: Selected as bench reserve for Wales B v France
Most improved International player last season: Wales centre Allan Bateman

	apps.
Wales B (1989/90)	1 rep

Suggestions to improve rugby: Recognise players as most important aspect of game
Other notable landmarks in rugby career: Played for Welsh Schools U-11s and full season for Wales Youth (1988/89)
Touchlines: DIY, tennis, golf

Sims, D.   England

Full Name: David Sims
International category: England U-21
Club: Gloucester
Positions: Lock, No.8
Height: 6'8" **Weight:** 16st 6lb
Occupation: Student
Born: Gloucester, 22.11.69
Family: Single
Family links with rugby:
Grandfather Thomas Price played for England (1948–49)
Former clubs: Longlevens, Sunnybank (Aus)
International debut: Netherlands 3, England U-21 24, 1990
Best moment in rugby: Putting on Gloucester senior shirt for first time
Worst moment in rugby: Watching 1990 Pilkington Cup final defeat to Bath from Gloucester replacements' bench
Most respected opponent: Gloucester lock John Gadd (in training)

	apps.	pts.
England U-21 **(1990)**		
Last Season	1 cap	0

Serious injuries: Damaged neck muscles
Other sporting achievements: Basketball for Gloucester Jets
Best memory last season: Winning England U-21 cap and playing all three divisional matches for South West
Most improved International player last season: England No.8 Mike Teague
Other notable landmarks in rugby career: Attended England Schools (16 Group) and Colts final trials. Played for South West U-21s before graduating to senior team. Won England Students cap against Combined Services and was replacement for England U-21s against French Armed forces. Played for Brisbane club Sunnybank last summer
Touchlines: Swimming, training, music

Skinner, M.G.   England

Full Name: Michael Gordon
Skinner
International category: England
Full
Club: Harlequins
Position: Blind-side flanker
Height: 6'4" **Weight:** 16st 7lb
Occupation: Freelance computer
consultant
Born: Newcastle upon Tyne,
26.11.58
Family: Single
Former clubs: Blaydon, Blackheath
International debut: France 10,
England 9, 1988
Five Nations' debut: As above
Best moments in rugby: Winning
first England cap. Harlequins
winning first of five successive
Middlesex Sevens titles at
Twickenham in my first season
with club (1986)
Worst moment in rugby:
Breaking nose in first line-out v
Ireland (1988) and continuing
Most embarrassing moment:
Playing blind-side for Barbarians v
NZ Barbarians (1987/88). Still
bound to scrum when Michael
Jones was scoring on blind side
burst from 10-yard scrum

	apps.	pts.
England B (1987)		
Last Season	1 cap	0
England (1988)		
Last Season	7 caps	4
Career	12 caps	4
1990	Tour to Argentina	
1991	World Cup squad	

Most respected opponent: 'Skippa', captain and No.8 of Ryton RFC – great
commitment and loyalty to club
Serious injuries: Knee operation – file and drill knee cap
Best memory last season: England beating France 26–7 at Parc des Princes
Most improved International player last season: Me
Suggestions to improve rugby: Better referees
Other notable landmarks in rugby career: Scored winning try on debut
for Blaydon at Stockton (1975/76) and received hero's welcome afterwards
on return from having eye stitched at hospital. Started career as centre at
school, and played No.8 and flanker for Northumberland Colts. Joined

Blackheath in 1979 and represented Kent in 1986 County Championship final. Became regular in London divisional team after moving to Harlequins. Made England B debut in 1987 match v France

Smith, B.A.   Ireland

Full Name: Brian Anthony Smith
International category: Ireland Full
Club: Leicester
Positions: Scrum-half, fly-half
Height: 5'10" **Weight:** 13st 7lb
Occupation: Student
Born: St George, Australia, 9.9.66
Family: Single
Family links with rugby: Brother and father are/were rugby league players
Former clubs: Wests (Brisbane), Manly (Sydney), Oxford University
International debut: Australia v South Korea, 1987
Five Nations' debut: Ireland 10, Scotland 13, 1990
Best moment in rugby: Scoring 26 points for Australia against a World XV in 1988 – including penalty goals with both left and right feet
Worst moment in rugby: Losing 1989 Varsity match with Oxford
Most respected opponent: New Zealand's Grant Fox – a points-scoring machine

	apps.	pts.
Australia (**1987**)	6 caps	8
Ireland (**1989**)		
Last Season	4 caps	10
Career	4 caps	10

Other sporting achievements: Track and field Blue at Oxford
Best memory last season: Oxford's victory over a World XV at Iffley Road
Most improved International player last season: England fly-half Rob Andrew – only now getting the credit he deserves
Suggestions to improve rugby: Relax amateur laws. Recognise South Africa and play them. Put rugby in the Olympics. Change laws to make game faster

Other notable landmarks in rugby career: Australian Schools (1983), Australia: Bledisloe Cup win over All Blacks, World Cup, tour of Argentina (1986–88), Oxford (1988–90), Ireland – playing against All Blacks again and in Five Nations' Championship for first time (1989/90)
Touchlines: Enjoy studying politics and attending theatre/movies at Oxford. Play all ball sports

Smith, I.R.   England

Full Name: Ian Richard Smith
International category: England B
Club: Gloucester
Position: Flanker
Height: 6' Weight: 13st 10lb
Occupation: Civil engineer
Born: Gloucester, 16.3.65
Family: Single
Family links with rugby: Father Dick was an England trialist who played for Gloucester and Barbarians
Former club: Longlevens
International debut: Basque XV 3, England B 63, 1989
Best moment in rugby: Reaching Twickenham with Gloucester in 1989/90 Pilkington Cup final
Worst moment in rugby: Losing final 6-48 to Bath
Most embarrassing moment: Above match – we were humiliated
Most respected opponent: Neath flanker Lyn Jones
Best memory last season: Beating Bath in English First Division

England B (**1989/90**)	Tour to Spain
England 1990	World Cup squad
1995	Development squad

Most improved International player last season: England hooker Brian Moore
Suggestions to improve rugby: Relax amateur laws
Other notable landmarks in rugby career: England 18-Group trialist. Played his 200th game for Gloucester in 1989/90 Pilkington Cup final. Spent

1988 Australian season playing in Wollongong. Selected to England's 1991 World Cup squad, having spent last summer on standby for Argentine tour
Touchlines: Shooting, squash

Smith, S.J. Ireland

Full Name: Stephen James Smith
International category: Ireland Full
Club: Ballymena
Position: Hooker
Height: 6' **Weight:** 16st
Occupation: Sportswear representative
Born: Belfast, 18.7.59
Family: Single
Family links with rugby: Brother Oliver plays for Ballymena
International debut: Ireland 10, England 21, 1988
Five Nations' debut: Ireland 21, France 26, 1989
Best moment in rugby: Selection for 1989 Lions
Worst moment in rugby: Having to leave field at Twickenham after damaging rib cartilage against England in 1990 clash
Most respected opponent: All Black hooker Sean Fitzpatrick
Serious injuries: Damaged rib cartilage

	apps.	pts.
Ireland (**1988**)		
Last Season	2 caps	0
Career	9 caps	4
Lions 1989		

Best memory last season: Helping Ballymena win Ulster League and Cup double for second consecutive season (first team to achieve feat since 1907)
Most improved International player last season: Scotland wing Tony Stanger
Suggestions to improve rugby: More professional approach away from field to match greater commitment being made by players

Other notable landmarks in rugby career: Called out to 1987 World Cup as Ireland's second replacement hooker but did not feature. Following season broke into Ireland team and became first Irishman to mark debut with a try since Hugo MacNeill in 1981. Represented Barbarians against 1988 Wallabies, 1989 Home Unions against France, and 1989 Lions in Australia, playing 5 games and scoring 2 tries. Toured South Africa with 1989 World XV and found experience awe-inspiring – a real eye-opener
Touchlines: Golf

Soden, P.J. Ireland

Full Name: Philip Joseph Soden
International category: Ireland U-21
Club: Constitution
Position: Loose-head prop
Height: 6'1" **Weight:** 16st 2lb
Occupation: Own dry-cleaning business
Born: London, 6.9.69
Family: Single
Former club: Christian Brothers College (Cork)
International debut (U-21): Ireland 13, New Zealand 13, 1989
Best moment in rugby: Playing in above match
Best memory last season: Winning regular place in Constitution team
Most improved International player last season: Ireland No.8 Noel Mannion
Other notable landmarks in rugby career: Played for Irish Schools (1986–88) and Munster at Schools and U-20 level, before graduating to U-21 team last season
Touchlines: Golf, swimming

	apps.	pts.
Ireland U-21 (**1989**)		
Last Season	1 cap	0

Sole, D.M.B.   Scotland

Full Name: David Michael Barclay Sole
International category: Scotland Full
Club: Edinburgh Academicals
Position: Prop
Height: 5'11" **Weight:** 16st 4lb
Occupation: Grain buyer
Born: Aylesbury, 8.5.62
Former clubs: Exeter University, Toronto Scottish, Bath
International debut: Scotland 18, France 17, Murrayfield, 1986
Five Nations' debut: As above
Best moment in rugby: Captaining Scotland to 1990 Five Nations' Grand Slam
Worst moment in rugby: Suffering broken nose and cheekbone playing in Bath's 12–3 win against Moseley in the 1987 John Player Cup quarter-final
Most respected opponents: Scotland's Iain Milne and France's Jean-Pierre Garuet – two of the world's strongest scrummagers. They don't bend the rules, but use their strength to succeed
Serious injuries: Broken nose, cheekbone

	apps.	pts.
Scotland B (**1983**)		
Last Season	0 caps	0
Scotland (**1986**)		
Last Season	8 caps	8
Career	27 caps	8
Lions 1989	3 caps	0

Best memory last season: Winning Five Nations' Grand Slam; helping British Lions to series win in Australia
Other notable landmarks in rugby career: 1987 John Player Cup winners' medal. Appointed Scotland captain (Scotland 38, Fiji 17, Murrayfield, 28 October 1989). Captained Lions against New South Wales B and the Anzacs during 1989 tour of Australia. Captained Barbarians against 1989 All Blacks. Captained Home Unions against Europe in April 1990. Captained Scotland in 1990 tour of New Zealand

Stanger, A.G.   Scotland

Full Name: Anthony George Stanger
International category: Scotland Full
Club: Hawick
Position: Wing
Height: 6'2" **Weight:** 13st 7lb
Occupation: Bank officer
Born: Hawick, 14.5.68
Family: Single
Family links with rugby: Peter (brother) plays for Hawick, Scotland U-18s
International debut: Scotland 38, Fiji 17, Oct 1989
Five Nations' debut: Ireland 10, Scotland 13, 1990
Best moment in rugby: Scoring try in Grand Slam decider against England
Worst moment in rugby: Getting dropped by Hawick in 1986/87 as an 18-year old
Most respected opponents: Rory Underwood and Arthur Emyr
Other sporting achievements:

	apps.	pts.
Scotland (1989)		
Last Season	8 caps	28
Career	8 caps	28

Hawick High School athletics champion (three times)
Best memory last season: Winning Grand Slam with Scotland
Most improved International player last season: Scotland prop Paul Burnell
Other notable landmarks in rugby career: Scored 6 tries in first 6 Internationals (2 on debut against Fiji, 3 against Romania and 1 against England in Grand Slam decider). Toured with Scotland in Japan (summer 1989), scoring 3 tries in 2 games, and to New Zealand last summer. Made debut for Hawick while 17-year-old student – 5 caps for Scottish Schools at centre in 1985/86, followed by 2 for Scotland U-21s

Full Name: James Staples
International category: Ireland B
Club: London Irish
Positions: Full-back, wing
Height: 6'2" **Weight:** 13st 7lb
Occupation: Commercial property
agent
Born: London, 20.10.65
Family: Single
Family links with rugby: Younger
brother plays for Westcombe Park
Former clubs: St Mary's,
Bromley, Sidcup
International debut (B): Scotland
22, Ireland 22, 1989
Best moment in rugby: Playing
for Irish Wolfhounds in 1988/89
Hong Kong Sevens
Worst moment in rugby: Missing
out on promotion to English First
Division with London Irish in
1988/89 after losing 22–21 to
last-minute dropped goal by
Blackheath, having led 21–0 at
half-time
Most embarrassing moment:
Missing flight home from Spain on
first senior trip

	apps.	pts.
Ireland U-25 (**1990**)		
Last Season	1 cap	0
Ireland B (**1989**)		
Last Season	1 cap	0

Most respected opponent: Scotland full-back Gavin Hastings – strong, fast
and always a threat
Other sporting achievements: Played in same forward line as Crystal Palace
FC's Ian Wright for Greenwich Borough
Best memory last season: Representing Irish province (Connacht) v All
Blacks
Most improved International player last season: England flanker Peter
Winterbottom – developed ball skills to match his power and aggression
Other notable landmarks in rugby career: Took over from former Ireland
full-back Hugo MacNeill at No.15 in London Irish team. Played twice for
Ireland U-25s before reaching B grade last season

Stephens, C.J.   Wales

Full Name: Colin John Stephens
International category: Wales B
Club: Llanelli
Position: Fly-half
Height: 5'7" **Weight:** 11st 8lb
Born: Morriston, 29.11.69
Family: Single
International debut (U-21):
Scotland 13, Wales 20, 1988
Best moment in rugby: Wales B
debut v France, 1989 (lost 15–28)
Worst moment in rugby: Pulling
hamstring at Lisbon Sevens last
summer
Most respected opponent:
Former Wales fly-half Paul Turner
Other sporting achievements:
Cricket for Dafen in South Wales
League
Best memory last season:
Selected as replacement for
Barbarians v New Zealand
**Most improved International
player last season:** England
scrum-half Richard Hill
Other notable landmarks in

	apps.	pts.
Wales B (1989)		
Last Season	2 caps	7

rugby career: Played two seasons for Welsh Schools (1986–87), touring
New Zealand, and went on to represent Welsh Universities and Colleges.
Scored 14 points on U-21 debut at Murrayfield. Toured Canada with
Wales B (1989)

Stott, F.H.   Scotland

Full Name: Fraser Hunter Stott
International category: Scotland U-21
Club: West of Scotland
Position: Scrum-half
Height: 5'10" **Weight:** 12st 1lb
Occupation: Quality assurance clerk
Born: Glasgow, 13.8.69
Family: Single
Family links with rugby: Father played for West of Scotland, Glasgow, and North & Midlands
Former clubs: Cambuslang, Glasgow High/Kelvinside, Napier (NZ)
International debut (U-21): Scotland 10, Wales 24, 1990
Best moment in rugby: Helping Napier (NZ) win trophy-treble (first team for twenty-seven years to achieve feat)
Worst moment in rugby: Being with David Millar in New Zealand when he broke his neck

	apps.	pts.
Scotland U-21 (**1990**)		
Last Season	1 cap	0

Most embarrassing moment: Trying to run ball out from under posts, while playing for GHK. Ran into team mate, spilled ball, and opposition scored
Most respected opponents: Scrum-halves Alan Tait (Melrose) and Bob Hogarth (Kelso)
Best memory last season: Winning first Scottish cap at Millbrae, Ayr
Most improved International player last season: Wales scrum-half Robert Jones – continues to get better and better
Suggestions to improve rugby: Get more youngsters involved to increase interest/support in game
Other notable landmarks in rugby career: Scottish trials at U-18 and U-19 level. U-21 squad member (1988/89) but only capped last season
Touchlines: Fishing, shooting

Sutton, A. Wales

Full Name: Andrew Sutton
International category: Wales B
(squad)
Club: Newbridge
Position: Lock
Height: 6'4" **Weight:** 18st
Occupation: Dispensing optician
Born: Tredegar, 27.3.65
Family: Married
Family links with rugby: Cousin
plays junior rugby
Former clubs: Abergavenny,
Saracens, Cardiff
Best moment in rugby: Touring
Canada with Wales B (1989)
Worst moment in rugby: Being
sent off playing for Abergavenny
and thus missing Youth cap against
South Africa
Most respected opponent:
Former England lock Maurice
Colclough

Wales B (**1989/90**)	Tour to Canada

Serious injuries: Broken collarbone
Other sporting achievements:
Accomplished judo exponent
Best memory last season: Touring Canada with Wales
Most improved International player last season: Wales lock Andy Allen
Suggestions to improve rugby: Increase emphasis on personal fitness
Other notable landmarks in rugby career: Played for Wales Youth in
1983/84 season
Touchlines: Having to put up with being good looking

Tayler, P.M.   England

Full Name: Peter Michael Tayler
International category: England B
Club: Rosslyn Park
Position: Flanker
Height: 6'1" **Weight:** 16st
Occupation: Marketing executive
Born: Folkestone, 14.2.64
Family: Single
Family links with rugby: Father
played for Combined Services
Former clubs: Old Meadonians,
Manly (Aus)
International debut: England B
12, Fiji 20, 1989
Best moment in rugby: Manly
beating Ranwick 33–3 in Sydney
Premiership competition
Most embarrassing moment:
Attempting a drop goal
Serious injuries: Broken nose
(three)
Best memory last season:
Winning first England B cap and
being selected as replacement for
England v Italy (won 33–15)

England B (1989)	apps.	pts.
Last Season	2 caps	0

**Most improved International
player last season:** England scrum-half Richard Hill
Suggestions to improve rugby: Differential penalties. Less points for lesser
crimes
Other notable landmarks in rugby career: Member of England Schools
squad but never capped. Played three times for England Colts (1982). Spent
1988 playing in Australia. Returned to win B recognition last season before
being put on England stand-by in Rovigo
Touchlines: Cycling

Teague, M.C.   England

Full Name: Michael Clive Teague
International category: England
Full
Club: Gloucester
Positions: No. 8, flanker
Height: 6'3" **Weight:** 16st 7lb
Occupation: Bricklayer
Born: Gloucester, 8.10.60
Family: Married
Family links with rugby:
Grandfather played for
Gloucestershire
Former clubs: Cardiff, Gloucester
Old Blues
International debut: France 32,
England 18, 1984
Five Nations' debut: As above
Best moment in rugby: 1989
Lions winning decisive third Test
against Australia
Worst moment in rugby:
England losing 1990 Grand Slam
decider to Scotland
Most embarrassing moment:
Giving Wales 3 seconds of hell and
then being carried off injured
(1989)
Most respected opponent: All
Black Murray Mexted
Serious injuries: Torn shoulder,
knee ligaments

	apps.	pts.
England B (**1981**)		
Last Season	1 cap	0
England (**1985**)		
Last Season	4 caps	0
Career	11 caps	4
1991	World Cup squad	
Lions 1989	2 Tests	0

Best memory last season: England beating France 26-7 in Paris
Most improved International player last season: England centre Will
Carling
Suggestions to improve rugby: Cannot improve the game that much, it's
improving itself
Other notable landmarks in rugby career: Represented England at U-23
and B levels. Also played for 1989 Lions in Australia, where voted 'man of
the series'
Touchlines: Motocross

Thomas, C.J.   Wales

Full Name: Ceri John Thomas
International category: Wales U-21
Club: Cardiff
Positions: Wing, full-back
Height: 5'10" **Weight:** 12st
Occupation: Civil Servant
Born: Tonyrefail, 8.3.69
Family: Single
Family links with rugby: Father played for Bridgend. Brother Mike played for Maesteg and Pontypridd
Former club: Tonyrefail
International debut (U-21): Scotland 10, Wales 24, 1990
Best moment in rugby: Playing for Cardiff against 1989 All Blacks
Worst moment in rugby: Tour-ending injury (knee ligaments) in second game of Wales U-19s 1987 New Zealand tour. Still finished top scorer with 5 tries

	apps.	pts.
Wales U-21 (**1990**)		
Last Season	1 cap	0

Most embarrassing moment: Chasing after contact lens which blew away in wind (found it)
Most respected opponent: Give all opponents equal respect
Serious injuries: Knee ligaments (out three months), concussion (twice)
Other sporting achievements: Soccer for Mid-Glamorgan Schools
Best memory last season: Playing for Wales U-21s in Scotland
Most improved International player last season: Wales fly-half David Evans
Suggestions to improve rugby: Wales must develop a pattern of play and stick to it. They must also improve communication between players on field, and introduce a more professional attitude to training
Other notable landmarks in rugby career: Won 6 caps for Wales Youth before moving to Wales U-20s in 1989, via U-19s, and onto U-21s last season
Touchlines: Sprinting, training, squash

Thomas, P.J.   Wales

Full Name: Phillip John Thomas
International category: Wales U-21
Club: Glamorgan Wanderers
Position: Flanker
Height: 5'11½" **Weight:** 13st
Occupation: Apprentice fitter
Born: Barry, 27.7.69
Family: Single
Former club: Llantwit Major
International debut (U-21): Scotland 10, Wales 24, 1990
Best moment in rugby: Playing for Wales U-21s
Worst moment in rugby: Losing front teeth playing for Llantwit Major, aged 17
Most respected opponent: Bridgend's Wales B flanker Mike Budd
Other sporting achievements: Welsh lifeguard team
Best memory last season: Beating Scotland U-21s in Ayr
Most improved International player last season: Bridgend's Welsh No.8 Owain Williams

	apps.	pts.
Wales U-21 (**1990**)		
Last Season	1 cap	0

Suggestions to improve rugby: Remove sin-bin. It gives referees and players an 'easy' option
Other notable landmarks in rugby career: Represented Wales Youth in three non-cap matches (1987/88) and Wales U-20s against North Wales U-23s. Helped Wales U-21s beat Combined Services U-21s 83–3
Touchlines: Lifeguard coaching

Thompson, G.J.   England

Full Name: Gavin John Thompson
International category: England
U-21
Club: Harlequins
Position: Centre
Height: 6' **Weight:** 13st 5lb
Occupation: Insurance underwriter
Born: Croydon, 30.8.69
Family: Single
Former club: Rosslyn Park
International debut (U-21):
Romania 13, England 54, 1989
Best moment in rugby: Scoring a
try on my Harlequins debut last
season v Bath
Worst moment in rugby: Being
hosed down with cold water after
my first game of mini-rugby aged
10, having got covered in mud
Most embarrassing moment:
Trying to go round behind posts
after crossing try line in a school
match and dropping ball
Most respected opponent:
England fly half Rob Andrew – he
can read and run a game as he likes
Other sporting achievements:
Represented Surrey at hockey and
cricket at U-15 and U-16 levels

	apps.	pts.
England U-21 (**1989**)		
Last Season	3 caps	12
England 1990	Tour to Argentina	
1995	Development squad	

Best memory last season: Scoring try for England U-21s in Romania
Most improved International player last season: Rob Andrew
Suggestions to improve rugby: Play League games on home and away basis.
Alter points system to make it less of an incentive to kick for goal
Other notable landmarks in rugby career: England 18-group, 4 caps
(1987). England Colts, 3 caps (1988). Toured Kenya with Penguins (1989).
Appointed England U-21 captain for their two Internationals and selected for
England tour of Argentina (1990). Scoring tries in each of three U-21
Internationals played
Touchlines: Reading, especially autobiographies

Thorburn, P.H.   Wales

Full Name: Paul Huw Thorburn
International category: Wales Full
Club: Neath
Position: Full-back
Height: 6' **Weight:** 13st 5lb
Occupation: Sales manager for telecom company
Born: Rheindalen, West Germany, 24.11.62
Family: Married with daughter
Family links with rugby: Father played for Cardiff 2nd XV. Brother had England Schools Trial
Former clubs: Swansea University, Ebbw Vale
International debut: France 14, Wales 3, 1985
Five Nations' debut: As above
Best moments in rugby: Kicking last-minute penalty which beat Australia 22–21 and gave Wales third place in 1987 World Cup. Scoring first ever try for Wales against Namibia last summer
Worst moment in rugby: Being dropped by Wales for 1988 game against England

	apps.	pts.
Wales B (1984)		
Last Season	1 cap	15
Wales (1984)		
Last Season	7 caps	57
Career	31 caps	256

Most embarrassing moment: Taking easy penalty kick for Neath against Sale. Scoreboard was directly behind posts and as I was about to strike ball it registered 3 extra points. I promptly missed
Most respected opponent: French full-back Serge Blanco
Serious injuries: Broken leg, collarbone. Dislocated shoulder
Other sporting achievements: Cricket for Hereford and Worcester
Best memory last season: Neath winning Welsh Cup
Most improved International player last season: England centre Will Carling
Suggestions to improve rugby: Make it easier for players to compete in events all over world by compensating employers for time away from work. Reckon I need fourteen weeks off for rugby between now and end of World Cup

Other notable landmarks in rugby career: Born in Europe, grew up in England, but played for Welsh Universities, UAU and Ebbw Vale before joining Neath. Record points scorer in Welsh rugby. Failed to score only twice in 29 appearances for Wales (v Scotland 1989 and Ireland 1990). Set Welsh record when scoring 52 points in 1986 Five Nations' Championship. Among other fondest memories are 70-yard penalty which helped Wales beat Scotland in 1986, and injury-time penalty that beat Ireland in 1988 to secure Welsh Triple Crown. Captained Wales four times
Touchlines: Waterskiing, squash, golf

Thorneycroft, H.S.　　　England

Full Name: Harvey Spencer Thorneycroft
International category: England U-21
Club: Northampton
Position: Wing
Height: 6' **Weight:** 14st 7lb
Occupation: Student
Born: Northampton, 22.2.69
Family: Single
Former club: Nottingham
International debut (U-21): Romania 13, England 54, 1989
Best moment in rugby: Scoring 3 tries for England Colts against Wales Youth at Neath in 1988
Worst moment in rugby: Running half length of pitch at Bath and dropping ball on try-line
Most embarrassing moment: Sent off playing in school game
Most respected opponent: England B wing Steve Hackney – mixes social life with commitment
Other sporting achievements: Sprinted for Midlands Schools

	apps.	pts.
England U-21 (**1989**)		
Last Season	3 caps	12

Best memory last season: Representing England U-21s against Netherlands and French Armed Forces

Most improved International player last season: England centre Jeremy Guscott

Suggestions to improve rugby: Follow approach of Dick Best (England U-21 and B coach). Only kick when need to kick to establish a more flowing game

Other notable landmarks in rugby career: Represented South England Public Schools. Collected 3 caps for each of England Colts, Students and U-21s

---

Thresher, D.B.   England

Full Name: David Bruce Thresher
International category: England B
Club: Harlequins
Position: Lock
Height: 6'5" **Weight:** 16st 7lb
Occupation: Financial futures trader
Born: Bromley, Kent, 17.8.64
Family: Single
Family links with rugby: Brother Stuart plays for Harlequins, London and England B
Former club: Oxford University
International debut: Spain 9, England B 31, 1989
Best moment in rugby: Making B debut on Spanish tour
Worst moment in rugby: Any bad injuries
Most respected opponent: Dean Richards – tremendous strength and influence
Best memory last season: Final whistle of last match
Most improved International player last season: England scrum-half Richard Hill

	apps.	pts.
England B (1989)		
Last Season	2 caps	0

Suggestions to improve rugby: Hang violent offenders. Improve quality of refereeing

Other notable landmarks in rugby career: Played for Welsh Universities, Kent and London Division

Titley, M.H. Wales

Full Name: Mark Howard Titley
International category: Wales Full
Club: Swansea
Position: Right wing
Height: 5'9" **Weight:** 12st
Occupation: Financial advisor
Born: Swansea, 3.5.59
Family: Single
Family links with rugby: Father
played for Swansea Schools
Former clubs: Bridgend, London
Welsh
International debut: Romania 24,
Wales 6, 1983
Five Nations' debut: France 14,
Wales 3, 1985
Best moment in rugby: Winning
first Welsh cap in Bucharest
Worst moment in rugby:
Swansea losing 16–18 at
'invincible' Pontypool in 1983/84
Welsh Cup after having try
disallowed in last minute
Most respected opponent:
Former Wales wing Adrian Hadley
Best memory last season:
Scoring try for Wales against France
**Most improved International
player last season:** Wales wing
Arthur Emyr

	apps.	pts.
Wales B (1982)		
Last Season	0 caps	0
Wales (1983)		
Last Season	2 caps	4
Career	15 caps	16

Suggestions to improve rugby: Increase points for tries and reduce worth of penalties
Other notable landmarks in rugby career: Started career as fly-half for East Wales Schools, moving to centre and then wing while playing for London Welsh and Surrey. Returned to Principality to join Bridgend and was Man of Match in 1982 Schweppes Cup final. Played for Wales B in same season.

Returned to Welsh team briefly last season for first time since 1986 tour to South Pacific
Touchlines: Golf (18-handicap)

Tukalo, I. Scotland

Full Name: Iwan Tukalo
International category: Scotland Full
Club: Selkirk
Position: Left wing
Height: 5'9" **Weight:** 13st
Occupation: Senior engineer with British Gas, Scotland
Born: Edinburgh, 5.3.61
Family: Susan (wife)
Former club: Royal High
International debut: Scotland 15, Ireland 18, 1985
Five Nations' debut: As above
Best moment in rugby: Beating England to win 1990 Grand Slam
Worst moment in rugby: Playing for South of Scotland v New Zealand (1983)
Most embarrassing moment: Running to listen to captain's instructions in Scotland's match v Fiji (1989) and arriving too late
Most respected opponent: Australia wing David Campese – electrifying pace over 5 yards and excellent side-step
Serious injuries sustained: Torn ligaments, ankle and knee. Torn hamstring

	apps.	pts.
Scotland B (1982)		
Last Season	0 caps	0
Scotland (1985)		
Last Season	6 caps	8
Career	23 caps	40

Best memory last season: Completing Grand Slam
Most improved International player last season: Scotland prop Paul Burnell
Other notable landmarks in rugby career: Played in 21 of Scotland's last 23 cap Internationals; played three times at scrum-half for Scottish Schools

in 1978–79, captaining side against France; toured with Scotland to Romania (1984), North America (1985), Spain and France (1986), Japan (1989) and New Zealand (1990); played in 13 of last 18 tour games
Touchlines: Squash, golf

Turnbull, D.J.   Scotland

Full Name: Derek James Turnbull
International category: Scotland Full
Club: Hawick
Position: Flanker
Height: 6' 3" **Weight:** 16st
Occupation: Police officer
Birthplace: Hawick, 2.10.61
Family: Single
Family links with rugby: Father past president of Hawick Trades RFC
Former clubs: Hawick PSA, Hawick Trades
International debut: New Zealand 30, Scotland 3, 1987
Five Nations' debut: Scotland 23, France 12, 1988
Best moment in rugby: Coming on as a replacement in the 1990 Grand Slam decider against England at Murrayfield
Worst moment in rugby: Losing to New Zealand in 1987 World Cup quarter-finals
Most embarrassing moment: Leading a Hawick Sevens side out at Gala Sports on 1 April, 1989. The rest of the side stayed in the dressing room until I was out onto the pitch myself – all by myself!
Most respected opponent: Willie Duggan – he knew how to cheat well
Other sporting achievements: Completed London Marathon in 1982
Best memory last season: Scotland's Grand Slam

	apps.	pts.
Scotland B (1982)		
Last Season	0 caps	0
Scotland (1987)		
Last Season	1 cap	0
Career	4 caps	0

Most improved International player last season: Scotland wing Tony Stanger

Suggestions to improve rugby: Don't allow anyone to kick the ball in opponents' half of the field

Other notable landmarks in rugby career: Scotland tours to North America (1985), France and Spain (1986), World Cup (1987), Zimbabwe (1988), Japan (1989) and New Zealand (1990)

Touchlines: Enjoy golf – especially the 19th hole

Turner, P.   Wales

Full Name: Paul Turner
International category: Wales B
Club: Newport
Positions: Fly-half, full-back
Height: 5'9" **Weight:** 11st 7lb
Occupation: Sales representative
Born: Newport, 13.2.60
Family: Married with son
Family links with rugby: Related to Mike Watkins through marriage
Former clubs: Newbridge, London Welsh
International debut: Wales 13, Ireland 19, 1989
Five Nations' debut: As above
Best moments in rugby: Playing in Hong Kong Sevens three times between 1985–88
Worst moment in rugby: Being summoned to touchline to replace injured Paul Thorburn on debut at Cardiff in 1989, and then Paul deciding to continue
Most embarrassing moment: As above
Most respected opponent: Former All Black Frano Botica (now Rugby League) in Sevens
Serious injuries: Popped rib cartilage

	apps.	pts.
Wales B (**1985**)		
Last Season	0 caps	0
1989	Tour to Canada	
Wales (**1989**)		
Last Season	0 caps	0
Career	3 caps	0

298

Other sporting achievements: Soccer for Ebbw Vale District (too small to make it professionally)

Most improved International player last season: England fly-half Rob Andrew

Suggestions to improve rugby: Alter whole curriculum of rugby calendar. Play game during summer months and take better care of pitches so that more games could be played in shorter space of time. Rugby days at present under used. Should be carnival atmosphere, like at Australian rugby league

Other notable landmarks in rugby career: Equally adept kicking off either foot. Hold season-scoring records at Newbridge (405 in 1983) and Newport (368 in 1986/87). Kicked 96 points in 13 matches for London Welsh, and have around 3,000 points in two spells at Newbridge. A Barbarian and the first Newbridge back to be capped by Wales. Returned to Newport last season

---

Ubogu, V.E. England

Full Name: Victor Eriakpo Ubogu
International category: England (development squad)
Club: Bath
Position: Loose-head prop
Height: 5'9" **Weight:** 16st
Occupation: Surveyor
Born: Lagos, Nigeria, 8.9.64
Family: Single
Former clubs: Moseley, Richmond
Best moment in rugby: Bath beating Toulouse last season
Worst moment in rugby: Not reaching last four with England in inaugural Student World Cup (1988) after losing to USSR and NZ
Best memory last season: Bath beating Gloucester 48–6 in Pilkington Cup final
Suggestions to improve rugby: There should be more regard for players. We tend to be ignored – not listened to enough

	apps.	pts.
England B (**1989/90**)	Rep 1	
England 1995	Development squad	

Other notable landmarks in rugby career: Played for Oxford in 10–15 loss to Cambridge in 1987 Varsity match

Underwood, R.   England

Full Name: Rory Underwood
International category: England Full
Club: Leicester
Position: Wing
Height: 5'9" **Weight:** 13st 7lb
Occupation: RAF pilot
Born: Middlesbrough, 19.6.63
Family: Married with child
Family links with rugby: Brother Tony plays for Leicester and England B
Former club: Middlesbrough
International debut: England 12, Ireland 9, 1984
Five Nations' debut: As above
Best moments in rugby: Scoring 2 tries for England in 34–6 defeat of Wales and first in 26–7 win over France in Paris (both last season)
Worst moment in rugby: England's 9-12 loss to Wales at Cardiff (1989)
Most embarrassing moment: Making error which led to Wales scoring crucial try against England in above match
Most respected opponent: French wing Patrice Lagisquet
Other sporting achievements: Swam and played cricket for Barnard Castle School, which England team-mate Rob Andrew also attended

	apps.	pts.
England B (**1982**)		
Last Season	0 caps	0
England (**1984**)		
Last Season	6 caps	36
Career	38 caps	88
1991	World Cup squad	
Lions 1986		
1989	3 Tests	0

Best memory last season: As above, and equalling Douglas Lambert's 82-year-old England record of 5 tries in an International (v Fiji)
Most improved International player last season: Rob Andrew

Suggestions to improve rugby: Continued improvement by Unions in looking after players and wives

Other notable landmarks in rugby career: Scored 2 tries for Leicester against Barbarians in 1983 – three months later was in England team. Missed tour to Argentina last summer, due to RAF commitments, having become England's most-capped back and highest try-scorer during 1989/90 season. Previously played for England Colts, U-23 and B teams. Toured Australia with 1989 Lions, playing in all three Tests

---

Underwood, T.   England

Full Name: Tony Underwood
International category: England B
Club: Leicester
Position: Wing
Height: 5'9" **Weight:** 12st 10lb
Occupation: Student
Born: Ipoh, Malaysia, 17.2.69
Family: Single
Family links with rugby: Brother Rory is England's record try-scorer
International debut: England B 12, Fiji 20, 1989
Best moments in rugby: Playing for Barbarians v 1989 All Blacks, and for Irish Wolfhounds in Hong Kong Sevens
Worst moment in rugby: Second half of 1989/90 when broke jaw, tore hamstring and damaged knee cartilage
Most respected opponents: Harlequins' England wing Andy Harriman and entire All Black XV
Serious injuries: As listed above
Best memory last season: Representing Barbarians in front of full house at Twickenham
Most improved International player last season: England fly-half Rob Andrew

	apps.	pts.
England B (1989)		
Last Season	1 cap	4
England 1990	Tour to Argentina	
1991	World Cup squad	
1995	Development squad	

Suggestions to improve rugby: Take necessary steps to prevent player drain to rugby league

Other notable landmarks in rugby career: Played for England Schools (18-Group) before graduating to England team for inaugural Student World Cup (1988). Gone on to represent Combined Students, England B, North of England and, latterly, England in 1990 summer tour of Argentina

Touchlines: Cricket and squash

Wainwright, R.I   Scotland

Full Name: Robert Iain Wainwright
International category: Scotland (Japan squad)
Club: Edinburgh Academicals
Position: Flanker
Height: 6'5" **Weight:** 15st 7lb
Occupation: Medical student
Born: Perth, 22.3.65
Family: Single
Family links with rugby: Father (J. F. Wainwright) a 1956 Cambridge Blue
Former club: Cambridge University
International debut (B): Italy 3, Scotland 26, 1988
Best moment in rugby: Watching Scotland win 1990 Grand Slam at Murrayfield
Worst moment in rugby: Cambridge Univ v Durham Univ (Jan 1988)
Most respected opponent: Scotland flanker John Jeffrey
Serious injuries: Broken cheek-bone (Jan 1990), ankle (Sept 1990)

	apps.	pts.
Scotland B (1988)		
Last Season	0 caps	0

Most improved International player last season: England centre Will Carling
Notable landmarks in rugby career: Cambridge Blue (1986), Barbarians Easter tour (1988), Hong Kong Sevens (1988,89), Scotland B (1988), touring Japan with Scotland – 2 games, 2 tries (1989)
Touchlines: Wildlife, fishing, photography, whisky

Wakeford, J.D.M.   Wales

Full Name: John Donald Marshall
Wakeford
International category: Wales B
Club: South Wales Police
Position: Lock
Height: 6'7" **Weight:** 17st 8lb
Occupation: Police Officer
Family: Single
Family links with rugby: Father is
former chairman of Glamorgan
Wanderers
Former club: Glamorgan
Wanderers
International debut: Wales 24,
Western Samoa 6, 1988
Best moment in rugby: Scoring
try on full debut against Samoans
Worst moment in rugby: Tearing
knee ligaments to miss 1989
Combined Services tour to New
Zealand
Most embarrassing moment:
South Wales Police's Welsh Cup
quarter-final defeat against
Llanharan in 1988/89
Serious injuries: Broken ribs, torn
knee ligaments

	apps.	pts.
Wales B (1989)		
Last Season	2 caps	0
Wales (1988)		
Last Season	0 caps	0
Career	2 caps	4

Other sporting achievements:
Former competitive swimmer
Best memory last season: The end of it
Most improved International player last season: Wales wing Arthur Emyr
Suggestions to improve rugby: More weight training and better all-round
fitness
Touchlines: Squash, swimming

Wareham, R.A.   England

Full Name: Richard Antony (Biff) Wareham
International category: England U-21
Club: Leicester
Position: Tight-head prop
Height: 5'11" **Weight:** 15st 10lb
Occupation: PE student
Born: Rugby, 24.1.68
Family: Single
Family links with rugby: Father (Gerald) played for Rugby Welsh
Former clubs: Sandal, Wakefield, Bradford & Bingley, Loughborough Students
International debut (U-21): Romania 13, England 54, 1989
Best moment in rugby: Winning UAU championship for third time with Loughborough (1990)
Worst moments in rugby: Dropped by Yorkshire U-21s in same season as playing for England 21s (1989). England Students losing 6-16 to Welsh in Cardiff (1989)

	apps.	pts.
England U-21 (**1989**)		
Last Season	1 cap	0
England 1995	Development squad	

Most embarrassing moment: Being tackled on rare occasion in possession and opposition running it back 75 yards for try
Most respected opponent: Rugby loose-head prop Andy Roda
Best memory last season: Playing for U-21s in Romania
Most improved International players last season: England front row men Paul Rendall and Brian Moore
Other notable landmarks in rugby career: Playing at Twickenham, Cardiff and Murrayfield in 1989. British Isles Select v Soviet Students (1988). Five caps for Combined England Students. Attending Loughborough – made more aware of requirements of game, how much fitness can improve performance

Full Name: Alan Michael Warwood
International category: Scotland U-21 (squad)
Club: London Scottish
Positions: Centre, full-back
Height: 6'1" **Weight:** 13st 12lb
Occupation: Life Assurance clerk
Born: Coventry, 2.4.69
Family: Single
Family links with rugby: Father is qualified RFU coach
Former clubs: Barkers Butts, Leicester
Best moment in rugby: Winning Colts County Championship twice with Warwickshire
Worst moment in rugby: Playing in Anglo-Scots team which lost 1989/90 Scottish Inter-District Championship decider 15–18 to Glasgow on last kick of game
Most respected opponent: Wales centre Mark Ring
Serious injuries: Broken nose (twice)

	apps.
Scotland U-21 (**1989/90**)	Rep 1

Other sporting achievements: County Schools cricket
Best memory last season: Making debut for Anglo-Scots against South of Scotland
Most improved International player last season: Scotland prop Paul Burnell
Other notable landmarks in rugby career: Former captain of Midlands Colts. Replacement when Scotland U-21s lost 10–24 to Wales at Millbrae, Ayr last season

Watkins, I.J.   Wales

Full Name: Ian John Watkins
International category: Wales B
Club: Cardiff
Position: Hooker
Height: 5'10" **Weight:** 14st 8lb
Occupation: Sales executive
Born: Blaina, 10.3.63
Family: Married with a son
Family links with rugby: Father
John played scrum-half for
Pontypool, Abertillery and Ebbw
Vale and captained Monmouth
Police and British Police
**Former clubs: RTB Youth,
Ebbw Vale**
International debut: England 3,
Wales 11, 1988
Five Nations' debut: As above
Best moment in rugby: Coming
on as last-minute replacement in
1988 at Twickenham
Worst moment in rugby: 1988
Welsh tour to New Zealand
Most embarrassing moment:
Being sent off v Pontypridd on
Boxing Day, 1990
Most respected opponent: New
Zealand hooker Sean Fitzpatrick –
excellent thrower-in of ball

	apps.	pts.
Wales B (**1986**)		
Last Season	1 cap	0
Wales (**1988**)		
Last Season	Rep 3	
Career	10 caps	4

Serious injuries: Knee ligaments, badly strained back
Other sporting achievements: Soccer trials for Coventry City
Best memory last season: Cardiff 15, New Zealand 25
**Most improved International player last season: England hooker Brian
Moore**
Suggestions to improve rugby: End midweek matches to allow players to
train harder during week
Other notable landmarks in rugby career: Started career as scrum-half
and centre before moving into pack at senior school. Scored try v Scotland
(1988) in first game he started. Captained 1988 Barbarians at Leicester
and on 1989 Easter tour. Younger half of only father and son combination
to play for Ebbw Vale. First hooker from Ebbw Vale to play for Wales
Touchlines: Weight training, golf

Webb, J.M.   England

Full Name: Jonathan Mark Webb
International category: England
Full (squad)
Club: Bath
Position: Full-back
Height: 6'2½" **Weight:** 13st 8lb
Occupation: Doctor
Born: London, 24.8.63
Former clubs: Northern, Bristol
International debut: England 6,
Australia 19, 1987 World Cup
Five Nations' debut: France 10,
England 9, 1988
**Other notable landmarks in
rugby career:** Educated in
Newcastle and played for Northern
before medical studies forced move
to West Country. Represented
England B before making England
debut as replacement for concussed
Marcus Rose in 1987 World Cup.
Returned to Australia on 1988
England tour. Lost England
full-back slot to Simon Hodgkinson
in May 1989. Joined Bath late last
season

	apps.	pts.
England B (1987)		
Last Season	0 caps	0
England (1987)		
Last Season	Rep 2	
Career	16 caps	102
1995	Development squad	

Webster, R.E.   Wales

Full Name: Richard Edward
Webster
International category: Wales
(World Cup squad)
Club: Swansea
Position: Flanker
Height: 6'2" **Weight:** 14st 7lb
Occupation: Sales representative
Born: Morriston, 9.7.67
Family: Single with daughter
Former club: Bonymaen
International debut: Wales 22,
Australia 21, 1987
Best moment in rugby: Winning
first Wales cap in World Cup third
place play-off
Worst moment in rugby: Getting
injured
Most respected opponent: All of
them
Serious injuries: Five operations
on knee
Best memory last season:
Coming on as replacement for
Swansea in Welsh Cup semi-finals
– first game back after two and a
half years out injured
**Most improved International
player last season:** England flanker Peter Winterbottom
Other notable landmarks in rugby career: Won 6 caps for Wales Youth
(1984–86). Selected for Wales' 1991 World Cup squad
Touchlines: Horse riding, weightlifting

	apps.	pts.
Wales (1987)		
Last Season	0 caps	0
Career	1 cap	0
1991	World Cup squad	

Weir, G.W.   Scotland

Full Name: George Wilson
(Doddie) Weir
International category: Scotland B
Club: Melrose
Positions: No.8, lock
Height: 6'7" **Weight:** 15st
Occupation: Agricultural student
Born: Edinburgh, 4.7.70
Family: Single
Family links with rugby: Father
played for Gala. Brother plays for
Stewart's-Melville School
International debut (B): Scotland
22, Ireland 22, 1990
Best moment in rugby: Being
picked for Scotland's tour to New
Zealand last season
Most respected opponent:
Scotland flanker John Jeffrey
Other sporting achievements:
Stow sprint champion. Completing
Thirlestone cross-country (horses)
Best memory last season:
Winning Scottish First Division
with Melrose
**Most improved International
player last season:** Scotland wing
Tony Stanger

	apps.	pts.
Scotland U-21 (**1990**)		
Last Season	1 cap	0
Scotland 1990	Tour to New Zealand	

Suggestions to improve rugby: Abolish conversions and instead increase
worth of tries
Other notable landmarks in rugby career: Toured New Zealand with
Scottish Schools (1988) and Scotland (1990). Represented South of Scotland
in Inter-District Championship, Scotland B and Scotland U-21s (v Wales,
1990). Played four games for Scotland in New Zealand last summer
Touchlines: Horse riding (one-day eventing), clay pigeon shooting

Wells, J.M.   England

Full Name: John Martin Wells
International category: England B
Club: Leicester
Position: Flanker
Height: 6'1" **Weight:** 13st 10lb
Occupation: Leisure property
consultant
Born: Driffield, Yorks, 12.5.63
Family: Married
Former clubs: Loughborough
Students, Newark
International debut: Spain 9,
England B 31, 1989
Best moment in rugby: 1988/89
Pilkington Cup final
Worst moment in rugby:
Leicester losing to Bath in
last-minute of above game
Most respected opponent: All
Black flanker Michael Jones
(Leicester v NZ Barbarians)
Serious injuries: Broken
collarbone, wrist, ribs and fingers.
Damaged knee ligaments and
cartilage
Best memory last season:
Playing for England XV in 33–15
win against Italy XV

	apps.	pts.
England B (1988)		
Last Season	1 cap	0
England XV 1989/90	1 app	0

Most improved International player last season: Scotland prop Paul
Burnell
Suggestions to improve rugby: Make necessary alterations to ensure that
players do not lose out financially for playing game
Other notable landmarks in rugby career: Represented England U-16s,
U-18s, Students and U-23s. Toured Spain with England B (1989)

White, A.   Ireland

Full Name: Aidan White
International category: Ireland U-21
Club: Corinthians
Position: Full-back
Height: 6'1" **Weight:** 13st
Occupation: Bank official
Birthplace: Galway, 23.9.68
Family: Single
Family links with rugby: Father
International debut (U-21):
Ireland 10, Italy 9, 1989
Best moment in rugby: Winning my first cap at Schools level against Scotland
Worst moment in rugby: Losing my first Senior Cup final with Corinthians
Serious injuries sustained: Dislocated shoulder and collarbone
Other sporting achievements: Soccer trials with Everton FC. Turned down soccer scholarship to USA

	apps.	pts.
Ireland U-21 (1989)		
Last Season	2 caps	3

Best memory last season: Tour to Italy with Irish U-21s
Most improved International player last season: Ireland full-back Kenny Murphy
Notable landmark in rugby career: First Connacht Schoolboy to play for Irish Schools
Touchlines: Soccer, golf, squash and snooker

White, D.B.   Scotland

Full Name: Derek Bolton White
International category: Scotland
Full
Club: London Scottish
Positions: No.8, lock, flanker
Height: 6'4½" **Weight:** 16st
Occupation: Sales manager
Born: Haddington, 30.1.58
Family: Married
Family links with rugby: Kenyan
(brother) plays for Harlequins
Former clubs: Dunbar,
Haddington, Gala
International debut: Scotland 16,
France 7, 1982
Five Nations' debut: As above
Best moment in rugby: Winning
1990 Grand Slam
Worst moment in rugby: 1989
Lions' first Test defeat (12–30) v
Australia

	apps.	pts.
Scotland B (**1982**)		
Last Season	0 caps	0
Scotland (**1982**)		
Last Season	8 caps	12
Career	26 caps	24
Lions 1989	1 Test	0

Most embarrassing moment:
Missing an opponent and hitting
John Jeffrey instead
Most respected opponent: Jock
Beattie. He combined strength,
skill, and a determination to win
with a really mean streak
Serious injuries: Severed medial
ligament in left knee (New Zealand
1981)
Best memory last season: All the fun we (Scotland) had!
Most improved International player last season: Scotland lock Chris Gray
Suggestions to improve rugby: Get the Unions into the 20th century.
Appoint team managers. Allow payments for books, articles, appearances etc
Other notable landmarks in rugby career: Toured with Scotland to New
Zealand (1981 and 1990), Australia (1982), France (1986) and World Cup
(1987), and went to Australia (1989) with Lions. Have played in each of back
five positions for country. Played in seven games for 1989 Lions, scoring 1
try. Scotland replacement 13 times. Have played Inter-District rugby for
Edinburgh, the South and Anglo-Scots

Williams, B.V.   Wales

Full Name: Brian Victor Williams
International category: Wales Full
Club: Neath
Position: Prop
Height: 6'1" **Weight:** 13st 10lb
Occupation: Farmer
Born: Penffordd, 9.7.62
Family: Married
Family links with rugby: Younger
brother played for Wales U-15s
Former club: Narberth
International debut: Wales 9,
Scotland 13, 1990
Five Nations' debut: As above
Best moment in rugby: Winning
first full cap, at Cardiff
Worst moment in rugby:
Dislocating shoulder three times
and needing two operations and
two years' away from game to solve
problem
Most respected opponent:
Ireland prop Des Fitzgerald
Serious injuries: Shoulder
dislocations
Best memory last season: Neath
beating Bridgend 16–10 to win
Schweppes Welsh Cup

	apps.	pts.
Wales B (1985)		
Last Season	0 caps	0
Wales (1990)		
Last Season	2 caps	0
Career	2 caps	0

Other notable landmarks in rugby career: Did not take up game until aged
17 when he joined Narberth. Spotted by Neath in Pembrokeshire team that
beat Japan. Won first and only B cap five years ago

Williams, D.A.   Wales

Full Name: David **Aled** Williams
International category: Wales Full
Club: Bridgend
Position: Scrum-half
Height: 5'5" **Weight:** 11st 2lb
Occupation: Surveyor
Born: Cardigan, 26.1.64
Family: Single
Former clubs: Llanelli, Swansea
International debut: Namibia 30,
Wales 34, 1990
Best moment in rugby: Wales
debut in second Test at Windhoek
Worst moment in rugby:
Bridgend losing 1990 Welsh Cup
final to Neath
Most respected opponent:
Australian half-back Mark Ella
Best memory last season:
Reaching Cup final and being
selected to tour Namibia
**Most improved International
player last season:** Wales centre
Allan Bateman
**Other notable landmarks in
rugby career:** Played for Welsh

Wales (1990)	apps.	pts.
Last Season	1 cap	0
Career	1 cap	0

Schools (U-18) and Welsh
Students. Included in Wales B squad but never played. Represented Wales
in Hong Kong Sevens
Touchlines: Golf, squash

Williams, O.L.   Wales

Full Name: Owain Llewellyn Williams
International category: Wales Full
Club: Bridgend
Position: No.8
Height: 6'6" **Weight:** 15st 7lb
Occupation: TV design student
Born: Bridgend, 10.10.64
Family: Single
Family links with rugby: Brother Gareth played for Bridgend and Wales. Father played for Pontypridd
Former clubs: Glamorgan Wanderers, Queensland (Aus)
International debut: Namibia 30, Wales 34, 1990
Best moment in rugby: Winning first cap in second Test at Windhoek
Worst moment in rugby: Bridgend losing 1990 Welsh Cup final
Most respected opponent: Neath's Wales No.8 Mark Jones
Other sporting achievements: Basketball and cross-country for Mid-Glamorgan Schools

	apps.	pts.
Wales (1990)		
Last Season	1 cap	4
Career	1 cap	4

Best memory last season: Walking out onto Cardiff Arms Park for first time – unbelievable noise
Most improved International player last season: French wing Patrice Lagisquet
Suggestions to improve rugby: Throw out half the rules: make game more simple and less technical
Other notable landmarks in rugby career: Represented Welsh Schools (U-18), Students and Academicals. Also played for Crawshays, Public School Wanderers and Barbarians (v Penarth). Played against England and New Zealand while with Queensland in 1988. Toured Namibia with Wales last season

Williams, S.M.   Wales

Full Name: Steven Michael Williams
International category: Wales U-21
Club: Swansea
Positions: No.8, flanker
Height: 6'5" **Weight:** 17st
Occupation: Trainee quantity surveyor
Born: Neath, 3.10.70
Family: Single
Former club: Bryncoch
International debut (U-21): Scotland 10, Wales 24, 1990
Best moment in rugby: Scoring try for Wales against Singapore in Hong Kong Sevens
Worst moment in rugby: Namibian tour – did not go as I had planned
Most respected opponent: Bath's England lock Nigel Redman – he gave me a good hiding in my first game for Swansea
Serious injuries: Torn ankle ligaments (1989/90)

	apps.	pts.
Wales U-21 (**1990**)		
Last Season	1 cap	0
Wales (**1989/90**)	Namibia squad	

Best memory last season:
Coming on as replacement for Wales in quarter-final win over Australia at Hong Kong Sevens
Most improved International player last season: England centre Will Carling
Suggestions to improve rugby: Change training times from evenings to mornings
Other notable landmarks in rugby career: Played for Welsh Schools and Welsh Tertiary Colleges. Captained Wales U-21s last season before touring Namibia with Wales

Williams-Jones, H.   Wales

Full Name: Hugh Williams-Jones
International category: Wales Full
Club: South Wales Police
Position: Prop
Height: 6' **Weight:** 16st 7lb
Occupation: Police officer
Former clubs: Bridgend,
Pontypridd
International debut: Scotland 23,
Wales 7, 1989
Five Nations' debut: As above
Best moment in rugby: Winning
first full cap
Worst moment in rugby: After
coming on as replacement against
Scotland, not being selected for
next match against Ireland
Most embarrassing moment:
South Wales Police's Welsh Cup
quarter-final defeat against
Llanharan in 1988/89
Most respected opponent:
Scotland prop David Sole
Other sporting achievements:
Glamorgan County Cricket U-15
cap
Best memory last season: Being
selected for third Full cap, against
Ireland

	apps.	pts.
Wales B (1989)		
Last Season	1 cap	0
Wales (1989)		
Last Season	2 caps	0
Career	3 caps	0

Most improved International player last season: Scotland wing Tony
Stanger
Other notable landmarks in rugby career: Winning 3 Welsh Youth caps
and 1 at B level. Have been on two Welsh tours

Wilson, D.J.   Scotland

Full Name: Duncan James Wilson
International category: Scotland U-21 (squad)
Club: Currie
Position: Tight-head prop
Height: 5'11" **Weight:** 17st
Occupation: Electrical control engineer
Born: Bathgate, 7.12.68
Family: Single
Former club: Livingston
International debut (U-21):
Scotland 21, Combined Services 4, 1990 (non-cap)
Best moment in rugby: Selection for Scotland U-21s
Most embarrassing moment: Being stripped by team mates after game on 17th birthday
Most respected opponent: Edinburgh Wanderers' loose-head (1988/89) – I had just moved from hooker to prop and he gave me a lesson

	apps.
Scotland U-21 **(1989/90)**	Rep 1

Best memory last season:
Currie's promotion to Scottish First Division
Most improved International player last season: Scotland prop Paul Burnell
Suggestions to improve rugby: Leave the laws alone!
Other notable landmarks in rugby career: Being the only person from my school year still to be playing rugby

Wilson, G.D.   Scotland

Full Name: Grant Douglas Wilson
International category: Scotland B
Club: Boroughmuir
Position: Prop
Height: 5'11" **Weight:** 16st 7lb
Occupation: Police officer
Born: Edinburgh, 10.11.66
Family: Single
Family links with rugby: Named after great Hawick rugby brothers of Jake, Oliver and Derrick Grant
Former club: Preston Lodge
International debut (B): Scotland 22, Ireland 22, 1989
Best moment in rugby: Being selected by Scotland at tight-head for non-cap Test v Japan in Tokyo (1989) in front of specialist tight-heads
Worst moment in rugby: Losing 9-31 to France B (1990)
Most embarrassing moment: Catching ball inside own 22, somebody else calling 'mark', and having to take resulting kick myself

	apps.	pts.
Scotland B (1989)		
Last Season	2 caps	0
Scotland (1989/90)	Rep 1	

Most respected opponents: Scotland props Iain Mine and David Sole
Other sporting achievements: 1989 Scottish Youth sprint and marathon canoeing champion
Best memory last season: Touring Japan with Scottish squad
Most improved International player last season: Scotland wing Tony Stanger
Suggestions to improve rugby: Establish a Scottish knock-out cup competition and reduce size of First Division from fourteen to ten clubs
Other notable landmarks in rugby career: Played for South of Scotland U-16s, Edinburgh and Scotland U-18s (1983–85), U-21s (1985–89), British Police, and Edinburgh District side. Last season represented Scotland XV v Japan, Scotland B v Ireland and France, and was on replacements' bench for Scotland v Fiji

Windo, A.J.   England

Full Name: Anthony John Windo
International category: England U-21
Club: Gloucester
Position: Loose-head prop
Height: 6' **Weight:** 15st 2lb
Occupation: Warehouse supervisor
Born: Gloucester, 30.4.69
Family: Married with son
Family links with rugby: Grandfather played
Former clubs: Longlevens, Gloucester Spartans
International debut: French Armed Forces 16, England U-21 23, 1990
Best moment in rugby: Being selected for England U-21s
Worst moment in rugby: Missing half of 1987 season with damaged knee ligaments
Most respected opponent: Gloucester's former England prop Malcolm Preedy (in training)
Serious injuries: Damaged knee ligaments (in plaster for seven weeks)

	apps.	pts.
England U-21 (**1990**)		
Last Season	1 cap	0

Other sporting achievements: Cricket for Gloucester Schools
Best memory last season: Making League debut for Gloucester against Saracens
Most improved International player last season: England centre Will Carling
Suggestions to improve rugby: None – happy with progress being made
Other notable landmarks in rugby career: Started career with Longlevens mini-section. Played two seasons for Gloucester Colts, captaining them through unbeaten 1986/87 season. Invited to tour Portugal with club (1987)
Touchlines: Weight training

Winterbottom, P.J.   England

Full Name: Peter James Winterbottom
International category: England Full
Club: Harlequins
Position: Flanker
Height: 6' **Weight:** 14st 10lb
Occupation: Inter-dealer Euro-bond broker
Born: Horsforth, Leeds, 31.5.60
Family: Single
Family links with rugby: Father played for Headingley and is past President
Former clubs: Fleetwood, Headingley, Exeter, Napier HS OBs (NZ), Hawkes Bay (NZ), Durban HS OBs (SA), Merolomas (Vancouver, Can)
International debut: England 15, Australia 11, 1982
Five Nations' debut: Scotland 9, England 9, 1982
Best moment in rugby: Making England debut against touring Wallabies
Worst moment in rugby: There has not been one
Most embarrassing moment: Being caught from behind by Gareth Chilcott, playing touch rugby

	apps.	pts.
England B (**1981**)		
Last Season	0 caps	0
England (**1982**)		
Last Season	8 caps	0
Career	37 caps	8
1990	Tour to Argentina	
1991	World Cup squad	
Lions 1983	4 Tests	0

Most respected opponent: Former French flanker Jean-Pierre Rives – a legend
Serious injuries: My brain
Other sporting achievements: School U-16 tennis champion
Best memories last season: Winning Middlesex Sevens for record seventh time with Harlequins. England's 26–7 defeat of France in Paris
Most improved International player last season: England fly-half Rob Andrew

Other notable landmarks in rugby career: Much travelled. Shot up the representative ranks following impressive displays for Yorkshire, and England against France in 1981 B International. Represented England Colts at No.8, before switching to flanker, where played for Yorkshire. Tours included New Zealand with 1983 Lions, and South Africa (1984) and World Cup (1987) with England. Played club rugby all over world

Wyllie, D.S. Scotland

Full Name: Douglas Stewart Wyllie
International category: Scotland
Full
Club: Stewart's Melville
Positions: Fly-half, centre
Height: 6'1" **Weight:** 13st 10lb
Occupation: Sports sales rep
Born: Edinburgh, 20.5.63
Family: Married
International debut: Scotland 12,
Australia 37, 1984
Five Nations' debut: Scotland 21,
Wales 25, 1985
Best moment in rugby: Winning
1982 Middlesex Sevens at
Twickenham with Stewart's
Melville as an 18-year-old
Worst moment in rugby: Playing in
Scotland XV which lost 1989 'Test'
24–28 to Japan in Tokyo – we took them for granted
Most embarrassing moment: As above
Most respected opponent: Former Scotland No.8 John Beattie – most aggressive player I have ever come up against
Serious injuries: Broken bone in foot (1987/88)
Other sporting achievements: Soccer for England U-13 Schoolboys
Best memory last season: Landing injury-time drop goal to beat Selkirk and keep Stewart's Melville in the First Division
Most improved International player last season: Scotland lock Chris Gray
Suggestions to improve rugby: Remuneration for working time lost to rugby. Allow players to benefit from off-field activities (e.g. speech-making) related to the game

Notable landmarks in rugby career: Called into Scotland senior squad aged 19, having twice represented Scotland B in 1982. Selected to Scotland bench in 1983. Spent early years in England, where educated at Dulwich College in south London, and also in Yorkshire. Did not take up rugby until aged 14. Ever-present for Scotland in 1987 World Cup, moving from centre to fly-half after John Rutherford broke-down in opening match

Touchlines: Golf (14-handicapper at Baberton GC). Hearts soccer fan (my company sponsor the club)

Late Entry:

Buchanan-Smith, G.A.   Scotland

Full Name: George **Adam** Buchanan-Smith
International category: Scotland Full
Club: Heriot's F.P.
Position: Flanker
Height: 6'2" **Weight:** 14st 2lb
Occupation: P.E. Teacher
Born: 26.7.64
Family: Single
Family links with rugby: Brother Stuart plays for London Scottish
Former club: London Scottish
International debut: Scotland 38, Fiji 17, 1989
Notable landmark in rugby career: Won first full cap against Fijians last season after coming on as 65th minute replacement for Graham Marshall. Toured New Zealand with Scotland last summer

Retirees

Anderson, W.A.   Ireland

Full Name: William Andrew Anderson
International category: Ireland Full
Club: Dungannon
Position: Second row
Height: 6'4½" **Weight:** 15st 10lb
Occupation: Regional Technical Officer for Irish Rugby Football Union
Born: Sixmilecross, 3.4.55
Family: Married with two sons
Family links with rugby: Brother played for Omagh
Former clubs: Kings' Scholars, Omagh
International debut: Ireland 9, Australia 16, 1984
Five Nations' debut: Ireland 9, Scotland 32, 1984
Best moments in rugby: Winning 1985 Triple Crown with Ireland. Captaining Ireland v 1989 All Blacks
Worst moment in rugby: Being dropped five times
Most embarrassing moment: Taking Argentine flag and getting arrested, in Buenos Aires on 1980 Penguins tour
Most respected opponent: Wales lock Bob Norster – one of the great line-out jumpers
Other sporting achievements: Represented Ulster at athletics
Best memory last season: Captaining Ireland v New Zealand
Most improved International player last season: Ireland flanker Pat O'Hara

	apps.	pts.
Ireland (**1984**)		
Last Season	3 caps	0
Career	27 caps	4

Suggestions to improve rugby: Because of time spent away for International training and matches, maybe a trip for girlfriends/wives and family at end of season

Other notable landmarks in rugby career: Playing for Ireland over last six years – won six Inter-Provincial titles and beaten five International teams. Retired from game midway through last season

Touchlines: Weight training, gardening, swimming, spending time with my family

---

Calder, F.   Scotland

Full Name: Finlay Calder OBE
International category: Scotland Full
Club: Stewart's Melville FP
Position: Flanker
Height: 6'1" **Weight:** 15st 7lb
Occupation: Grain shipper
Born: Haddington, 20.8.57
Family: Married with two children
Family links with rugby: Jim (twin brother) capped by Scotland and Lions; John (brother) capped Scotland B and was third Calder on 1982 Australia tour; Gavin (eldest brother) played at district level
Former club: Melrose
International debut: Scotland 18, France 17, 1986
Five Nations' debut: As above
Best moment in rugby: Winding up John Jeffrey prior to the 1990 Grand Slam decider
Worst moment in rugby: Being referred to as 'Buftie' by younger members of club
Most respected opponent: New Zealand flanker Michael Jones – quite simply the best

	apps.	pts.
Scotland B (**1983**)		
Last Season	0 caps	0
Scotland (**1986**)		
Last Season	7 caps	4
Career	28 caps	8
Lions 1989	3 Tests	0

Other sporting achievements: Birdie 3 at second hole at Lauder Golf Club
Best memory last season: Winning Grand Slam
Most improved International player last season: Ireland full-back Kenny Murphy
Suggestions to improve rugby: Don't take yourself or the game too seriously – it's supposed to be played for fun
Other notable landmarks in rugby career: 1989 Scotland captain. Captained 1989 British Lions to 2-1 Test series win in Australia (Lions first for fifteen years). Scored second International try in 21–0 defeat of France last season. Retired from game after Scotland's end-of-season tour to New Zealand (1990)

Davies, C.   Wales

Full Name: Carwyn Davies
International category: Wales Full (squad)
Club: Llanelli
Position: Wing
Height: 5'10" **Weight:** 13st 3lb
Occupation: Farmer
Born: Llangadog
Family: Married
Former club: Llandovery
International debut: Wales 24, Western Samoa 6, 1988
Five Nations' debut: Scotland 23, Wales 7, 1989
Best moment in rugby: Breaking Llanelli try-scoring record with 45 in 1987/88
Most respected opponent: Former Australia wing Peter Grigg
Serious injuries: Sprung shoulder joint on full debut against Western Samoa
Best memory last season: Scoring 100th try for Llanelli and becoming only 14th player to do so

	apps.	pts.
Wales B (1988)		
Last Season	0 caps	0
Wales (1988)		
Last Season	Rep 2	
Career	4 caps	4

Most improved International player last season: England centre Jeremy Guscott
Reason for retiring: Taking over farm from parents
Suggestions to improve rugby: More consideration for players. Unions expect so much (time off etc)
Other notable landmarks in rugby career: Fly-half in formative years. Had trials with Wales Youth. Joined Llanelli after playing against Scarlets for Llandovery in Welsh Cup. In addition to full Wales honours, also represented Wales B
Touchlines: Cricket

Dean, P.   Ireland

Full Name: Paul Dean
International category: Ireland Full/Lions
Club: St Mary's College
Position: Fly-half
Height: 5'9½" **Weight:** 12st 6lb
Occupation: Sales representative
Born: Dublin, 28.8.60
International debut: South Africa 23, Ireland 15, 1981
Five Nations' debut: Ireland 20, Wales 12, 1982
Serious injuries: Torn lateral cartilage in right knee (after 20 minutes of 1989 Lions' opening match against Western Australia)
Reasons for retiring: Serious knee injury, business commitments
Other notable landmarks in rugby career: Represented Ireland Schools (1977–78). Played in Ireland's two Triple Crown winning teams, 1987 World Cup, and with Barbarians and Lions (Senior International on 1989 tour)

	apps.	pts.
Ireland (1981)		
Last Season	0 caps	0
Career	32 caps	19
Lions 1989		

Devereux, J.   Wales

Full Name: John Devereux
International category: Wales Full
Former club: Bridgend
New Club: Widnes RLFC
Position: Centre
Height: 6'1" **Weight:** 14st 2lb
Occupation: Surveyor
Born: Pontycymmer, 30.3.66
International debut: England 21,
Wales 18, 1986
Five Nations' debut: As above
Serious injuries: Accident prone
**Other notable landmarks in rugby
career:** Made international debut
against England aged just 19 and went
on to collect 21 caps in three years
before 'heading North' to join Widnes

	apps.	pts.
Wales (**1986**)		
Last Season	To Rugby League	
Career	21 caps	20
Lions 1989		

Ellis, K.S.   Wales

Full Name: Kevin Stewart Ellis
International category: Wales B (squad)
Former club: Bridgend
New club: Warrington RLFC
Position: Scrum-half
Height: 5'9" **Weight:** 13st
Born: Bridgend, 29.5.65
Family: Single
Best moments in rugby: Helping Bridgend beat Wales XV 24-17 and reach Schweppes Cup final (both 1989/90)
Worst moment in rugby: Fracturing cheekbone in a Bridgend trial
Most respected opponent: Wales wing Arthur Emyr
Serious injuries: Fractured cheekbone
Other sporting achievements: Four Welsh lifesaving caps. Green belt in karate
Best memory last season: Scoring hat-trick of tries for Wales B in 52–13 defeat of Alberta (Canada)

Wales B (**1989/90**)	Rep 1
1989	Tour to Canada
	To Rugby League

Most improved international player last season: England No.8 Mike Teague
Suggestions to improve rugby: Make game more family-orientated to encourage increased support. Clubs and committees must treat players with more respect. Players should receive fringe benefits as in New Zealand to promote more enthusiasm and dedication
Other notable landmarks in rugby career: Played in three games on Wales B's Canadian tour (1989). Replacement for Wales B v France B (1989/90). Switched codes to Warrington RLFC in £100,000 deal at end of last season
Touchlines: Lifesaving, swimming, golf

Young, D.   Wales

Full Name: David Young
International category: Wales Full
Former club: Cardiff
New club: Leeds RLFC
Position: Tight-head prop
Height: 6'1" **Weight:** 16st 5lb
Born: Aberdare, 27.6.67
International debut: Wales 16,
England 3, 1987
Five Nations' debut: England 3,
Wales 11, 1988
**Other notable landmarks in
rugby career:** Bizarre introduction
to Welsh senior team, being
recruited to play v England in 1987
World Cup quarter-final, having
only travelled to tournament as a
spectator. Instantly became
first-choice and impressed Lions
management enough to earn invite
on 1989 tour where played in all
three Tests. Former captain of
Wales Youth, U-15 and U-16
teams, who also played for
Aberaman Youth and Swansea.
Switched codes to Leeds RLFC in
£150,000 deal last season

	apps.	pts.
Wales (1987)		
Last season	To Rugby League	
Career	12 caps	0
Lions 1989	3 Tests	0

International Results

The 1989/90 'season', as recognised in this book, runs from 13 May 1989 to 4 August 1990. Details are given of every International match played during the season (at or above U-21 level). In the case of tours, results, appearances (signified by the relevant match number after the player's name) and scorers have been logged. 'R' indicates an appearance as a replacement.

Romania 3, England 58
Bucharest, 13 May 1989

England: S Hodgkinson; R Underwood, S Halliday, J Guscott, C Oti; R Andrew (capt), S Bates, P Rendall, B Moore, G Chilcott (J Probyn 2), W Dooley, P Ackford, M Teague, P Winterbottom, D Richards (G Rees 25).

Scorers – Tries: Guscott 3, Oti 4, Probyn. **Conversions:** Hodgkinson 8. **Penalty goal:** Hodgkinson. **Dropped goal:** Andrew.

Romania U-21 13, England U-21 54
Bucharest, 13 May 1989

England: S Pilgrim (capt); P Hull, P de Glanville, G Thompson, D Essien; D Pears (H Thorneycroft 35), R Moon; M Hynes, N Killick, R Wareham, M Poole, S Shortland, M Harris, N Back, T Rodber.

Scorers – Tries: Moon, de Glanville 2, Back 3, Essien, Thompson, Thorneycroft, Killick.

Conversions: Pears, Pilgrim 6.

ENGLAND B TO SPAIN
May 1989: 3 games

PARTY: J Callard (1,2,3), **E Davis** (1), **N Heslop** (2,3), **S Hackney** (1,2,3), **R Lozowski** (1,3), **G Hartley** (1,2), **S Irving** (1R,2,3R), **M Hamlin** (1,3), **G Ainscough** (2,3), **G Doggart** (1,3), **C Luxton** (2), **A Sharp** (1,2,3), **M Linnett** (2,3), **A Mullins** (1,3), **K Dunn** (1), **N Hitchen** (2,3), **J Etheridge** (1,2), **R Kimmins** (2,3), **J Morrison** (1,3), **J Wells** (1,2R,3), **I Smith** (2), **D Pegler** (capt) (1,3), **D Ryan** (1,2), **D Thresher** (2,3).

Results: (1) Basque XV 3, England B 63 (7 May, San Sebastian); (2) Spanish

Select 15, England B 32 (10 May, Villa Joyosa); (3) **Spain 9, England B 31** (14 May, Madrid).

Scorers: Hamlin 26 (10c, 3p), Hackney 16 (4t), Ainscough 12 (3c, 2p), Hartley 12 (3t), Callard 12 (3t), Lozowski 8 (2t), Linnett 8 (2t), Heslop 4 (1t), Wells 4 (1t), Dunn 4 (1t), Luxton 4 (1t), Hitchen 4 (1t), Pegler 4 (1t), Doggart 4 (1t), Morrison 4 (1t).

Record: P3, W3, L0, F126, A27.

Spain 9, England B 31
Madrid, 13 May 1989

England B: J Callard; N Heslop, R Lozowski, G Ainscough (S Irving), S Hackney; M Hamlin, G Doggart; A Sharp (M Linnett), N Hitchen, A Mullins, J Morrison, R Kimmins, J Wells, D Pegler (capt), D Thresher.

Scorers – Tries: Pegler, Doggart, Morrison, Linnett, Callard, Hackney. **Conversions:** Hamlin 2. **Penalty goal:** Hamlin.

SCOTLAND TO JAPAN
May 1989: 5 games

Japan record their first ever victory over an International Board country when they beat error-prone Scotland on a convincing five-one try count in Tokyo's Chichibu Stadium. Despite fielding 11 capped players, there are no caps to be won as Scotland choose not to recognise the match as a full international.

PARTY: I Ramsey (2,4), C Glasgow (1,3,5), M Duncan (1,3,4,5), A Stanger (2,4), I Tukalo (1,2,3,5), B Edwards (1,4), S Lineen (1,2,3,5), R Maclean (1R,2,3,4,5), D Wyllie (1,3,5), M Walker (2,4), S Jardine (2,4), G Oliver (1,3,5), A Brewster (capt) (1,3,4,5), D Milne (2), G Wilson (2,4,5), P Wright (1,3), J Hay (1,3,5), I Corcoran (2,4), D Cronin (2,3,4,5), C Gray (1,2,3,5), S Munroe (1,4), G Marshall (1,4,5), A Buchanan-Smith (2,3,4), D Turnbull (1,3,5), R Wainwright (2,4), I Paxton (1,2,3,5).

Results: (1) Kanto 8, Scotland XV 91 (14 May, Tokyo); (2) Kyushu 0, Scotland XV 45 (17 May, Fukuoka); (3) Japan U-23 25, Scotland XV 51 (21 May, Osaka); (4) Kansai 12, Scotland XV 39 (24 May, Najoya); (5) **Japan 28, Scotland XV 24** (28 May, Tokyo).

Scorers: Glasgow 66 (3t, 21c, 4p), Ramsey 24 (5c, 4p), Tukalo 24 (6t), Duncan 24 (6t), Oliver 17 (1c, 5p), Maclean 12 (3t), Stanger 12 (3t), Gray 12 (3t), Walker 10 (1t, 3c), Wainwright 8 (2t), Buchanan-Smith 8 (2t), Wyllie 7 (1t, 1dg), Paxton 4 (1t), Lineen 4 (1t), Brewster 4 (1t), Edwards 4 (1t), Turnbull 4 (1t), Corcoran 4 (1t), Hay 4 (1t).

Record: P5, W4, L1, F251, A73.

WALES B TO CANADA
May-June 1989: 6 games

PARTY: P Thorburn (capt) (1,3,4,5,6), S Ford (1,3,4,6), A Emyr (1,2,3,4,5,6), D Griffiths (2,5), C Jones (1,2,4,6), D Evans (2,3,4), C Laity (3,5,6R), M Ring (1,2,4R,5,6), C Stephens (1,3,4,6), P Turner (2,3R,4), C Bridges (1,4,6), K Ellis (2,3,5), R Evans (1,3,5), L Delaney (1,4,6), S Jones (2,4,6), H Williams-Jones (2,3,5), I Watkins (1,2,4,6), P John (3,5), J Wakeford (1,2,4,5,6), Gareth Llewellyn (1,3,4,6), A Sutton (2,3,5,6R), M Jones (1,2,4), D Hopkins (2,3,5), M Budd (1,3,4,6), D Bryant (1,2,4,5,6), I Jones (3,5,6).

Results: (1) Nova Scotia 3, Wales B 70 (Halifax, 24 May); (2) Ontario 10, Wales B 23 (Toronto, 27 May); (3) Saskatchewan 0, Wales B 47 (Regina, 31 May); (4) CANADA 29, WALES B 31 (Edmonton, 3 June); (5) Alberta 13, Wales B 53 (Calgary, 6 June); (6) British Columbia 21, Wales B 21 (Vancouver, 9 June).

Scorers: P Thorburn 56 (1t, 14c, 8p), S Ford 48 (12t), A Emyr 36 (9t), K Ellis 16 (4t), M Jones 12 (3t), D Bryant 12 (3t), M ring 12 (3t), C Laity 12 (3t), P Turner 11 (1c, 3p), C Stephens 10 (2t, 1c), C Bridges 4 (1t), M Budd 4 (1t), R Evans 4 (1t), C Jones 4 (1t), penalty try (4).

Record: P6, W5, D1, L0, F245, A76.

Canada 29, Wales B 31
Edmonton, 3 June 1989

Wales B: P Thorburn (capt); S Ford, C Jones, D Evans (M Ring), A Emyr; C Stephens, C Bridges; S Jones, I Watkins, L Delaney, G Llewellyn, J Wakeford, M Budd, D Bryant, M Jones (**sent off for stamping**).

Scorers – Tries: Stephens, Ford, Emyr, C Jones, Thorburn. **Conversions:** Thorburn 4.

Penalty goal: Thorburn.

BRITISH LIONS TO AUSTRALIA
June-July 1989: 12 games

PARTY: G Hastings (2,3,5,7,9,10,12), P Dods (1,4,6,8,11), I Evans (1,2,4R,5,7,9,10,12), M Hall (3,4,6,7,8,11), C Oti (2,4,5), A Clement (11,12R), R Underwood (1,3,5R,6,7,8,9,10), J Devereux (2,3,5,11,12), J Guscott (2,4,5,8,9,10), S Hastings (1,3,5R,6,8,9,10,11R,12), B Mullin (1,4,6,7,11,12), C Chalmers (1R,2,3,5,7,11,12), P Dean (1), R Andrew (4,6,8,9,10,12), G Armstrong (2,4,6,8,11), R Jones (1,3,5,7,9,10,12), M Griffiths (2,4,5,8,11,12R), D Sole (1,3,6,7,8R,9,10,12), G Chilcott

(2,4,6,8,11), **D Young** (1,3,5,7,8R,9,10,12), **B Moore** (1,3,5,7,9,10,12), **S Smith** (2,4,6,8,11), **D Lenihan** (1,4,8,11), **W Dooley** (2,4,6,8,9,10), **P Ackford** (2,3,5,6,7,9,10,12), **R Norster** (1,3,5,7,11,12), **J Jeffrey** (2,4,6,8,11), **A Robinson** (2,4,6,8,11,12), **M Teague** (1,3,5,9,10,12), **F Calder (capt)** (1,3,5,7,9,10), **D Richards** (2,3,5,7,9,10), **D White** (1,4,6,7,8,11,12).

Manager: C Rowlands (Wales). **Coach:** I McGeechan (Scotland). **Assistant coach:** R Uttley (England).

Results: (1) Western Australia 0, Lions 44 (10 June, Perth); (2) Australia B 18, Lions 23 (14 June, Melbourne); (3) Queensland 15, Lions 19 (17 June, Brisbane); (4) Queensland B 6, Lions 30 (21 June, Cairns); (5) New South Wales 21, Lions 23 (24 June, Sydney); (6) New South Wales B 19, Lions 39 (27 June, Dubbo); (7) **Australia 30, British Lions 12** (first Test: 1 July, Sydney); (8) Australian Capital Territory 25, Lions 41 (4 July, Canberra); (9) **Australia 12, British Lions 19** (second Test: 8 July, Brisbane); (10) **Australia 18, British Lions 19** (third Test: 15 July, Sydney); (11) New South Wales Country 13, Lions 72 (19 July, Newcastle); (12) Anzac XV 15, Lions 19 (23 July, Brisbane).

Scorers: G Hastings 66 (2t, 2c, 17p, 1dg), Dods 66 (1t, 19c, 8p), Chalmers 28 (1t, 7dg), Mullin 28 (7t), Armstrong 20 (5t), Underwood 16 (4t), Andrew 16 (5c, 1p, 1dg), Jeffrey 16 (4t), Hall 12 (3t), S Hastings 12 (3t), Dooley 8 (2t), Evans 8 (2t), Smith 8 (2t), Robinson 8 (2t), Devereux 8 (2t), White 4 (1t), Moore 4 (1t), Jones 4 (1t), Oti 4 (1t), Norster 4 (1t), Sole 4 (1t), Guscott 4 (1t), Chilcott 4 (1t), Clement 4 (1t), penalty try (4).

Record: P12, W11, L1, F360 (50t, 26c, 27p, 9dg), A192.

First Test: **Australia 30, British Lions 1**ⁿ
Sydney, 1 July 1989
British Lions: G Hastings (Scotland); I Evans (Wales), M Hall (Wales), B Mullin (Ireland), R Underwood (England); C Chalmers (Scotland), R Jones (Wales); D Sole (Scotland), B Moore (England), D Young (Wales), P Ackford (England), R Norster (Wales), D White (Scotland), F Calder (Scotland, capt), D Richards (England).

Scorers – Penalty goal: G Hastings 2, Chalmers. **Dropped goal:** Chalmers.

Second Test: **Australia 12, British Lions 19**
Brisbane, 8 July 1989

British Lions: G Hastings (Scotland); I Evans (Wales), S Hastings (Scotland), J Guscott (England), R Underwood (England); R Andrew (England), R Jones (Wales); D Sole (Scotland), B Moore (England), D Young (Wales), W Dooley

(England), P Ackford (England), M Teague (England), F Calder (Scotland, capt), D Richards (England).

Scorers – Tries: G Hastings, Guscott. **Conversion:** Andrew. **Penalty goals:** G Hastings, Andrew. **Dropped goal:** Andrew.

Third Test: **Australia 18, British Lions 19**
Sydney, 15 July 1989

British Lions: G Hastings (Scotland); I Evans (Wales), S Hastings (Scotland), J Guscott (England), R Underwood (England); R Andrew (England), R Jones (Wales); D Sole (Scotland), B Moore (England), D Young (Wales), P Ackford (England), W Dooley (England), M Teague (England), F Calder (Scotland, capt), D Richards (England).

Scorers – Try: Evans. **Penalty goals:** G Hastings 5.

IRELAND TO NORTH AMERICA (no caps awarded)
August-September 1989: 4 games

PARTY: F Dunlea (2,3,4), P Danaher (1,3,4R), P Purcell (3), P Haycock (3), J Sexton (1,2,4), M Kiernan (1,2,3,4), P Clinch (1,2,4), K Crossan (1,2,4), N Barry (1R,2,3), B Smith (1,4), F Aherne (1,2,4), M Bradley (2R,3,4R), T Clancy (2R,3), N Popplewell (1,2,4), J McDonald (1,2,4), T Kingston (3,4R), G Halpin (3), J McCoy (1,2,4), W Anderson (capt) (1,2,3,4), N Francis (1,3), B Rigney (2,4), P O'Hara (1,3,4), D McBride (2), P Matthews (1,2,4), P Kenny (3), N Mannion (1,2,3,4)

Results: (1) British Columbia 18, Ireland XV 21 (30 Aug, Vancouver); (2) **Canada 21, Ireland XV 24** (2 Sept, Victoria); (3) Mid West 6, Ireland XV 58 (6 Sept, Chicago); (4) **US Eagles 7, Ireland XV 32** (9 Sept, New York).

Scorers: Kiernan 61 (1t, 12c, 11p), Bradley 12 (3t), Dunlea 8 (2t), Mannion 8 (2t), Purcell 8 (2t), O'Hara 4 (1t), Sexton 4 (1t), Francis 4 (1t), Kingston 4 (1t), Clancy 4 (1t), Halpin 4 (1t), Haycock 4 (1t), Crossan 4 (1t), Danaher 3 (1dg), Smith 3 (1dg).

Record: P4, W4, L0, F135, A52.

Canada 21, Ireland 24
Victoria, 2 September 1989

Injury-time try by John Sexton prevents Ireland becoming first IB country to lose to Canada. British Columbia provide entire Canadian team for first time in their 100-year history.

Canada: M Wyatt; S Gray, B Ross, T Woods, S Brown; G Rees, J Graf; E Evans, D Spiers, P Zsabo, J Robertsen, J Hadley, R Radu, G McKinnon, G Ennis (capt).

Scorers – Penalty goals: Wyatt 6. **Dropped goal:** Rees.

Ireland: P Dunlea; J Sexton, P Clinch, M Kiernan, K Crossan; N Barry, F Aherne; N Popplewell, J McDonald, J McCoy, W Anderson (capt), B Rigney, P Matthews, D McBride, N Mannion.

Scorers – Tries: Dunlea, Sexton. **Conversions:** Kiernan 2. **Penalty goals:** Kiernan 4.

US Eagles 7, Ireland 32
New York, 9 September 1989

Ireland: F Dunlea (P Danaher); J Sexton, M Kiernan, P Clinch, K Crossan; B Smith, F Aherne (M Bradley); N Popplewell, J McDonald (T Kingston), J McCoy, W Anderson (capt), B Rigney, P Matthews, P O'Hara, N Mannion.

Scorers – Tries: Dunlea, Mannion, Crossan, Bradley. **Conversions:** Kiernan 2. **Penalty goals:** Kiernan 3. **Dropped goal:** Smith.

Italy U-21 9, Ireland U-21 10
Treviso, 30 September 1989

Ireland: A White (I Gallagher); J Harley, D Lynagh, J Clarke, W Kearns; E Elwood, R Saunders (capt); B Barrett, A Adair (B Browne), A McKeen, E O'Sullivan (V Costello), D Bursey, K O'Connell, K Gallick, R Finegan.

Scorers – Try: Lynagh. **Penalty goals:** Lynagh 2.

France 27, Home Unions 29
Paris, 4 October 1989

France: S Blanco; B Lacombe, P Sella, M Andrieu, P Lagisquet; D Camberabero, P Berbizier (capt); M Pujolle, D Bouet (H Chabowski 61), L Seigne, T Devergie, G Bourguignon, P Benetton, O Roumat, L Rodriguez.

Scorers – Tries: Blanco, Benetton, Camberabero. **Conversions:** Camberabero 3. **Penalty goals:** Camberabero 3.

Home Unions: G Hastings (Scotland); S Hastings (Scotland), B Mullin (Ireland), J Guscott (England), R Underwood (England); R Andrew (England, capt), R Jones (Wales); M Griffiths (Wales), S Smith (Ireland), J Probyn (England), P Ackford (England), D Cronin (Scotland), P Matthews (Ireland), A Robinson (England), D Egerton (England).

Scorers – Tries: R Andrew, G Hastings 2. Conversion: G Hastings. **Penalty goals:** G Hastings 4. **Dropped goal:** Andrew.

NEW ZEALAND TO WALES AND IRELAND
October-November 1989: 13 games

Results: (1) Cardiff 15, NZ 25 (Oct 14, Arms Park); (2) Pontypool 6, NZ 47 (18 Oct, Pontypool Park); (3) Swansea 22, NZ 37 (21 Oct, St Helen's); (4) Neath 15, NZ 26 (25 Oct, The Gnoll); (5) Llanelli 0, NZ 11 (28 Oct, Stradey Park); (6) Newport 9, NZ 54 (31 Oct, Rodney Parade); (7) **Wales 9, New Zealand 34** (4 Nov, Cardiff); (8) Leinster 9, NZ 36 (8 Nov, Lansdowne Road); (9) Munster 9, NZ 31 (11 Nov, Musgrave Park); (10) Connacht 6, NZ 40 (14 Nov, Galway); (11) **Ireland 6, New Zealand 23** (18 Nov, Dublin); (12) Ulster 3, NZ 21 (21 Nov, Ravenhill); (13) **Barbarians 10, New Zealand 21** (25 Nov, Twickenham).

Record: P13, **W**13, L0, F406, A119.

Wales 9, New Zealand 34
Cardiff, 4 November 1989

Wales: P Thorburn; M Hall, M Ring, D Evans, M Emyr; A Clement, R Jones (capt); M Griffiths, K Phillips, D Young, P Davies, G Llewellyn, P Pugh, G Jones, M Jones.

Scorers – Penalty goals: Thorburn 3.

Ireland 6, New Zealand 23
Dublin, 18 November 1989

Ireland: P Rainey; K Hooks, (P Danaher), B Mullin, D Irwin, K Crossan; B Smith, F Aherne; N Popplewell (D Fitzgerald), S Smith, J McCoy, D Lenihan, W Anderson (capt), P Matthews, P O'Hara, N Mannion.

Scorers – Penalty goals: Smith 2.

Barbarians 10, New Zealand 21
Twickenham, 25 November 1989

Barbarians: G Hastings (Scotland); T Underwood (England B), S Hastings (Scotland), J Guscott (England), R Underwood (England); T Clement (Wales), N Farr-Jones (Australia); D Sole (Scotland, capt), B Moore (England), D Young (Wales), W Dooley (England), P Ackford (England), P Matthews (Ireland), G Rees (England), P Davies (Wales).

Replacement: B Mullin (Ireland) for Guscott.

Scorers – Try: Matthews. **Penalty goals:** G Hastings 2.

Scotland 38, Fiji 17
Murrayfield, 28 October 1989

Scotland: G Hastings; A Stanger, S Hastings, S Lineen, I Tukalo; C Chalmers, G Armstrong; D Sole (capt), K Milne, P Burnell, C Gray, D Cronin, J Jeffrey, G Marshall (A Buchanan-Smith 66), D White.

Replacements: P Dods, C Glasgow, G Oliver, I Corcoran.

Scorers – Tries: Stanger 2, G Hastings, Tukalo, Milne, Gray. **Conversions:** G Hastings 4. **Penalty goals:** G Hastings 2.

England B 12, Fiji 20
Headingley, 31 October 1989

England B: S Pilgrim; T Underwood, S Irving, F Clough, E Davis; P Hull, D Morris; J Leonard, K Dunn, J Probyn, S O'Leary, R Kimmins, P Tayler, D Pegler (capt), D Thresher.

Scorers – Try: Penalty try. **Conversion:** Pilgrim. **Penalty goals:** Pilgrim 2.

England 58, Fiji 23
Twickenham, 4 November 1989

England: S Hodgkinson; R Underwood, J Guscott, W Carling (capt), M Bailey (S Halliday 78); R Andrew, R Hill; M Linnett, B Moore, A Mullins, W Dooley, P Ackford, M Skinner, P Winterbottom (G Rees 27), D Egerton.

Replacements: J Webb, S Bates, P Rendall, J Olver.

Scorers – Tries: Underwood 5, Skinner, Bailey, Linnett, Ackford, Guscott. **Conversions:** Hodgkinson 5, Andrew. **Penalty goals:** Hodgkinson 2.

France B 28, Wales B 15
La Teste, 12 November 1989

Wales B: M Rayer; A Harries, A Davies, A Bateman, A Edmunds; C Stephens (S Lewis 58), A Booth; J Rowlands, P John, H Williams-Jones, A Allen, J Wakeford, M Budd, M Edwards, D Bryant (capt).

Scorers – Penalty goals: Davies 4. **Dropped goal:** Stephens.

Ireland U-21 13, New Zealand U-21 13
Donnybrook, 19 November 1989

Ireland: A White; J Harley, R Moloney, J Clarke, W Kearns; N Barry, A Matchett; P Soden, B Browne, A McKeon, K O'Connell (capt), E O'Sullivan, D Bursey, K Gallick, R Finegan.

Replacements: D Lynagh, E Elwood, R Saunders, P Hogan, J Lennon, A Adair.

Scorers – Try: O'Sullivan. **Penalty goals:** Barry, White. **Dropped goal:** Barry.

Scotland B 22, Ireland B 22
Murrayfield, 9 December 1989

Scotland B: D Barrett; A Moore, B Edwards, I Jardine, S Porter; D Shiel, D Bryson; G Graham, K McKenzie, G Wilson, J Richardson, A MacDonald, J Macklin (capt), D Busby, D Leckie.

Scorers – Tries: Moore, Busby. **Conversion:** Shiel. **Dropped goals:** Shiel 3. **Penalty goal:** Barrett.

Ireland B: K Murphy; J Staples, J Hewitt, P Clinch, P Murray; P Russell, A Rolland; B McKibben, J McDonald, P Clohessy, B Rigney, M Galwey (P Johns), P Collins (capt), P Kenny, B Robinson.

Scorers – Tries: Murray, Kenny. **Conversion:** Russell. **Penalty goals:** Russell 4.

Scotland 32, Romania 0
Murrayfield, 9 December 1989

Scotland: G Hastings; A Stanger, S Hastings, S Lineen, L Renwick; D Wyllie, G Armstrong; D Sole (capt), K Milne, P Burnell, C Gray, D Cronin, D Jeffrey, F Calder, D White.

Replacements: P Dods, C Glasgow, G Oliver, G Marshall, A Brewster, I Corcoran.

Scorers – Tries: Stanger 3, White, Sole. **Conversions:** G Hastings 3. **Penalty goals:** G Hastings 2.

England B 18, Soviet Union 10
Northampton, 23 December 1989

England B: S Langford; F Packman, F Clough, J Buckton, E Davis; D Pears, S Bates; M Linnett, J Olver, A Mullins, D Baldwin, J Etheridge, M Skinner, D Pegler (capt), M Teague.

Scorers – Tries: Clough 2. **Conversions:** Pears 2. **Penalties:** Pears 2.

Scottish Trial: Blues 45, Reds 4
Murrayfield, 6 January 1990

Blues: G Hastings; T Stanger, S Hastings, S Lineen, L Renwick; D Wyllie, G Oliver; D Sole (capt), K Milne, P Burnell, C Gray, D Cronin, D Turnbull, A Buchanan-Smith, G Marshall (J Macklin 33).

Scorers – Tries: Oliver, Marshall, Buchanan-Smith, G Hastings, Gray, Macklin, S Hastings 2. **Conversions:** G Hastings 2. **Penalty goals:** G Hastings 2. **Dropped goal:** Wyllie.

Reds: P Dods; A Moore, P Rouse (B Edwards 54), I Jardine, I Tukalo; C Glasgow, S Jardine; G Graham, J Allan, I Milne, J Richardson, A MacDonald, J Jeffrey, F Calder (capt), C Hogg.

Scorer – Try: Moore.

England 23, Ireland 0
Twickenham, 20 January 1990

England: S Hodgkinson; R Underwood, J Guscott, W Carling (capt), M Bailey; R Andrew, R Hill; P Rendall, B Moore, J Probyn, W Dooley, P Ackford, M Skinner, P Winterbottom, D Egerton.

Replacements: S Halliday, M Teague, S Bates, M Linnett, J Olver, A Buzza.

Scorers – Tries: Probyn, Egerton, Underwood, Guscott. **Conversions:** Hodgkinson 2. **Penalty goal:** Hodgkinson.

Ireland: K Murphy; M Kiernan, B Mullin, D Irwin, K Crossan; P Russell, F Aherne; D Fitzgerald, S Smith (J McDonald), G Halpin, N Francis, W Anderson (capt), P Matthews, P O'Hara, N Mannion.

Replacements: N Popplewell, M Bradley, P Collins, B Smith, P Murray.

Referee: P Robin (France).

Wales (13) 19, France (9) 29
Cardiff, 20 January 1990

Wales: P Thorburn, M Titley, M Ring, M Hall, A Emyr; D Evans, R Jones (capt); M Griffiths, K Phillips, D Young (H Williams-Jones), A Allen, K Moseley, P Davies, G Jones, M Jones.

Scorers – Try: Titley. **Penalty goals:** Thorburn 4. **Dropped goal:** Evans.

France: J-B Lafond; M Andrieu, P Sella, D Charvet, P Lagisquet; D Camberabero, P Berbizier (capt); P Ondarts, L Armary, J-P Garuet, T Devergie, D Erbani, E Champ, L Rodriguez, O Roumat.

Scorers – Tries: Lafond, Sella, Camberabero, Lagisquet, Rodriguez. **Conversions:** Camberabero 3. **Penalty goals:** Camberabero.

Referee: F Howard (England).

France B 31, Scotland B 9
Oyonnax, 21 January 1990

Scotland B: D Barrett; A Moore, P Rouse, B Edwards, S Porter; J Breckenridge, D Bryson; G Graham, I Corcoran, G Wilson, J Richardson, S Munroe, J Macklin (capt), D Busby, A MacDonald.

Replacements: C Redpath, C Glasgow, S Jardine, S Reid, B Robertson, J Allan.

Scorers – Penalty goals: Barrett 3.

France B 15, England B 15
Paris, 3 February 1990

England B: A Buzza; J Fallon, B Barley, J Buckton, N Heslop; D Pears, D Morris; J Leonard, N Hitchen, A Mullins, D Baldwin, S O'Leary, P Tayler, D Pegler (capt), T Rodber.

Scorers – Penalties: Pears 5.

France (0) 7, England (13) 26
Paris, 3 February 1990

France: S Blanco; M Andrieu, P Sella, D Charvet, P Lagisquet; F Mesnel, P Berbizier (capt); P Ondarts, L Armary (P Marocco), J-P Garuet, T Devergie, D Erbani, E Champ, L Rodriguez, O Roumat.

Replacements: P Marocco, M Pujolle, A Carminati, H Sanz, D Camberabero, J-B Lafond.

Scorers – Try: Lagisquet. **Penalty goal:** Charvet.

England: S Hodgkinson; R Underwood, J Guscott, W Carling (capt), M Bailey; R Andrew, R Hill; P Rendall, B Moore, J Probyn, W Dooley, P Ackford, M Skinner, P Winterbottom, M Teague.

Replacements: S Halliday, F Clough, S Bates, M Linnett, J Olver, D Egerton.

Scorers – Tries: Underwood, Guscott, Carling. **Conversions:** Hodgkinson 2. **Penalty goals:** Hodgkinson 4.

Referee: O Doyle (Ireland).

Ireland (7) 10, Scotland (0) 13
Dublin, 3 February 1990

Ireland: K Murphy, M Kiernan, B Mullin, D Irwin, K Crossan; B Smith, F Aherne; J Fitzgerald, J McDonald, D Fitzgerald, D Lenihan, W Anderson (capt), P Matthews, P O'Hara (P Collins), N Mannion.

Scorers – Try: McDonald. **Penalty goals:** Kiernan 2.

Scotland: G Hastings; A Stanger, S Hastings, S Lineen, I Tukalo; C Chalmers, G Armstrong; D Sole (capt), K Milne, P Burnell, C Gray, D Cronin, J Jeffrey, F Calder, D White.

Scorers – Tries: White 2. **Conversion:** Chalmers. **Penalty goal:** Chalmers.

Referee: C Norling (Wales).

England (16) 34, Wales (0) 6
Twickenham, 18 February 1990

England: S Hodgkinson; S Halliday, J Guscott, W Carling (capt), R Underwood; R Andrew, R Hill; P Rendall, B Moore, J Probyn, W Dooley, P Ackford, M Skinner, P Winterbottom, M Teague.

Scorers – Tries: Underwood 2, Carling, Hill. **Conversions:** Hodgkinson 3. **Penalty goals:** Hodgkinson 4.

Wales: P Thorburn; M Titley, M Ring, M Hall, A Emyr; D Evans, R Jones (capt); M Griffiths, K Phillips, L Delaney, A Allen, G Llewellyn, P Davies, R Collins, M Jones.

Scorers – Try: Davies. **Conversion:** Thorburn.

Referee: D Leslie (Scotland).

342

Scotland (3) 21, France 0
Murrayfield, 18 February 1990

Scotland: G Hastings; A Stanger, S Hastings, S Lineen, I Tukalo; C Chalmers, G Armstrong; D Sole (capt), K Milne, P Burnell, C Gray, D Cronin, J Jeffrey, F Calder, D White.

Scorers – Tries: Calder, Tukalo. **Conversions:** Chalmers 2. **Penalty goals:** Chalmers 2, G Hastings.

France: S Blanco; P Hontas, P Sella, F Mesnel, P Lagisquet; D Camberabero, H Sanz; M Pujolle, L Armary, P Ondarts, T Devergie, O Roumat, J-M Lhermet, A Carminati, L Rodriguez.

Referee: F Howard (England)

France (12) 31, Ireland (6) 12
Paris, 3 March 1990

France: S Blanco (M Andrieu 20); P Hontas, P Sella, F Mesnel, P Lagisquet; D Camberabero, H Sanz; M Pujolle, L Armary, P Ondarts, J Condom, T Devergie, O Roumat, J-M Lhermet (E Melville 18), L Rodriguez (capt).

Scorers – Tries: Mesnel 2, Lagisquet. **Conversions:** Camberabero 2. **Penalty goals:** Camberabero 5.

Ireland: K Murphy; K Hooks, M Kiernan, P Danaher, K Crossan; B Smith, F Aherne; J Fitzgerald, T Kingston, D Fitzgerald, D Lenihan (capt), N Francis, D McBride, P O'Hara, N Mannion.

Scorers – Penalty goals: Kiernan 4.

Referee: K McCartney (Scotland).

Wales (3) 9, Scotland (10) 13
Cardiff, 4 March 1990

Wales: P Thorburn; M Hall, M Ring, A Bateman, A Emyr; D Evans, R Jones (capt); B Williams, K Phillips, J Pugh, G Llewellyn, P Davies, M Perego, R Collins, M Jones.

Scorers – Try: Emyr. **Conversion:** Thorburn. **Penalty goal:** Thorburn.

Scotland: G Hastings; A Stanger, S Hastings, S Lineen, I Tukalo; C Chalmers, G Armstrong; D Sole (capt), K Milne, P Burnell, C Gray, D Cronin, J Jeffrey, F Calder, D White.

Scorers – Try: Cronin. **Penalty goals:** Chalmers 3.

Referee: R Hourquet (France).

Ireland U-25 (9) 12, US Eagles (0) 10
Limerick, 10 March 1990

Ireland U-25: J Staples; J Clarke, P Danaher, V Cunningham, P Murray; P Henebry, A Blair; N Popplewell, J O'Rearden, G Halpin, K O'Connell, P Johns, M Galwey, B Robinson, D McBride.

Scorers – Try: Cunningham. **Conversion:** Hennebry. **Penalty goals:** Hennebry 2.

Scotland (9) 13, England (4) 7
Murrayfield, 17 March 1990

Scotland: G Hastings; A Stanger, S Hastings, S Lineen, I Tukalo; C Chalmers, G Armstrong; D Sole (Capt), K Milne, P Burnell, C Gray, D Cronin, J Jeffrey, F Calder, D White (D Turnbull 30).

Scorers – Try: Stanger. **Penalty goals:** Chalmers 3.

England: S Hodgkinson; S Halliday, J Guscott (M Bailey 64), W Carling (Capt), R Underwood; R Andrew, R Hill; P Rendall, B Moore, J Probyn, W Dooley, P Ackford, M Skinner, P Winterbottom, M Teague.

Scorers – Try: Guscott. **Penalty goal:** Hodgkinson.

Referee: D Bishop (New Zealand).

Ireland (10) 14, Wales (0) 8
Dublin, 24 March 1990

Ireland: K Murphy, M Kiernan, B Mullin, K Crossan; B Smith, M Bradley (F Aherne 40); J Fitzgerald, T Kingston, D Fitzgerald, D Lenihan (capt), N Francis, D McBride, P O'Hara, N Mannion.

Scorers – Tries: Smith, McBride, Kingston. **Conversion:** Kiernan.

Wales: P Thorburn (A Clement 22); S Ford, M Ring, A Bateman, A Emyr; D Evans (A Edmunds 57), R Jones (capt); B Williams, K Phillips, H Williams-Jones, G Llewellyn, A Allen, R Collins, M Morris, M Jones.

Scorers – Tries: Ford, Llewellyn.

Referee: D Bishop (New Zealand).

	P	W	D	L	F	A	Pts
Scotland	4	4	0	0	60	26	8
England	4	3	0	1	90	26	6
France	4	2	0	2	67	78	4
Ireland	4	1	0	3	36	75	2
Wales	4	0	0	4	42	90	0

Home Unions 43, Europe 18
Twickenham, 22 April 1990

Home Unions: G Hastings (Scotland); A Stanger (Scotland), J Guscott (England), W Carling (England), R Underwood (England); R Andrew (England), R Hill (England); D Sole (Scotland, capt), B Moore (England), M Griffiths (Wales), D Cronin (Scotland), N Francis (Ireland), J Jeffrey (Scotland), P Winterbottom (England), N Mannion (Ireland).

Replacements: C Chalmers (Scotland) for Carling, D Turnbull (Scotland) for Mannion.

Scorers – Tries: Carling 2, Cronin, Jeffrey, Guscott, Andrew, Hastings. **Conversions:** Hastings 6. **Penalty Goal:** Hastings.

Europe: M Toader (Romania); M Dancia (France), G Langlade (France), N Fulina (Romania), P Lagisquet (France); B Capatini (France), A Heuber (France); M Pujolle (France), P Dintrans (France, capt), G Rossi (Italy), M Cecillon (France), S Clorascu (Romania), T Janeczek (France), H Dumitras (Romania), A Tikhonov (USSR).

Replacements: I Mironov (USSR) for Dancia, F Gaentaniello (Italy) for Lagisquet, P Capdevielle (France) for Rossi, K Tapper (Sweden) for Tikhonov.

Scorers – Tries: Fulina, Mironov, Tikhonov, Langlade. **Conversion:** Toader.

Referee: F Howard (England)

Scotland U-21 10, Wales U-21 24
Ayr, 28 April 1990

Scotland U-21: C Redpath; C Henderson, R Adam, G Shiel, D Macrae; S Nichol, F Stott; J Couper, S Brotherstone, G McKee, G Mackay, G Weir (D Jackson), S Reid, C Brown, C Hogg (capt).

Replacements: M Moncrieff, A Warwood, G Farquharson, L Dow, S Paul.

Scorers – Try: Macrae. **Penalty goals:** Shiel 2.

Wales U-21: L Evans; C Thomas, R Sheppeard, M Egan, M Yendle; A Davies, P John; T Orrell, A Lamerton, L Mustoe, P Arnold, S Roy, M Lloyd, P Thomas, S Williams (capt).

Replacements: A Lewis, B Haywood, M De-Maid, G Richards, R Shaw, N Jones.

Scorers – Tries: Lloyd 2, Davies. **Conversions:** Evans 2, Davies. **Penalty goal:** Evans.

Dropped goal: Davies.

Netherlands 3, England U-21 24
Hilversum, 29 April 1990

Netherlands: M Marcker; B Verhofstadt, S Hadinegoro, E van der Laan, B Wisse; M Michelsen, M Eman; W van der Kley, M Visser, G de Vries, R Broers, E Berendsen, M van Loon, Y Kummer (capt), W van Altena.

Scorer – Penalty goal: Michelsen.

England U-21: W Kilford; L McKenzie, P de Glanville, G Thompson (capt), H Thorneycroft; G Gregory, J Davis; G Baldwin, S Davies, N Lyman, N Ashurst (E Peters), M Poole, D Sims, N Back, A Milward.

Scorers – Tries: Thorneycroft 2, Thompson. **Conversions:** Gregory 3. **Penalty goals:** Gregory 2.

Italy XV 15, England XV 33
Rovigo, 1 May 1990

Italy: L Troiani; E Venturi, G Morelli, S Barba, M Cuttita; M Bonomi (D Tebaldi), F Pietrosanti (I Francescati); G Gespan, C Pratichetti (G Pivetta), A Piazza, R Favaro, P Pedroni, R Saetti, P Reale, C Covi (capt).

Scorers – Try: Cuttita. **Conversion:** Troiani. **Penalty goals:** Troiani 3.

England: S Hodgkinson (Nottingham); N Heslop (Orrell), W Carling (Harlequins, capt), J Buckton (Saracens), C Oti (Wasps); R Andrew (Wasps), S Bates (Wasps); M Linnett (Moseley), B Moore (Nottingham), J Probyn (Wasps), R Kimmins (Orrell), W Dooley (Preston Grasshoppers), J Wells (Leicester), N Back (Nottingham), D Cusani (Orrell).

Replacements: J.Olver (Harlequins) for Moore, F.Clough (Wasps) for Carling. P Tayler.

Scorers – Tries: Oti, Buckton, Back, Andrew. **Conversions:** Hodgkinson 4. **Dropped goal:** Andrew.

French Armed Forces 16, England U-21 23
Fontainebleau, 12 May 1990

F.A.F.: L Pommies; E Artiguste, R Frenzel (capt), L Nardi, S Weller (M Fiart 20); E Berdeu, O San Nicolas; G Racine, P Miriski, C Calzolari, M Milovic (G Rossi 65), T Fontanillas, M Lievremont, R Reynet, J Lagrande.

Scorers – Try: Rossi. **Penalty goals:** Pommies 3. **Dropped goal:** Pommies.

England U-21: W Kilford; L McKenzie, L Boyle, G Thompson (capt), H Thorneycroft; A Lee, N Summers; A Windo, S Davies, G Baldwin, M Poole, A Milward, N Ashurst, N Back, E Peters.

Scorers – Tries: Kilford 2, Thompson. **Conversion:** Lee. **Penalty goals:** Lee 3.

WALES TO NAMIBIA
May-June 1990: 6 games

PARTY: P Thorburn (2,4,6), **M Rayer** (1,3,5), **S Ford** (1,2,4,6), **A Emyr** (2,3,4,6), **S Bowling** (1,3,5), **M Ring** (1,3,4,5,6), **A Bateman** (1,2,4,6), **S Parfitt** (2,3,4R,5), **A Clement** (2,3R,4,5,6), **A Williams** (1,3,5,6R), **C Bridges** (2,4,6), **S Fealey** (1,3,5), **J Pugh** (2,5), **I Buckett** (1,3,5), **M Griffiths** (2,4,6), **P Knight** (1,3,4,6), **K Phillips (capt)** (1,2,4,6), **K Gregory** (3,5), **P Arnold** (1,2,4,6), **G Llewellyn** (1,3,4,5,6), **O Williams** (1,3,5,6), **R Phillips** (1,2,5), **S Williams** (2,5), **M Jones** (2,3,4,6), **A Reynolds** (1,3,4,5R,6R), **M Morris** (2,3,4,5,6).

Results: (1) Welwitschia 0, Wales 73 (23 May, Swakopmund); (2) Namibia B 18, Wales 35 (26 May, Windhoek); (3) Central Region 6, Wales 43 (30 May, Windhoek); (4) **Namibia 9, Wales 18** (first Test: 2 June, Windhoek); (5) North Region 9, Wales 67 (6 June, Tsumeb); (6) **Namibia 30, Wales 34** (second Test: 9 June, Windhoek).

Scorers: Rayer 64 (2t, 19c, 6p), Thorburn 44 (1t, 8c, 8p), Emyr 20 (5t), A Williams 19 (3t, 2c, 1dg), Parfitt 16 (4t), Fealey 16 (4t), O Williams 16 (4t), Ford 8 (2t), Ring 8 (2t), Morris 8 (2t), Reynolds 8 (2t), Bridges 4 (1t), Llewellyn 4 (1t), R Phillips 4 (1t), S Bowling 4 (1t), Buckett 4 (1t), Bateman 4 (1t), K Gregory 4 (1t), S Williams 4 (1t), Pugh 4 (1t), Clement 3 (1dg), penalty try (4).

Record: P6, W6, L0, F270, A72.

First Test: **Namibia 9, Wales 18**
Windhoek, 2 June 1990

Namibia full-back Andre Stoop becomes the third player to be sent off by English referee Fred Howard when he is dismissed for head-butting in the 21st minute. Paul Thorburn caps an outstanding performance with 14 points and his first try in 30 Internationals for Wales.

Namibia: A Stoop; G Mans (capt), J Deysel, V du Toit, B Schwartz; S McCulley, B Buitendag; C Derks, S Smidt, M Grobler, S Losper, A Van der Merwe, J Barnard, A Skinner, T Oosthuizen.

Scorers – Try: Mans. **Conversion:** McCulley. **Penalty goal:** McCulley.

Wales: P Thorburn; S Ford, M Ring, A Bateman, A Emyr (S Parfitt); A Clement, C Bridges; M Griffiths, K Phillips (capt), P Knight, G Llewellyn, P Arnold, M Morris, A Reynolds, M Jones.

Scorers – Tries: Thorburn, Bridges. **Conversions:** Thorburn 2. **Penalty goals:** Thorburn 2.

Second Test: **Namibia 30, Wales 34**
Windhoek, 9 June 1990

Wales almost throw match away, having led by 15 points with 20 minutes remaining, but hold on to end six-match tour unbeaten. Owain Williams marks his debut with one of the visitors' 4 tries.

Namibia: J Coetzee; G Mans (capt), J Deisel, V du Toit, B Schwartz; S McCulley, B Buitendag; C Derks, S Smidt, M Grobler, S Losper, A Van der Merwe, J Barnard (J Coetzee), A Skinner, T Oosthuizen.

Scorers – Tries: Mans, Schwartz 2. **Conversions:** McCulley, Coetzee 2. **Penalty goals:** McCulley 2, Coetzee. **Dropped goal:** Coetzee.

Wales: P Thorburn; S Ford (A Williams), M Ring, A Bateman, A Emyr; A Clement, C Bridges; M Griffiths, K Phillips (capt), P Knight, G Llewellyn, P Arnold, O Williams, M Morris, M Jones (A Reynolds).

Scorers – **Tries:** Emyr 2, O Williams, penalty try. **Conversions:** Thorburn 3. **Penalty goals:** Thorburn 3. **Dropped goal:** Clement.

SCOTLAND TO NEW ZEALAND
May-June 1990: 8 games

PARTY: G Hastings (2,4,6,8), **P Dods** (1,3,5,7), **A Stanger** (2,4,6,8), **S Porter** (1,3,7), **I Tukalo** (2,4,5,6), **A Moore** (1,3,5,7,8), **S Hastings** (2,4,5,6,7R,8), **S Lineen** (1,4,6,8), **C Redpath** (1,3,7), **G Shiel** (2,3,5,7), **C Chalmers** (1,4,6,8), **D Wyllie** (2,3,5,7), **G Armstrong** (2,4,6,8), **G Oliver** (1,3,5,7,8), **D Sole** (capt) (1,2,4,6,8), **A Brewster** (3,5,7), **P Burnell** (2,3,5,7), **I Milne** (1,4,6,8), **K Milne** (1,4,7,8), **J Allan** (2,3,5,6), **D Cronin** (2,3,4,6,7R,8), **C Gray** (1,4,6,8), **J Richardson** (2,5,7), **G Weir** (1,3,5,7), **F Calder** (1,4,6,8), **D Turnbull** (1,2R,3,5,7), **J Jeffrey** (2,4,6,8), **A Buchanan-Smith** (2,3,5,7), **D White** (2,4,6,8), **G Marshall** (1,3,5,7).

Results: (1) Poverty Bay/East Coast 0, Scotland 45 (30 May, Gisborne); (2) Wellington 16, Scotland 16 (2 June, Wellington); (3) Nelson Bays/Marlborough 6, Scotland 23 (6 June, Nelson); (4) Canterbury 12, Scotland 21 (9 June, Christchurch); (5) Southland 12, Scotland 45 (12 June, Invercargill); (6) **New Zealand 31, Scotland 16** (first Test: 16 June, Dunedin); (7) Manawatu 4, Scotland 19 (19 June, Palmerston North); (8) **New Zealand 21, Scotland 18** (second Test: 23 June, Auckland).

Scorers: P Dods 58 (2t, 13c, 8p), G Hastings 39 (6c, 9p), Moore 16 (4t), Marshall 12 (3t), S Hastings 8 (2t), K Milne 8 (2t), Lineen 8 (2t), Wyllie 6 (2dg), Allan 4 (1t), Buchanan-Smith 4 (1t), Oliver 4 (1t), Chalmers 4 (1t), Stanger 4 (1t), Turnbull 4 (1t), Sole 4 (1t), Gray 4 (1t), Calder 4 (1t), Shiel 4 (1t), Richardson 4 (1t), penalty try (4).

Record: P8, W5, D1, L2, F203, A102.

First Test: **New Zealand 31, Scotland 16**
Dunedin, 16 June 1990

Scotland are cleaned out in the line-out as the World champion All Blacks recover from a less than convincing first half to dispatch the European champions. Birthday boy Grant Fox pockets 15 points.

New Zealand: K Crowley; J Kirwan, J Stanley, W Little, T Wright; G Fox, G Bachop; S McDowell, S Fitzpatrick, R Loe, I Jones, G Whetton, A Whetton, M Brewer, W Shelford (capt).

Scorers – Tries: Crowley, Fox, Jones, Kirwan 2. **Conversions:** Fox 4. **Penalty goal:** Fox.

Scotland: G Hastings; T Stanger, S Hastings, S Lineen, I Tukalo; C Chalmers, G Armstrong; D Sole (capt), J Allan, I Milne, C Gray, D Cronin, J Jeffrey, F Calder, D White.

Scorers – Tries: Lineen, Gray, Sole. **Conversions:** G Hastings 2.

Second Test: **New Zealand 21, Scotland 18**
Auckland, 23 June 1990

Scotland come within 8 minutes of beating New Zealand and levelling series only for Grant Fox's fifth penalty goal to save the All Blacks' blushes.

New Zealand: K Crowley; J Kirwan, J Stanley, W Little, T Wright; G Fox, G Bachop; S McDowell, S Fitzpatrick, R Loe, I Jones, G Whetton, A Whetton, M Brewer, W Shelford (capt).

Scorers – Try: Loe. **Conversion:** Fox. **Penalty goals:** Fox 5.

Scotland: G Hastings; A Stanger, S Hastings, S Lineen, A Moore; C Chalmers, G Armstrong (G Oliver 69); D Sole (capt), K Milne, I Milne, C Gray, D Cronin, J Jeffrey, F Calder, D White.

Scorers – Tries: Stanger, Moore. **Conversions:** G Hastings 2. **Penalty goals:** G Hastings 2.

ENGLAND TO ARGENTINA
July-August 1990: 7 games

PARTY: S Hodgkinson (2,4,5,7), **J Liley** (1,2R,4,6), **N Heslop** (1,3,5,7), **C Oti** (1,2,3,5,6,7), **T Underwood** (2,4,6), **J Buckton** (1,2,4,5,7), **W Carling (capt)** (1,3,5,7), **G Childs** (4,6), **G Thompson** (2,3,6), **P Hull** (3,4,6), **D Pears** (1,2,3,5,7), **R Hill** (1,3,4,5,7), **D Morris** (2), **S Bates** (6), **J Leonard** (2,3,5,7), **M Linnett** (1,4,6), **J Probyn** (2,5,7), **V Ubogu** (1,3,4,6), **B Moore** (1,4,5,7), **J Olver** (2,3,6), **W Dooley** (2,3,5,7), **R Kimmins** (1,4,6), **M Poole** (1,4,6), **N Redman** (2,3,5,7), **A Robinson** (1,4,6), **D Ryan** (2,3,5,7), **M Skinner** (1,4,5,7), **P Winterbottom** (2,3,5,7), **D Egerton** (1,3,6,7R), **T Rodber** (2,4,6).

Results: (1) Banco Nacion 29, England 21 (14 July, Buenos Aires); (2) Tucuman Selection 14, England 19 (18 July, Tucuman); (3) Buenos Aires Selection 26, England 23 (21 July, Buenos Aires); (4) Cuyo Selection 22, England 21 (24 July, Mendoza); (5) **Argentina** 12, **England** 25 (first Test: 28 July, Buenos Aires); (6) Cordoba Selection 12, England 15 (31 July, Cordoba); (7) **Argentina** 15, **England** 13 (second Test: 4 August, Buenos Aires).

Scorers: Hodgkinson 56 (1t, 2c, 16p), Pears 18 (3c, 4p), Liley 15 (1t, 1c, 3p), Heslop 8 (2t), Kimmins 8 (2t), Ryan 8 (2t), Oti 4 (1t), Carling 4 (1t), Buckton 4 (1t), Olver 4 (1t), Robinson 4 (1t), Egerton 4 (1t).

Record: P7, W3, L4, F137, A130.

First Test: **Argentina 12, England 25**
Buenos Aires, 28 July 1990

Argentina: A Scolni; H Vidou, M Loffreda (capt), D Cuesta Silva, S Salvat; R Madero, E Gomez; A Rocca, J-J Angelillo, L Molina, E Branca, A Lachetti, P Garreton, M Bertranou, M Baeck.

Scorers – Penalty goals: Vidou 4.

England: S Hodgkinson; N Heslop, W Carling (capt), J Buckton, C Oti; D Pears, R Hill; J Leonard, B Moore, J Probyn, N Redman, W Dooley, M Skinner, P Winterbottom, D Ryan.

Scorers – Tries: Ryan, Oti. **Conversion:** Hodgkinson. **Penalty goals:** Hodgkinson 5.

Second Test: **Argentina 15, England 13**
Buenos Aires, 4 August 1990

Argentina: A Scolni; H Vidou, M Loffreda (capt), D Cuesta Silva, S Salvat; R Madero, E Gomez; M Aguirre, J Angelillo, D Cash, D Branca, A Lachetti, P Garreton, M Baeck, M Bertranou.

Scorers – Penalty goals: Vidou 5.

England: S Hodgkinson; N Heslop, W Carling (capt), J Buckton, C Oti; D Pears, R Hill; J Leonard, B Moore, J Probyn, N Redman, W Dooley (D Egerton), M Skinner, P Winterbottom, D Ryan.

Scorers – Tries: Hodgkinson, Heslop. **Conversion:** Hodgkinson. **Penalty goal:** Hodgkinson.

Appendix

England's Development Squad

(Other players selected by England as training party for 1995 World Cup)

BLACKETT, Peter Mofield. Club: Bath; Position: Wing; Height: 5' 10",
Weight: 13st 10lb; Born: Bath, 26.2.64.

BLACKMORE, Andrew George. Club: Bristol; Position: Lock; Height: 6'7",
Weight: 18st; Born: Bristol, 1.11.65.

DEAR, Simon James. Club: Rosslyn Park; Position: Lock; Height: 6'8",
Weight: 17st 4lb; Born: Peterborough, 30.1.63.

DUNSTON, Ian Charles. Club: Wasps; Position: Tight-head prop; Height:
5'10", Weight: 15st 12lb; Born: Essex, 11.6.68.

HUNTER, Ian. Club: Northampton; Position: Full-back; Height: 6'2",
Weight: 14st 12lb; Born: London, 15.2.68.

McGAULEY, Conor Francis. Club: Rosslyn Park; Position: Prop; Height:
6'3", Weight: 17st 7lb; Born: Beckenham, 6.5.65.

MacNAUGHTON, Robert Carlo. Club: Liverpool St Helens; Position:
Centre; Height: 6', Weight: 13st; Born: Guildford, 21.9.65.

PARTON, Andrew Richard. Club: Coventry; Positions: Wing, full-back;
Height: 6'3", Weight: 14st; Born: Coventry, 31.1.68.

POTTER, Stuart. Club: Nottingham; Position: Centre; Height: 5'11", Weight
13st 7lb; Born: Lichfield, 11.11.67.

ROBERTS, Harry. Club: Wasps; Position: Hooker; Height: 5'11", Weight:
15st 8lb; Born: Lusaka, Zambia, 3.12.60.

STEELE, John David. Clubs: Northampton and Army; Position: Fly-half;
Height: 5'10", Weight: 12st 5lb; Born: Cambridge, 9.8.64.

TAYLOR, Roger John. Club: Nottingham; Position: Hooker; Height: 6',
Weight: 15st 7lb; Born: Chatham, 23.6.67.

THACKER, Troy Anthony. Club: Leicester; Position: Hooker; Height: 5'8",
Weight: 14st 3lb; Born: Kettering, 17.5.65.

International Season 1990/91

1990

September 8:   Ireland U-25 v Spain
        29:   The National Power Centenary Match:
              England v Barbarians (Twickenham)
              England Colts v Canada (Twickenham)
October 6:   Wales v Barbarians (Cardiff)
        20:   Ireland B v Argentina (Thomond Park)
        27:   Ireland v Argentina (Dublin)
        29:   England U-21 v Ireland U-21 (Moseley)
November 3:   The National Power International:
              England v Argentina (Twickenham)
         9:   Welsh Districts v Sweden (Aberavon)
        10:   Scotland v Argentina (Murrayfield)
        17:   Barbarians v Argentina (Cardiff)
December 1:   Wales B v France B (tba)
        22:   Ireland B v Scotland B (Ravenhill, Belfast)
        27:   Welsh U-18 v Australia U-18 (Cardiff)

1991

January 5:   Scottish Trial (Murrayfield)
        19:   The British Gas Challenge:
              Wales v England (Cardiff)
              France v Scotland (Paris)
February 2:   The Royal Bank International:
              Scotland v Wales (Murrayfield)
              Ireland v France (Dublin)
        16:   The Save & Prosper International:
              England v Scotland (Twickenham)
              Wales v Ireland (Cardiff)
March 2:   Ireland v England (Dublin)
              France v Wales (Paris)
              Scotland B v France B (Glasgow)

9:	Welsh Youth v French Juniors (Whitland)
15:	England Colts v Italian Youth (Cambridge)
16:	The Royal Bank International:
	Scotland v Ireland (Murrayfield)
	The Save & Prosper International:
	England v France (Twickenham)
23/24:	Cathay Pacific Hong Kong Bank Sevens
30:	Ireland U-18 v England U-18 (Dublin)
	Scotland U-18 v Netherlands U-18 (tba)
	Wales U-18 v France U-18 (Angoulême)
April 3:	England U-18 v France U-18 (Northampton)
6:	Wales U-18 v Ireland U-18 (tba)
	England Colts v Wales Youth (Fylde)
9:	England U-18 v Scotland U-18 (Aspatria)
10:	Scotland U-21 v English Students U-21 (South of Scotland)
13:	Wales U-18 v England U-18 (Colwyn Bay)
20:	Scotland Colts v England Colts (tba)
27:	Wales U-21 v Scotland U-21 (tba)
	Wales U-18 v Scotland U-18 (tba)
April/May	France Juniors v England Colts (tba)
May 11:	Sweden v Welsh Districts (Stockholm)
July 20:	Fiji v England (Suva)
27:	Australia v England (Sydney)
September 7:	Scotland v Barbarians (Murrayfield)

Fixtures

League Season 1990/91

England:
Courage Clubs Championship.

September 22, 1990
October 6
October 13
October 20
October 27
November 10
November 17
January 12, 1991
February 9
March 9
March 23
April 13
April 20

Ireland:
All Ireland League.

October 6, 1990
October 13
November 3
November 10
November 17
November 24
January 5, 1991
January 12
January 26
Round robin play-offs:
February 9
February 23
March 9

Wales:
Heineken National League.

September 22, 1990
September 29
October 13
October 20
October 27
November 3
November 10
November 24
December 8
December 15
December 22
January 12, 1991
February 9
March 9
March 23
April 13
April 20
April 27

Scotland:
McEwans National League.

September 22, 1990
September 29
October 6
October 13
October 20
October 27
November 3
November 17
January 12, 1991
January 26
February 9
February 23
March 9

Fixtures

Representative Season 1990/91

England
ADT Security Systems Divisional Championship.

December 1, 1990:	London v North, Midlands v South West
December 8:	London v Midlands, North v South West
December 15:	North v Midlands, South West v London

Ireland
Irish Inter Provincial Championship.

December 1, 1990:	Munster v Connacht, Ulster v Leinster
December 8:	Connact v Leinster, Munster v Ulster
December 15:	Leinster v Munster, Ulster v Connacht

Scotland
McEwans Inter District Championship.

November 24, 1990:	Edinburgh v Glasgow, North/Mids v South
December 1:	South v Anglo-Scots, North/Mids v Edinburgh
December 8:	Edinburgh v Anglo-Scots, Glasgow v North/Mids
December 15:	Anglo-Scots v North/Mids, Glasgow v South
December 29:	South v Edinburgh, Anglo-Scots v Glasgow

Full List of Entries

England

Ackford, P.J.
Ainscough, G.C.
Andrew, C.R.
Ashurst, N.
Back, N.A.
Bailey, M.D.
Baldwin, D.N.
Baldwin, G.P.S.
Barley, B.
Bates, S.M.
Blackett, P.M.
  (Development Squad)
Blackmore, A.G.
  (Development Squad)
Boyle, L.S.
Buckton, J.R.
Buzza, A.J.
Callard, J.E.B.
Carling, W.D.C.
Chilcott, G.J.
Childs, G.C.
Clarke, B.B.
Clough, F.J.
Collings, P.
Cusani, D.A.
Davies, S.L.
Davis, E.
Davis, J.
De Glanville, P.R.
Dear, S.J. (Development Squad)
Doggart, G.
Dooley, W.A.
Dunn, K.A.
Dunston, I.C.
  (Development Squad)
Egerton, D.W.
Essien, D.N.

Excell, S.C.
Fallon, J.A.
Gregory, G.D.
Guscott, J.C.
Hackney, S.T.
Halliday, S.J.
Hamlin, M.P.
Hannaford, M.P.
Harriman, A.T.
  (Development Squad)
Harris, M.A.
Harrison, M.E.
Hartley, G.J.
Heslop N.J.
Hill, R.J.
Hitchen, N.
Hodgkinson, S.D.
Horrobin, J.K.
Hull, P.A.
Hunter, I. (Development Squad)
Hynes, M.P.
Kilford, W.A.
Killick, N.J.
Kimmins, R.
Langford, S.R.
Lee, A.J.
Leonard, J.
Liley, J.G.
Linnett, M.S.
Lozowski, R.
Luxton, C.T.
Lyman, N.M.
McGauley, C.F.
  (Development Squad)
McKenzie, L.
MacNaughton, R.C.
  (Development Squad)
Milward, A.W.

Moon, R.H.StJ.B.
Moore, B.C.
Morris, C.D.
Morrison, J.S.C.
Mosses, G.B.
Mullins, A.R.
O'Leary, S.T.
Olver, C.J.
Oti, C.
Packman, F.
Parton, A.R. (Development Squad)
Pears, D.
Pegler, D.J.
Peters, E.W.
Pilgrim, S.J.
Poole, M.D.
Potter, S. (Development Squad)
Povoas, S.J.
Probyn, J.A.
Redman, N.C.
Rees, G.W.
Rendall, P.A.G.
Richards, D.
Roberts, H. (Development Squad)
Robinson, R.A.
Rodber, T.A.K.
Ryan, D.
Sharp, A.V.
Shortland, S.M.
Sims, D.
Skinner, M.G.
Smith, I.R.
Steele, J.D. (Development Squad)
Tayler, P.M.
Taylor, R.J. (Development Squad)
Teague, M.C.
Thacker, T.A.
   (Development Squad)
Thompson, G.J.
Thorneycroft, H.S.
Thresher, D.B.
Ubogu, V.E.
Underwood, R.
Underwood, T.
Wareham, R.A.
Webb, J.M.

Wells, J.M.
Windo, A.J.
Winterbottom, P.J.

Ireland

Aherne, L.F.P.
Anderson, W.A. (Retiree)
Barry, N.
Blair, A.G.
Bradley, M.T.
Bursey, D.J.W.
Clinch, P.D.
Clohessy, P.
Collins, P.C.
Crossan, K.D.
Cunningham, V.J.G.
Danaher, P.P.A.
Dean, P. (Retiree)
Dinneen, L.M.
Dunlea, F.J.
Finegan, R.A.J.
Fitzgerald, D.C.
Fitzgerald, J.J.
Francis, N.P.
Gallick, K.
Galwey, M.J.
Halpin, G.F.
Harley, J.R.
Haycock, P.P.
Hennebry, P.J.
Hewitt, J.A.
Hooks, K.J.
Irwin, D.G.
Johns, P.S.
Kearns, W.P.P.
Kenny, P.
Keyes, R.P.
Kiernan, M.J.
Kingston, T.J.
Lenihan, D.G.
Lynagh, D.J.
McBride, W.D.
McCoy, J.J.
McDonald, J.P.
McKeen, A.J.W.

McKibbin, B.M.
Mannion, N.P.S.
Matchett, W.D.A.
Matthews, P.M.
Moloney, R.J.
Mulcahy, W.J.M.
Mullin, B.J.
Murphy, K.J.
Murray, P.V.
O'Connell, K.
O'Hara, P.T.
O'Sullivan, E.T.
Popplewell, N.
Rainey, P.I.
Rigney, B.J.
Riordan, J.C.
Robinson, B.F.
Rolland, A.C.P.
Russell, P.
Saunders, R.
Sexton, J.F.
Smith, B.A.
Smith, S.J.
Soden, P.J.
Staples, J.
White, A.

Scotland

Adam, D.R.W.
Allan, J.
Armstrong, G.
Barrett, D.
Breckenridge, G.M.
Brewster, A.K.
Brown, C.J.
Bryson, D.
Buchanan-Smith, G.A. (p. 323)
Burnell, A.P.
Busby, J.D.
Calder, F. (Retiree)
Chalmers, C.M.
Corcoran, I.
Couper, J.A.
Cronin, D.F.

Dods, M.
Dods, P.W.
Dow, J.L.
Duncan, M.D.F.
Edwards, B.
Farquharson, G.C.
Glasgow, I.C.
Graham, G.
Gray, C.A.
Hastings, A.G.
Hastings, S.
Hay, J.A.
Henderson, W.M.C.
Hogg, C.D.
Jackson, D.A.
Jardine, I.C.
Jardine, S.
Jeffrey, J.
Leckie, D.E.W.
Lineen, S.R.P.
MacDonald, A.E.D.
McKee, G.T.
McKenzie, K.D.
Mackay, G.T.
Macklin, A.J.
Maclean, R.R.W.
Macrae, D.
Marshall, G.R.
Milne, I.G.
Milne, K.S.
Moncrieff, M.
Moore, A.
Munroe, D.S.
Nichol, S.A.
Oliver, G.H.
Paul, S.W.
Paxton, I.A.M.
Peterson, G.L.
Redpath, A.C.
Renwick, W.L.
Richardson, J.F
Robertson, G.B.
Rouse, P.R.
Shiel, A.G.
Shiel, D.K.
Sole, D.M.B.

Stanger, A.G.
Stott, F.H.
Tukalo, I.
Turnbull, D.J.
Wainwright, R.I
Warwood, A.M.
Weir, G.W.
White, D.B.
Wilson, D.J.
Wilson, G.D.
Wyllie, D.S.

Wales

Allen, A.G.
Arnold, P.
Bateman, A.G.
Booth, A.H.
Bridges, C.J.
Bryant, D.J.
Buckett, I.
Budd, M.
Clement, A.
Collins, R.G.
Davies, C. (Retiree)
Davies, J.D.
Davies, N.G.
Davies, P.T.
Davies, W.S.M.
De Maid, M.W.
Delaney, L.
Devereux, J. (Retiree)
Edmunds, D.A.
Edwards, M.W.
Ellis, K.S. (Retiree)
Emyr, A.
Evans, D.W.
Evans, I.C.
Evans, I.L.
Evans, R.L.
Fealey, S.
Ford, S.P.
Goodey, R.
Griffiths, M.
Hall, M.R.

Harries, A.
Hayward, B.
Hopkins, D.S.
Jenkins, G.R.
John, P.
Jones, C.J.
Jones, G.
Jones, M.A.
Jones, R.N.
Jones, S.N.
Jones, S.T.
Knight, P.
Laity, C.
Lamerton, A.E.
Llewellyn, G.
Llewellyn, G.D.
Lloyd, M.J.
Lloyd, S.J.
Mason, J.
Morgan, M.
Morris, M.S.
Moseley, K.
Mustoe, L.
Norster, R.L.
Orrell, T.
Parfitt, S.A.
Perego, M.A.
Phillips, K.H.
Phillips, R.D.
Pickering, D.F.
Pugh, J.D.
Pugh, P.
Rayer, M.A.
Reynolds, A.D.
Richards, D.G.
Ring, M.G.
Roberts, G.J.
Rowlands, J.
Sheppeard, R.
Silva, M.A.
Stephens, C.J.
Sutton, A.
Thomas, C.J.
Thomas, P.J.
Thorburn, P.H.
Titley, M.H.

Turner, P.
Wakeford, J.D.M.
Watkins, I.J.
Webster, R.E.
Williams, B.V.

Williams, D.A.
Williams, O.L.
Williams, S.M.
Williams-Jones, H.
Young, D. (Retiree)